MW00780987

CITY OF SERPENTS

HOW TO GET OVER BETRAYALS & ABUSE

2ND EDITION

CHRIS JOSH

WWW.CHRISJOSH.COM

Be the first to know about new releases and exclusive offers.

Subscribe to the emails at ChrisJosh.com/Subscribe

www.ChrisJosh.com

Copyright © 2024 by Chris Josh

All rights reserved.

No part of this book may be reproduced in any form or by any electronic or mechanical means, including information storage and retrieval systems, without written permission from the author, except for the use of brief quotations in a book review.

Serpent
Slayer

COS BY CJ

CONTENTS

I dedicate this book to all those who stand for truth, justice, peace, honor and love. And to those who seek knowledge and spread it freely. Those masterful teachers who came before, those who are here now and those who will come. To the builders of our past, present and future; builders of hope and advancement. To those who seek the cure rather than perpetual profit. And to those who defend the weak and help the needy, even when they're struggling themselves. To the humble ones who don't expect anything in return, save the pleasure of the Most High. To the ones who will give you the shirt off their backs. All of you aforementioned therein are the most honorable ones in the eyes of God. You are the ones who shine so brightly and glamorously, that not even the most brilliant diamond can compare. You are wholesomely needed and appreciated.

Thank you

INTRODUCTION

Allow me to introduce myself; my name is Chris Josh and boy do I have a story to tell. The book you have now is the 2ⁿᵈ edition of "City of Serpents." The current subtitle is "How To Get Over Betrayals & Abuse." However, the subtitle of the 1ˢᵗ edition was "Conquer Your Mind & Walk In Your Power." I wanted the new subtitle to target its intended audience better. The cover of the 1ˢᵗ edition had the same artwork design, except it was red instead of green. The new color represents both love and serpents. And serpents represents both healing and betrayers. Ironically, the betrayers ultimately led to my healing journey, and they tested my unconditional love along the way. On a side note, my name in Arabic means green, sage, wisdom, and love. In this book, I will show you how to overcome all types of betrayals and abuse by narcissists.

I eliminated many passages for this edition. So, it's about 25% shorter in print length. And new in this edition is the appendix, entitled, "The Shadow Self Workbook," found at the end of the book. It consists of important self-healing questions to address the pain caused by a betrayal and is intended to help you unburden yourself from the memories.

When I went over the 1st edition of "City of Serpents" during the audiobook production, some things stuck out to me, and I decided to make some changes for a better reading experience. The overall message of the book has not been compromised. However, the book has been greatly improved and even more enjoyable to read than the 1st edition. And the added appendix provides more value by helping you dive deep into the issues surrounding a betrayal, in order to heal fully.

Prior to the 1st edition of "City of Serpents," the book was originally called, "Rising Above the Abyss: a Story of Resilience, Faith and Triumph." I was on the cover of that book and the characters in that version didn't have names. I set out to make the story more memorable, marketable and easier to read. While this book is 100% based on a true story, the real names weren't used because I didn't want to give those people any publicity. I will tell you that the names used all correlate with the original names in that they start with the same letters and some rhyme or sound like the originals. While the names in this book are English, the original ones are Arabic and/or Islamic. The main characters were all born Muslim, including Chris (more about the name later in the book).

In this book, I will be sharing the powerful story of a little boy who grew up in a broken home, surrounded by an abusive, narcissistic mother (Sally), a hateful brother (Milton), and an absent, self-absorbed father (Neuman). The story covers the devastating impact of these circumstances throughout his childhood, teenage, and adult years. It's important to note that I have had to omit many events from this book or else it would be 1000 pages long. This person's story is nothing short of miraculous because what he endured would have broken even the strongest of individuals. It would have been enough to cause most people to lose all hope and consider suicide, let alone persevere steadfastly until the age of 43. It's important to recognize the immense difficulty of enduring such traumatic experiences. Many individuals who have gone through similar circumstances would likely have struggled with thoughts of suicide or even lost their sanity. Even for those who managed to persevere, it's understandable that they might harbor deep-seated feelings of bitterness and regret, be mistrustful of others, and be unable to find joy or humor in life. The effects of such trauma can be far-reaching and long-lasting, impacting nearly every aspect of a person's life.

It's nothing short of miraculous that he not only survived the traumatic circumstances of his childhood but also remained committed to his faith throughout his life. At just 7 years old, he began practicing fasting in accordance with Islamic tradition, and at 12, he started performing the Islamic 5x daily prayer. Despite facing significant health challenges in adulthood, including fibromyalgia, he refused to give up or succumb to despair. Instead, he continued to seek knowledge, learn new skills, and uphold his unwavering moral code. What's truly remarkable is that despite being let down by those closest to him, he never lost his capacity for love, compassion, and positivity. He became a beacon of hope and inspiration to everyone he met, spreading happiness wherever he went. It's a testament to the incredible resilience of the human spirit and a reminder that even in the darkest of times, there is always a glimmer of hope.

Although he had every RIGHT to quit, kill himself, treat others harshly, be negative, disrespectful, violent, become a liar and a cheat, and so on - he kept pushing and remained in a loving spirit. It is no doubt that love is what got him through it. In his darkest hours, alone, he was still nurturing others and offering free life-changing advice to those he saw needed it. I wrote this book because we are going through some difficult times here in America as of June 2022. People are losing their investments with high gas prices and everything going up. I know many people are depressed and anxious. By sharing the story of this young boy, who happens to be me, the author, I aim to help others dig themselves out of the bottomless pit.

I'll share actual events that happened to me - none of it is stretched or exaggerated. Nothing was added to this book to make the story "better." I'm only sharing what I went through. And for some, it may be hard to grasp how 1 human can go through all of that and come out looking unscathed - looking 20 years younger than I actually am. And how at the end of the 2nd narcissist relationship I had (ex-wife, Zina – pronounced Zin-na), I elevated myself into a completely different and healed version of myself. As of this writing, I am in the best shape ever. I'm more excited about life today than even when I was a child. I am living proof that with God (love), you can weather any storm and still come out looking better than your peers who had an easy life. Now, I understand the topic of God can be a turn-off for many. I get it; talking about God can be off-putting for some. I've been there myself, questioning whether there is any higher power in the face of all the suffering and tragedy throughout history. But hear me out. I've learned that unfortunate and difficult events help us grow and realize our full potential. We need to be worked on, whether by external forces or by us, to shine like a diamond.

I am grateful for everything in the past. Would I relive it? A part of me says, "HECK NO," but then another (crazy) part of me says, "I wouldn't be who I am if I didn't." Seriously. I wouldn't even relieve 1 month of what I endured if it wouldn't make me the man I am today. But I'm grateful because it made me who I am today. It strengthened, wisened, and helped me become a great problem solver. I learned to surrender and be extremely patient (endless, unconditional patience). I've come to embrace the power of unconditional love and living in the present moment, every moment of the day.

I tell my inner child he's a warrior; I'm proud of him and glad he didn't kill himself. I tell him I'm proud of him for not laying a finger on his mom, despite the daily abuse that lasted nearly 20 years. He, in turn, tells me that he's so proud of me and puts me on a pedestal. He can't believe who I've become. No one can believe it. Everyone wrote me off as the weird butt of all jokes. Picked last at everything. Never invited to go anywhere. Not a single call from anyone. They didn't know I was autistic, had ADHD, and was abused at home. I didn't know I was autistic or had ADHD, either. However, I never told anyone what I was going through with my mother. I was too ashamed. I felt worthless and that if I told people, I would prove to them that I was a weird, unlovable joke.

What's incredible is that when people ask me how I did it, I tell them it was God (love). They dismiss it. "No, really, how'd you do it?" If I tell them I did it through patience, consistent work, continuous learning, and sheer willpower and discipline, they'll deny it and chalk it up to luck. So, unfortunately, neither God nor I have gotten the credit we deserve so far. That will change because the type of people who receive this message will understand there's no way it was luck.

In this book, I will take you through hell without any flames coming near you. You will come to know what I went through. I wrote this book because many people face challenges and don't know if they can get through it all. I want to inspire you by showing that if I can survive the challenges I faced, you can too. It's a bit like an Olympic track record - the 100m has been held by Usain Bolt since 2012, with no one yet able to break his time of 9.63 seconds. However, once someone breaks the record, others will be inspired to do so too, knowing it's possible.

In the same way, I want you to see all that I went through and think to yourself, "If Chris can overcome that, so can I. You have power. It's called patience, love, compassion, and faith. And although your situation will be different from mine. Maybe your situation is even more intense but for a much shorter time. Even so, you can get through it.

I will also show you how to heal from your past trauma and get it out of your system. I will show you how to lead a happier and more fulfilling life. Love, or what I call God, has helped me heal and persevere. My gift to the world is to share this message, as I believe love has the power to transform and bring about a new era of peace, healing and abundance.

As a side note, keep in mind I started writing this book in 2022, possibly late 2021, and finished it in 2023. My memory doesn't serve me well. As a result, you'll see some discrepancies in the ages of my children as well as the length of me working out, amongst other things. And at times, you may feel like I'm repeating myself, but each time I'm revealing more details. Everything was done with purpose and intent. Throughout the entire time, I was progressing from my cognitive impairment and a shattered heart towards the more healed version of myself. My memory was severely impaired. I had no one during the entire process. No parents, no siblings, no cousins, no aunts or uncles, no real friends...no one. I was all alone, broken. There was no one there to tell me, "Chris, wake up. Time to power through the day. Time to write your book. Do this or do that." All I had was my intuition nudging me in the right direction.

Now, allow me to take you on a journey through my eyes and see how love exists in hell too.

THE GENESIS

*I*t was 1979; I was on a plane with my parents to the good ole USA. I couldn't see all the other passengers because I was in my mother's womb. I was made in Lebanon and born in New York City. Little did I know, I was in for a horrifying experience - a nightmare that would have taken out the toughest of men at a young age. That's how effed up things were!

Eventually, the plane landed, and we moved in with my uncle and his wife in New York City. There were lots of arguing and fighting, and yes, I can still vividly remember some things when we lived in that apartment in Chelsea, New York City. We lived there until I was 3 years old. So, to remember things that young is remarkable for me. I remember standing in front of our building, looking up, and seeing the towering buildings. They looked so much bigger and extraordinary back then. I was dumbfounded and had no idea what I was looking at.

At the time, I didn't know it, but Sally was disappointed with my pregnancy. She was very young. She was 15 when she got married and 16 when I was born. My parents fled the Lebanese Civil War and sought refuge and a better life in the United States of America. She was disappointed because she didn't want to be tied down by a baby. And because of that, she always had it out for me. She quite literally blamed me for everything, including the pregnancy itself. I became the scape-goat; I wasn't looked at as a human being. I was looked at as the problem. And the only way to solve it was to physically beat, criticize, and humiliate me.

If you can imagine yourself at the age of 15, I don't think you'd be excited about having a child. However, I don't think you'd blame the child. No normal person would. A normal person would say, "it's my responsibility." So, every time Sally would look at me, she'd be reminded that I was the one who took away her freedom and happiness. She failed to see that I was a source of happiness as I was always cheerful and cracking jokes. She was more enamored by her Lebanese friends, telling her how much fun they had at the club.

A child could walk into a store and buy cigarettes at that time. So, guess what I did at 3 years old? I'd cross the street, walk into the bodega with an empty pack of cigarettes in my hand, look at the clerk, point at the empty package, and give him the money. In turn, he gives me a new pack which I cross the street back home and give it to my mother. Yes, you read that right. Crossing the street solo at 3 years old in Chelsea, NYC, with busy car traffic. Did I come up with the idea? No. Sally did. Did it occur to her that I could be hit by a car or kidnapped? Probably. She probably wanted me to die or get kidnapped. But The Creator/God/Universe had me protected.

At age 4, my parents moved to West New York, New Jersey. I remember always going to the store to buy her cigarettes there too. Back then, I wasn't much of an eater. I didn't have much of an appetite. I don't know if it was due to trauma or depression, but I didn't have life in me to want to eat. So, one day, when I refused to eat her spaghetti, she took a big pot full of warm pasta and dumped everything all over my head simply because I didn't want to eat. Rather than taking me to the doctor, I don't know why she thought this would be the solution.

A year later, I learned something that broke me down and made me feel worthless. She recalled the day I was born. She told me that when the nurse brought me to her, she screamed in horror/disgust and told the nurse, "get him away from me!" Luckily my uncle was there, and he had his eye on me. This uncle eventually moved far away from Sally and his siblings to avoid their drama. Back to what I heard from my mother; I was speechless when she told me this. Imagine at the age of 5 years old being told by the one person that should have uncondi- tional love for you, essentially betray you and then boast about it in front of you. It was devastating.

Being the oldest, I never had anyone to confide in or complain to. Neuman was there but not really there. He was there because he was still married to Sally and came home every night to sleep, but he never talked to me or gave me life lessons or advice. The things he should have taught me, I had to learn on my own. When Sally physically abused me to the point I couldn't take it anymore, I'd grab his wrist and beg him to please do something about it. I would tell him, "please, talk to her; she keeps hitting me." He would look at me, and without a word, he'd walk away and leave the apartment. I was left defeated and deflated, angry and embarrassed. I didn't have anyone to talk to or ask for help.

Sally abused me physically, emotionally, and mentally consistently and daily, multiple times a day. She would tear me down and tell me I was no good. At the age of 7, she'd tell me, "look at so and so, he's a doctor, and he's married. What are you doing with your life? You're a loser. When are you going to get married? You're a man already!" And I'm sitting there dumbfounded. Does this lady expect me to get married in the 2nd grade? She didn't want to parent - not me, not my siblings. Rather, she wanted me to set the example (without being taught by grownups) and raise my siblings for her. So, from early on, I had to be my own parent. I mean that, literally. I had to sit in the corner with belt marks on my body and tears rolling down my eyes, getting sleepy from all the crying, trying to make sense of what was happening, and wondering when it (the nightmare) would stop.

When I say I was abused, I mean daily. Multiple times on many days. I was constantly berated and humiliated with hurtful words. I was under CONSTANT criticism. I'm not exaggerating when I say that nothing I did, including my breathing, went without criticism. My creativity was frowned upon, and she did all she could to silence me. There was a makeshift belt hook on the wall near the bathroom. There, she had a selection of different belts. Some had regular buckles, and some had heavy buckles. And depending on how badly she wanted to beat me, she'd stand in front of the belt hook and look momentarily to see which belt she would use. A whooping with the radio power cord was just as devastating as a whooping from a buckle. She'd yank it out of the radio, fold it, and whip my legs and back like I was Kunta Kinte. In her eyes, all I was *was* her property.

It was a never-ending nightmare, truly, through and through. I didn't think I'd ever get out of it. I thought I was stuck in a really bad dream. I had no one to complain to, and part of me felt so embarrassed to let anyone else besides Neuman know. Neuman is very silent. It's not that he's an introvert; he uses silence as a manipulation tactic. He's not famous, but he knows many people, and many people know him. He's respected by many. To the public, it seemed like he was surely a great father. But no one knew he'd walk away without a word when I'd begged him to stop Sally from abusing me. He'd walk out of the apartment. Leaving me stuck with the psycho. And yes, she is a psycho. I don't say that to insult her. She's a textbook narcissist who needed/needs serious medical help.

In 1979, I was born, but so was the Iranian Revolution. And with that, Shi'ite Islam spread to Lebanon and was revitalized. Everyone from my parent's village at that time was drinking alcohol. But when Ayatollah Khomeini gained power, conservative Islam was revived in that village as well as many other villages in South Lebanon. Sally portrayed herself to others as an ultra-conservative religious woman. Far from it, in my book. She casted spells on her siblings, me, Neuman, and my siblings. You name it. Just a lot of hate, envy, and jealousy. She needed an outlet to vent and express her frustrations, and I was her outlet. I was her punching bag. And because she KNEW with 100%

certainty that I would never hit her back due to my morals, she kept going. She picked me as the scapegoat because I was the strongest and most creative of her children. I've been sliced with a butcher knife. She once swung a shovel repeatedly at my knees outside my parent's house in Lebanon, where I spent the summer there in the mid-2000s, which I dodged by jumping as high as possible while bending my knees. I've been hit with rock-stuffed baseball bats. I used to fill my wiffle baseball bat with rocks and store it in the bathroom behind the tub (the old-school tub had spacing around it).

My younger brother, 2 ½ years younger than me, was a ROYAL pain in my ass. We'll call him Milton. I had two other siblings who were younger than him - they were chilled out, but Milton was a certified hater. We'll call the other two siblings Hannah and Houston. I was a bright child and creative as well. Throughout this book, I refer to myself as being bright and creative and this might sound arrogant and boastful but know that I attribute this brightness and creativity to my intuition, which is my communication line to the Divine. My ego does not take credit for being bright and creative nor does it write off others as sub-par or unworthy. I am forever humbled by the Almighty God. I pray everyone is blessed with great gifts from the Universe.

Being bright and creative made Milton furious. He'd literally almost suffocate. It was like he had so many burdens stressing him out like he had 5 kids and had just lost his job. Big mad! We fought a lot. I used to cut him a lot of slack, but I'd fight him when he got out of line. Our last fistfight was when I was about 22 years old. I whooped him real good. He never tried me again. Oh, how I wish I could kick my mom in the face with a pair of construction steel-toe boots for all the hell she put me through. She's lucky I'm merciful and obedient to God. I almost didn't write this book because I didn't want to write about her negatively, but the reality is, I'm just stating facts. And I know this book will help people get through their hard times.

I want people to know what I went through and be the source of their strength until they finally discover a way to be strong without my help. I'm not going to sugarcoat it. What I went through is extreme; quite honestly, no one can get through it unless The Creator is on their side - not even me. It sure took a lot of strength, but The Universe instilled an innate feeling of well-being in me with a good feeling from love. This helped me weather the storm, but I still had to be strong. I would always say, "that's ok, I still have my bicycle, and I just had a good meal," whenever she abused me and made me cry. I would talk myself out of that misery by looking at the bright side. No one taught me how to do that. I just did it.

2

HELL BEGINS

The abuse started early. I don't even remember when exactly the physical abuse started. I was either 4 or 5 years old, and it lasted till I was about 20 years old. One day, I came home for the weekend from college. Milton (prior to the final ass whooping) started to play wrestling with me, and then it got serious; Sally threw a BMX bike at us, and the metal part that the pedal connects (elbow part of metal) hit me right in the middle of the forehead. I had never felt pain like that. It's a miracle my head didn't split - nor did my skin. Truly a miracle. There's just no way you'll ever grasp what I went through.

I cried myself to sleep so many days - even during the afternoon. I'd wake up with a headache, confused about the time. At night, I was scared to fall asleep. I felt like something really bad was going to happen. I also felt like I was going to fall into a bottomless pit.

Now you might think I must have been doing something wrong. And, of course, as any child, I was misbehaving sometimes, but that was according to her stringent standards. She wanted me to stand like a soldier in formation without saying one word and without moving a centimeter. Seriously. So, of course, I was "misbehaving." I was a hyper kid. Always laughing and smiling, running around the house and the neighborhood.

At the time of this writing, I have 2 children. My daughter, Felicity, the oldest, was a hyper child too. Neuman was bewildered at how hyper she was, and he told me I was nowhere as hyped as Felicity. My children have never been so much as spanked on the behind. As hyper as my daughter was and as much as she drove me up the wall, I never spanked her. Felicity's mother, Zina, said she was surprised I don't abuse our children because I was abused. That's the thing, if I was abused here and there, I would think it's ok to hit my children here and there too. But since I was abused to the extreme, I completely empathize with my children and don't want them to deal with that type of trauma.

Because what was going on at home affected me at school and on the playground. As the saying goes, hurt people hurt people. And I was always negative and ready to fight. I had up to 3 physical fights a day regularly in grammar school, sometimes 4; before school started, at lunchtime, and after school. I fought kids 2 grades above me. Not proud of this at all, but this happens when you're not loved and, even worse, abused and neglected. When my 2nd-grade teacher went around the class asking what word starts with each letter, I got the letter F and guess what I blurted out? "F*ck!" All the kids in the school adored me because of that, and my mother's friends would laugh and ask me again what starts with the letter F, and I'd say "fruit" after they had urged me to say "fruit" next time the teacher asks.

See, I had a funny relationship with my so-called "friends." They liked my boldness and how I helped my older cousin when I was in kindergarten during his fight. He was on the other side of the gate and losing the fight. I looked around, found a broomstick, and passed it to him, throwing it under the gate. He used it to defend himself and save himself from his opponent. From that day, I was a legend. But 90% of these "friends" would pick on me for no reason. They hated me for the same reason Milton did. They were very competitive. I didn't understand what was happening because they'd have me over at their house but still bullied me. I didn't stop hanging out with them because I needed to be out of the house. Sally didn't want me in the house. She didn't mind if I played outside from 7 am to 9 pm at the age of 5. And because the bullying wasn't continuous all day, though it still occurred daily from the same kids, I settled for their "friendship."

And by bullying, I mean getting socked in the face occasionally but more so joking at my expense and shaming me. I was their piñata. There was no one else to take their insults but me. Over time, it wasn't as bad in high school - I was still being ridiculed now and then. I put up with them because they had my back. Not all of them ridiculed me, but about 60% did then. We were a really big crew in high school. We didn't refer to ourselves as a gang, but that's exactly what we were. We had big rumbles 1-2 times a day. It was wild. Drivers would get punched in the face if they honked their horns at us while we were busy rumbling or jumping someone. I don't understand how only 1 of us from the crew got expelled from the school. I put up with them because I felt invincible during my high school years. Everyone knew who I was, and they knew who I rolled with.

To me, these friends were way better than my experience at home. You may never know the feeling of walking around an entire town solo and not being afraid of the troublemakers because your crew was infamous. To me, the high school days restored my will to live. Yes, I was often torn down and criticized, and made fun of, but I felt like a popular gangster at the time. It was more fun than "home."

3

BEATING THE ODDS

*W*riting this book was difficult for me because it meant having to portray my own mother in a negative light. While part of me didn't want to do that, the reality is that I didn't have a positive relationship with her. While I am grateful for the gift of life, I didn't always feel that way growing up. Despite the challenges, I rebuilt my life and cut off toxic people, including every single family member. Today, I am grateful for the strength and resilience that allowed me to overcome these obstacles and lead a more fulfilled life.

But I'm telling you, it's a miracle I'm here today. I had suicidal thoughts for the majority of my life. I'm now almost 43 years old. It's only been about a year since I've let go of the suicidal thoughts and have fully embraced life with happiness and joy. Hardly anyone can survive 42 years of narcissistic abuse from 2 different women (Sally and Zina) and live to tell about it with a positive attitude. I'm here to prove it's possible with God's love. Not only that, God rebuilt me right in front of my abusers, to their utter shock and dismay. The first abuser was my mother, and it lasted 20 years. Then for about two years, she was out of the picture, and by the end of the 2 years, I got married to the second narcissistic abuser, which lasted 20 years also.

It bothered my mother that I was so happy. It bothered her because she wasn't happy and despised me for being born because that took away most of her freedom. If I was 16 years old, I'd be upset with being a parent so young, too. I certainly wouldn't blame the child or abuse them. She was extremely controlling, critical, disrespectful, and forceful. She didn't have the smooth talker trait, so she did everything through yelling, screaming, and hitting. She disrespected Neuman A LOT. Oh, how I used to wish he'd crack her jaw with a mean right hook, and I'd call her an ambulance, all giddy and satisfied.

Near the bathroom, there was a long hook on the wall holding several unique belts. Some were thinner than others. And some had heavier buckles than others. So, whenever she decided it was time for a beating, which was daily, she'd walk up to the hook and analyze what belt to use as if she was trying to pick out an outfit for a baby shower. After she picked it out, I had to pray she wasn't about to use the buckle! But of course, she did - not every time, but it happened a lot more than it should.

When she was really angry at me, she'd take the electrical cord out of the stereo, whip me with it, and leave marks all over my back, torso, and legs. It was pure hell; I was trapped in a crammed-up train track-style apartment with a heartless psycho. I was young and dependent on my parents. I had no choice but to stay in that apartment. The very same thing she hated me for- my love, my loving spirit, my happy spirit - got me through it all. And it wasn't till I was in my late 30s that I understood that love is God and God is love. I got emotional when I realized this and was extremely happy and honored that God was with me all along. It sent chills down my spine, and the hairs on my arms stood up. I clearly remember the feeling of God (love) throughout my upbringing - I just didn't know it was God Himself!

I got made fun of for believing in God. The kids would say that I was an Islamic sheikh because of my faith and obedience and that I would pray 5 times a day. I was more gullible than the average person back then, so when I heard of God, I just believed in Him instantly. It made sense because I thought it was logical that something made us humans.

In my 20s, Sally pressured me to make millions of dollars and didn't care how I made it - even if it was haraam (forbidden in Islam). I told her I would never do something haraam, and she said I couldn't walk around with the Quran in my hand out in the real world. I was confused. What was I being taught here? Did she want me to follow the religion or not? She just wanted to show her friends, "look at my son, he's rich, and he does his 5 daily prayers."

It was obvious she never gave a rat's ass about me. The real reason she wanted me to become wealthy was for her gain. She would get status in her community because she could then boast about how her son is a rich millionaire and how much she loves and is proud of me. That's what narcissistic parents do - they use their kids as trophies to show off to their friends and family. She pressured me as hard as possible by insulting, sham- ing, and making me feel less than others. She would ask me, "why do you carry yourself like that? You carry yourself as if you've got a lot of money, but you don't." I would tell her I'm grateful all my bills are being paid and I have extra to save up. That wasn't good enough for her. Therefore, she had no real respect for me. When I tell you this woman was impossibly unbearable, I just wanted to beat her viciously but always controlled myself. I controlled myself because, according to Prophet Muhammad, PBUH, you can't even make a frustrated sound towards your mother, let alone lay your hands on her. So, I just stayed there absorbing all the shots and beatings, crying so much that I'd fall asleep no matter what time it was.

4

ENVY AT HOME

*W*hat's worse is that Milton added tremendously to my suffering. He's had mental health issues since he was young. I don't know what he has exactly because he never shared it with me when he saw a psychiatrist. He had great envy towards me. Extremely jealous - even though he had a queen-sized bed, and I was sleeping on a run-of-the-mill mattress on the floor. I slept on that same mattress for 16 years, yet he was jealous of me. Because of that, he would irritate me, and I'd fight him. He admitted that he was jealous of me in his 20s.

In our younger days, we would wrestle for fun. Then, we started wrestling with intensity during our teenage years and with the intent to beat the other person up. And later, at 22 years old, we had a fistfight in our last fight, and I whooped him so good he never tried me again until a couple of years later. I thought I needed to get rid of this asshole. Lucky for him, I wasn't about to do a long bid to get rid of him. I eventually moved away from my parents and siblings and left the family business. That's the only way to get rid of them!

When I tell you Milton was a ROYAL PAIN IN THE ASS. Boy, oh boy!!! He was a sibling from hell. He deserved many ass-whoopings from me, but I showed him a lot of mercy. I didn't want to break his bones - I really didn't - because I'm an empath. I can feel what that's like in my root chakra, and I don't want anyone to go through that pain. My empathy got me into trouble. I cared too much. I should have kneed him in the nose and ended it early on.

I can't begin to tell you how much agony Milton caused me. What made things exponentially worse was that Sally always made excuses for him. I'm 2 years older than him, yet I was always seen as an adult from as young as 7 years old. "You're the oldest, and he's younger than you. You should be the one setting the example." Sally sent me to the supermarket daily, yet she never made Milton go. And if she did, it was probably once every 5 years. I had to fold the laundry every single day. Milton never folded the laundry, ever.

Because he saw he got unconditional support from her, he purposely pushed my buttons and treated me with a hateful heart. When he caught wind of me helping my father with his business, the brother from hell came to inject more crap into my life by coming to Neuman's store every day and picking fights with me, the workers, and the customers.

I honestly kept patient in those days. I was taught by Islamic teachers that I have to respect my parents. I can't talk back. I have to do what they say. I didn't want to shift the burden on

Neuman, so I tried to keep my cool. It was so hard working at Neuman's store. It was a wholesale & retail shop. Why's this so bad? First off, he never put the prices on the merchandise. It wasn't like we were quoting customers different prices randomly based on how we felt toward them. We had two prices per product: the retail price and the wholesale price. He just didn't want to spend money on the pricing gun and tags. In turn, to save a few bucks, the workers and I had to endure a never-ending battle with customers, many of whom were from the pits of the ghettos of the neighboring boroughs but also from all parts of the country and the world. Their attitudes were not inviting. They were rude and dramatic, always ready to fistfight. Very obnoxious and aggressive.

The customers would try to fool us by asking one of us what's the wholesale price of an item and then walking to the register with only 1 unit, which was considered retail. The minimum for wholesale pricing was 6 pcs per item. Then I had to explain to them that they needed to buy 5 more units if they wanted that price. And then all hell breaks loose. They start acting like they don't know this already - trying to get me to give in to them. But I never did unless the person was in a tough spot. On many days, hundreds of people would walk into the shop, and I'd have the same stupid argument about the wholesale and retail price over 250 times a day on average. Going to work was like going to war. I had to prep my mind for it each day.

In the 2000s, our market had a lot of foot traffic. This meant the store would get packed like a can of sardines, and that's when the thieves would strike. Now, I was working the register with angry, impatient customers in front of me, people arguing about the wholesale price, while simultaneously looking out for shoplifters. Sometimes two men would walk in and inquire about the baseball caps on the shelves behind the register. They'd try to distract me by asking me to see model after model. This way, the other guy could steal without my awareness, since I was so busy showing his accomplice 20 different caps. After the first time, I caught on to that scheme and never fell for it again.

Furthermore, the NYPD hated the entire market because it was filled with Arabs, Blacks, Africans, Indians, and Pakistanis. They would ticket us for the most trivial thing. So, I had to watch out for them. In dealing with all this pressure, I had to deal with my cock-sucking brother. He would piss me off. He just wanted to fight with me for whatever reason. And the crazy thing is, I won every fight we ever had. I always held back from giving him a can of ass-whooping because Islam taught me not to anger my parents. I always figured feeding him a knuckle sandwich would bring my parents a lot of stress and agony.

He REALLY hated the fact that I was always independent and would figure everything out on my own, like grabbing the right bus to NYC at the age of 7 or 8 by myself. That independence was something I developed because I was the oldest and was always being physically abused. I was left to deal with it all on my own. I had to figure out how to sort through my emotions. No one taught me. It took a long time for me to figure it out. Most people, not just Milton, frequently looked at my strengths and envied me for them. But they don't know how much turmoil I underwent to gain my strength. They didn't know I have two points on my spine that are painful to the touch. My back always feels like it needs to be cracked, even after it's cracked. There are painful points all over my ribs because the muscles around the area are spasmed. They don't understand that I had to reach deep within myself to find a way to cope with the constant pain.

They don't know the agony I've been going through and still do regarding bruxism or jaw clenching. The constant headaches as a result. Imagine holding your arm up for a prolonged time. How tired would your shoulder be? Exactly. Now imagine the same thing with my jaw. Because a disc is stuck in my jaw, it's technically always partially opened, and the muscles are always engaged to support it. It's exhausting, tiring, and achy. I still deal with this today. I've seen several orthodon-tists, including oral surgeons, who said repositioning the disc is pointless as it will get stuck again. I constantly live with jaw tension and back tension.

Part of the deal while working for Neuman was that I'd be the buyer for all the merchandise in his store. I would be in charge of bringing in products that people will actually buy and are profitable. I didn't get paid for it.

I'd visit fashion trade shows in different parts of the country while attending Rutgers University. These events were sporadic throughout the year. In turn, I took the corner where the cash register was and put some baseball caps up for sale. I used my own money that I had saved up. I had invested $15,000, my entire life savings, into inventory. The first day that they were available for sale, I didn't get one sale. Neither the second, third, nor sixth. I started panicking. I thought I just threw 15 grand in the dumpster. Finally, after a week, someone bought 6 caps. Boy, was I relieved! My daughter was under a year old at the time. I was freaking out because I was counting on the merchandise to sell through to pay our bills.

Things started to take off, and guess who took notice? You guessed it. Milton. He was sad. He was angry. He was crying. He was yelling. I thought to myself, "Good lord! Will you shut up? You hater ass bitch and do something with your life?" When I later had a clothing business in the area while working in Neuman's store, he would lament, "but why does he have two streams of income, and I only have one?" This came out of the mouth of a 21-year-old. He is so dependent on others; it's pathetic. He can't do anything for himself. He felt like he was entitled to everything without working for it. I later found out that Neuman would go grocery shopping for him and his wife.

When Sally went back to her country, I was 22 years old at the time. A year prior, I went to Lebanon with Neuman. It was only supposed to be for a couple of weeks. However, when I tried to leave, the airport called the military and told me I wasn't allowed to because my freaking father purposely didn't get me a visa. He wanted me to stay there. When I finally came up with a bullshit medical excuse to give to the army of Lebanon, they said, "you can leave, but you can never come back." I said, "done deal. You don't have to say that twice!"

When I arrived at Neuman's new home near West New York, NJ, I noticed a shiny new gray BMW 3 series parked in the garage. This starkly contrasted the old rented apartment where we had lived for 16 years. I looked out at my 12-year-old unreliable Nissan Maxima that wouldn't go into reverse. I looked back into the garage.

They bought it for him so he wouldn't complain that Sally had left the country - that was the excuse they gave me. Can you believe that BS? I didn't mind driving a 12-year-old Maxima, but I did mind when I had to parallel park, and it wouldn't grab reverse. I was old enough to support myself and get my own car, which I did. At that time, I got the latest Nissan Maxima. What was my obsession with Maximas? I don't know! I didn't know that much about cars back then.

5

BLAMED FOR BEING BORN

My mother's resentment towards me stemmed from blaming me for her pregnancy and the responsibilities that came with motherhood. She couldn't understand how I could remain cheerful despite having very little and envied me for it.

However, she was always open to receiving my favors, errands, and chores. You would think she'd let me live since I was buying cigarettes for her since I was 3 years old!

Later on, the demands grew. I had to shop for food, fold the laundry, work, and give her my daily earnings. My work was having my lemonade stand, shoveling snow, and raking leaves for many years; I bagged groceries at a local supermarket. I didn't mind working for my money. It just sucked that I had to give everything to her. The supermarket gig…99% of the time, I didn't want to go to work because the owners were assholes and weren't even paying me; I was collecting tips from customers! The nerve of these guys. Karma got them, and they were investigated for food stamp fraud and lost their business and the property. I'd get to the supermarket as early as 6 am and wait outside in the cold for the doors to open because whoever came first got to choose which cash register they worked at. I was superstitious, thinking one lane/register was more abundant than the other. The worst feeling is that after being forced to go to work, standing there all day bagging groceries and delivering them to those who requested them, I had to hand over all my earnings to Sally.

She said the money would be used to build a house in Lebanon. I was gullible and went along with it. A few years later, we ended up building that house, but clearly, I wasn't welcome in that house because I was met with brute force the few times I visited. I got a full-size shovel swung at my knees repeatedly, and all I could do was jump as high as I could to avoid the devastating strikes. Each time I jumped higher and higher until I got the sense to jump backward and get out of there!

I had no idea what peace and stability looked like up until that point. I was always in fight or flight mode. I was constantly insecure. That is because I was harshly criticized for every little thing I did. I lacked trust in what I was doing. I was always told to stand there and not say a single word - that if I talked, I would look lame. You have no idea how embarrassed and ashamed I was all my life. The one woman I thought would be my support was my hell on Earth.

What did I do to her, you might ask. Narcissists are psychotic and usually pick on one person to abuse and take out all their frustrations. She had no empathy toward me. When she charged at me with a big kitchen knife and slashed my wrist, she wasn't concerned; she was disappointed that it was just one slash on my wrist. All of this left me angry inside. It was like the movie "Groundhog Day." Every day was predictable - wake up, catch hell, and deal with it.

I was lactose intolerant back then, and she knew it. Guess what, though? She still fed me cereal and milk for breakfast every day, to which my stomach started gurgling on the way to school, and I had to run to the bathroom to relieve myself. Did I tell her? Yes, every day. Did she give a damn? Not one single concern was given. A brutal human being. She put up a facade in front of everyone that she was ultra-religious/conservative, but behind closed doors, she was a mean child abuser. As I said, all of this left me hurt and angry, and I behaved accordingly when I was out of the house.

6

FIGHTING WAS A LIFESTYLE

The mental, emotional, and physical abuse left me broken and lonely. As a result, I was problematic in school. My grades suffered, and my teachers and principal were always disciplining me. I was ready for battle at a moment's notice. In grammar school, I had physical fights before school started, at lunchtime, and after school (and sometimes during school). Yes, 3-4 fights a day! I remember walking on Bergenline Avenue in West New York, NJ (where we lived for 16 years), and a girl from school was walking with her mother, and she said hi to me, and I blurted out, "f you!" She was embarrassed. Years later, I was completely embarrassed at what I'd done, but I was only 5-6 years old at the time and angry at the world. Her name is Jackie R. I will never forget her name or kind gesture - no one had ever said hi to me the way she did - it was sincere. She didn't deserve that from me. I was lost in the wilderness with no compass or sense of direction. When I became an adult and recalled that day, tears rolled down my eyes for cursing at that girl like that. "What was I thinking," I asked myself. I felt so deflated, and I sincerely apologize for what I said.

If having 3-4 fights a day and being put in the corner or out in the hallway by your teachers for half the day wasn't enough, there was always that short evil mother of mine ready to pounce at me as soon as I got home. The abuse I endured was so severe that I often cried myself to sleep in the middle of the afternoon. At night, the fear of falling into a deep pit consumed me, making it difficult to drift off. I lacked effective communication skills and had no one to turn to for support. Despite my constant complaints to Neuman, he never took the time to listen and offer me help. For years, I believed Neuman to be a good man trapped in an unhealthy marriage, but after four decades, I realized that he was a manipulative narcissist who used silence and niceness (politics) to control others.

He gaslit me on numerous occasions, even until this year. I will explain later in the book how he was the biggest betrayal of my life. This man is generally respected by many and portrays an image of himself as a model citizen/human being. However, behind closed doors - apart from paying the rent ($600/month), food (we ate the same thing for 3 days in a row), and clothes (barely had any) - he never sat with me and corrected any of my behaviors - he never guided me to be a man - he never even taught me how to shave. He opted to hang out with friends, at night and play cards instead of helping me grow into an independent man. I'm not saying he shouldn't have any fun. And I'm grateful he provided a roof over our heads and put food on the table.

Do I blame Neuman? I used to cut him and Sally slack

because they had me so young, and they came to America with nothing. That was my thinking back then, but when I became a parent, I stopped making excuses for them. Nevertheless, between the two, I gravitated towards Neuman more just because he didn't hit me, criticize me, or reprimand me. I erroneously assumed that his quiet demeanor meant he was a good person. Now, I don't believe anyone is 100% bad. Both parents had good in them, but the bad outweighed the good.

Because I gravitated toward Neuman, I wanted to be around him. So, at 7-8 years old, I started taking the bus from West New York, NJ, to Washington Heights, NY, with no Google Maps, Waze, or GPS. All I knew was to read the destination on the bus' destination sign, flag it down, hop on, and pay the fare. When I got to the bus terminal, I would look for the signs regarding which street I wanted to walk onto. It is incredible that I wasn't hurt or kidnapped all those times I went to NY alone. I encountered a lot of mentally ill people and drug addicts. The kicker is both of my parents knew I was doing this, and they didn't bar me from doing so.

All I wanted was a father who would teach me how to play sports, take me on joy rides, teach me, and protect me - but I didn't get any of those. It was the same ole story. Dad comes home after work; Sally is waiting by the door; she starts berating him; he walks out the door immediately, only to come home at 1 am, go straight to his mattress, and fall asleep (they didn't sleep in the same bed). This was the daily pattern - hence why I only saw Neuman when he was asleep as I went to the bathroom in the middle of the night. He and I slept on the floor in the same room while my spoiled, bratty brother, Milton, slept between us on a full-size bed. I slept on the floor for 16 years on the same mattress. So many tears seeped through that mattress. I am grateful for that mattress as it was my only source of comfort - even if it was on the floor.

7

BATTLING HEALTH ISSUES

I can't remember when I was just happy and pain-free. Unfortunately for me, Sally smoked heavily during my pregnancy. This caused me a lot of issues with my ear, lungs, and allergies, and it had a negative effect on my nerves. Besides getting bullied in school (I will give more details in this book) and being physically/emotionally/mentally abused at home, I had to deal with excruciating ear pain, which left me lying on the couch, moaning in agony for years. I suffered from asthma to the point I needed to be sent to the ER. I often thought it was my time to go and that there was no way I could take another breath in!

My allergies were so bad, the mere thought of dust would shock my body and swell up my eyes. Because my allergies were affecting me so much, I saw an allergy doctor. I would get approximately 5 allergy injections in each arm every week. At the time, it only cost $30 for a visit (we had no health insurance).

Thirty dollars is a small price to pay, so your child doesn't have to suffer anymore. Wouldn't you agree? People were earning a decent living back then but with fewer expenses. But guess what? Sally and Milton blamed me for mishandling the family's finances by visiting this doctor. They said I was causing the family to go bankrupt. I believed them, but my math senses told me it didn't make sense. Nevertheless, I was hurt by these words.

I can't tell you how I would have murdered Sally and Milton. I thought long and hard about it, and there are many exhilarating ways to see them go. My mother would curse me day and night. She had me confused. I'd see her do her salaat (Islamic prayer), yet at the end, she made a du'a (asking Allah/God for things you want or need after prayer); she would start asking God to destroy me, destroy her siblings and to take my uncle's money away and to give it to her instead.

So many times, I would run to the corded phone while she was hitting me so I could call the police to help me, but she would rip the phone off the wall and disconnect the line from the phone jack. And I would feel deflated and helpless; it was very hard, and I had no one on my side. Milton was aggravating me daily, and my mother made me her punching bag to vent her frustrations.

8

BECOMING INFAMOUS

*E*veryone knew me in West New York, NJ. I became a mini-celebrity when in first or second grade, the teacher went around the classroom asking each student to give her a word that starts with the letter she gave them. So it started with A, then B, then C, and finally it was my turn, and my letter was F. So my teacher asked me, "what word starts with the letter F?" To which I blurted out, "f*ck!"

And the crowd went wild!! I didn't intend to, but I was just being honest. That was the first word that came to mind. The kids were joyous and filled with laughter. They all became my friends. My mother's friends laughed about it too and told me to tell the teacher "fruit" next time. I agreed with them but knew the teacher wouldn't ask us again because we had finished that lesson. So the joke was on them.

I was in first or second grade, and the other students and I were outside witnessing a fight. They were in the school's yard, and we were on the other side of the tall gate. Look who it was!

My second cousin. And he wasn't doing too well. The other kid was kicking his ass and smothering him. I started thinking about what I could do to help him. I spotted a broomstick a few feet away. I grabbed it off the floor and rolled it under the gate for him. I yelled out, "take the stick and hit him!"

And the crowd went wild again. The kids adored me. I was a legend from that day on. "Chris is crazy!" That's what the kids would chant. Everyone talked about it till my high school days. I got my respect that way. Unfortunately, I was hurt at home. And hurt people hurt people. Hurt people don't understand when someone is joking around. Because I mistook jokes as insults, I ended up in many unnecessary fights, costing me all those friends I gained.

Hurt people can't take anymore, so they're ready to fight. At least I was. I had lots of school fights. I fought practically every single student. There wasn't anyone left to fight, so I had to start the process of fighting everyone all over again for a 2nd time and a 3rd time, etc.

The kids saw there was something off about me. They didn't know I was autistic. No one did. They also didn't know I had ADHD. And they didn't know I was being violently abused at home. They noticed how I would always take things to heart and give them a reaction. So, they would constantly tease and bully me as a result. They knew they'd get a reaction out of me. These were my so-called "friends." They hurt me. I was embarrassed about my life. Did I continue to hang out with those kids? Yes. Why? Because it was still better than "home," and I needed an escape. It's not like I can go to the neighboring town and start making new friends there. Besides, hurt people hurt people. So, no matter where I would've gone, it would have played out the same way. I understand that now.

As early as I can remember, I always had pronounced and profound fear and anxiety in me throughout a great deal of my life. I was caught in a loop. I'd be in fear, and something would manifest that would keep me in fear. That was the cause of my hell. Many nights I would fear falling asleep because I had the feeling I would fall hundreds of feet into a dark pit. The thing that balanced out my fears was my fun, loving and bold heart.

One of the fears I used to have was Sally not picking me up from school when I wasn't feeling well. It was a crapshoot, but I'd go to the nurse's office, and the nurse would call Sally to pick me up. 99% of the time, she would yell at me over the phone and tell me to finish the day even though I had an upset stomach or a bad headache because I was getting sick. I can't explain how I thought all this was normal. I thought other kids had mothers like mine until I started visiting my friends' homes. No. Other mothers weren't like her at all. The complete opposite!

9

SURROUNDED BY NARCISSISTS

*I*t pains me to acknowledge that my mother was a deeply troubled individual. She exhibited textbook narcissistic behavior, a term that may be overused but, sadly, is all too common. While I could have followed in her footsteps, I consciously decided to take a different path. I chose to live my life with authenticity, honesty, and integrity, even when it seemed like those around me were not. I was determined to find a better way to live a life that aligned with my values and beliefs.

It is what it is. That was my fate. To be abused by several narcissists: Sally, Neuman, Milton, and Zina. *And* to be bullied by dozens of kids and disrespected by many adults. To protect my body against the belt whoopings and fight off every kid with something slick to say. If "all my life, I've been struggling" was a person, that would be me. People often look at me and think I was handed everything. There's no way anyone can still be loving, caring, and positive after all I've gone through. Logically, their brain says, "he's spoiled." Another reason is I'm 43 years old, but I look like I'm 23 years old, according to many. Many say there's no way I went through all that and look the way I do.

The truth is, I looked 43 years old at 30 years old. God worked many miracles in my life, and when I came across The Holy Quran, I came across a passage that states that there is light and guidance in The Holy Bible. So, I became interested in the teachings of the Bible and, of course, most importantly, The Holy Father, Jesus Christ, and the Holy Spirit. Once I accepted Christ as Lord and Son of God, the miracles accelerated. At the age of 42, after understanding who Christ is, I started healing from all my childhood traumas and the ongoing divorce (at the time of this writing). He guided me on what to do step by step every moment of the day. How to eat, how to workout, how to carry myself, how to speak, how to live, how to sleep, how to wash my face, how to use my intuition, how to be calm and relaxed in any situation, and how to heal myself with my thoughts - amongst many other things. Just about the same time, he healed me from severe fibromyalgia. Above all, God warned me, "remain humble, or I'll take it all away from you!" I complied without question.

God elevated me in my darkest time. I had just left my wife of 20 years due to her aggressive (covert) narcissistic behavior causing me lots of mental distress - to the point where I had brain fog, very poor concentration, very poor memory, inability to make decisions, inability to have a conversation with anyone, inability to create, and unable to give myself the self-care I deserved. She purposely started drama or brought drama into our lives. There was a period when I couldn't even walk!

Emotional abuse is so misunderstood and underrated. People chalk it off like it's wuss talk. They don't understand that it's worse than physical abuse!!! I'm not the world heavyweight boxing champ, but even he would confirm what I'm saying if he had undergone emotional abuse by a sneaky evil covert narcissist who has a severe mental illness and is just enamored with the idea of having total dominant control over everyone in her life.

My two main abusers were Sally and Zina. Both appeared as religious and pious women in their community, a village in South Lebanon. Sally had to persuade the community of her piousness because her parents weren't sayyids (people who claim to be descendants of Prophet Muhammad, which the community blindly respected just for that fact). On the other hand, Zina came from a family who claimed to be sayyids. Because of this and her father's family image of being religious, everyone assumed Zina was also pious and religious. Narcissists *love* to portray themselves as perfect to the outside world, but they always have one person they abuse. I knew who they (Sally and Zina) were. These weren't godly women. They were great bullshitters. Smooth talkers. Evil demons. They'll tell you whatever you want to hear as long as you validate them and stroke their egos. My mother vented by giving me a right hook to my chin. Luckily, she never knocked me out or broke one of my teeth, but it still hurt because it would be spontaneous and come out of nowhere. I think she might be the only one to give Floyd Mayweather a loss if she could just put enough power into that speedy punch. He'd be out early in round one.

The people around me loved the drama. They couldn't get enough of it. As if our family didn't have enough drama, Sally needed to know everyone else's drama - mainly the people of her village in Lebanon, including her family. She had to share the bad news with me, of course. I didn't understand how I might have been going through all this. I was very good at math, and I loved statistics as well. I would ponder on the possibility of all the events in my life lining up so horribly. How can that be? I'd understand if I dealt with just an abusive mother but all this other stuff too? Come on; I thought this had to be a prank by the universe. God is messing with my head. Surely this can't be real. Oh my God, it is! Holy shit, how do I get out of this? Think. Think! *starts thinking of ways to kill himself*

I can't tell you the number of times I thought of suicide. I thought about it all day, every day. I never flat-out admitted it to Sally or Zina, but I always said, "screw this life. I wish I were gone. I wish God would kill me already." I was only a child when the thoughts started right around 9 years old. At that age, I already knew about Allah and how suicide was a major sin that would send me straight to hell. Allah is absolutely correct! You see, when you have thoughts of suicide, your life becomes a living hell. Everything manifests so negatively that it perpetuates the thoughts of suicide and even amplifies them. I didn't understand this back then. I thought hell was a place you went to after you died, according to Islam. The truth is heaven and hell exist now. To get to heaven, you need to allow Christ (Christ consciousness) to guide you. No man can guide you. Only a higher consciousness, one that is much more knowledgeable than any human being, can guide you to the pearly white gates of heaven. There's too much information you need for your journey, and God gives it to you in the most efficient and enjoyable way possible through your inner voice, intuition, and thoughts.

I am extremely grateful now for all of my past. I see clearly now everything had to happen that way for me to become who I am today. The person I am today is someone my inner child not only admires, loves, and respects but is shocked at who we've become! From a place where we once wished for death to end our pain, we now cherish every moment of every day. This includes all the different versions of myself throughout the years. When I reminisce about past events, my mind shifts to that particular time and brings out that version of me. While I've learned to manage this tendency, as some try to use my past against me, I will no longer allow anyone to tear me down. I know who I am now; no one can convince me otherwise. My sense of self is unwavering, and I am firmly rooted in my identity.

I thought of how I'd commit suicide, but then I remembered Allah forbade it. So, I obliged. I can't say I was ever as detailed with my dream revenge on my abusers. In that sense, they got off easy. I just let God handle the situation. After the big betrayal I'll describe later in the book, God ordered me not to have any negative thoughts about them. Asked me not to seek revenge. He said, "relax, be at peace. I am fighting your battles. I am hitting them harder than you can ever hit them. Just forgive them and be joyous." This was told to me over and over and over after I left Zina. What great advice from the Most High! How you feel dictates how you're going to live. If I didn't release those negative emotions, I would go to hell again, which is the lower frequency. Instead, He wanted me to elevate to the higher frequencies and stay there while He handled the situation on my behalf. After all, I was the one betrayed after showing the utmost love, respect, and support whenever requested or needed to those around me.

Due to my loving nature, some think it's a facade until they really find out. Others think, "he's stupid." But see, I'm playing chess, and they're playing checkers. They're only thinking of one move. I was able to see several moves ahead. I could see how my love was coming back to me in the form of rewards and protection. I can feel how great I felt by keeping it real with God and trying to follow the rules.

My my my, I finally understood why people are so enthusiastic about Christ and the Bible. My faith gave me an unshakable knowledge that sustained me through unimaginably difficult times. God's love permeated my body, mind, and soul and helped me endure endless struggles. Love has been a soothing and transformative force, quenching the flames of anger and regret within me. It has enabled me to persevere in the face of adversity.

You might ask, "hold up a minute; is Chris Muslim or Christian?" The answer is both. I'm an omnist. I understand them both as well as Judaism (the gist), Hinduism, Buddhism, etc...Of course, some will say you can't do that and I once thought like that too. However, I understand how everything is true and related. This is a whole topic I can write a book on.

10

PERMANENT STATE OF FEAR

*B*oth of my children are honor roll students, and my daughter graduated high school as the salutatorian of her class. She got a full ride to NYU, majoring in chemistry. I know for a fact that my children would not be so successful in school if I treated them the same way my mother did, and I'm grateful for that. My daughter is a certified genius - so brilliant! All of her teachers love her. She would have daily phone conversations at home with her chemistry teacher as well as other teachers. That speaks volumes.

My mother didn't like that I was always happy and had a vibe that I was satisfied with being alive with what little I had. This was because, as she saw things, everything was horrible. My parents' arrival in the United States at such an early age was challenging. I can't imagine traveling at such a young age with hardly any money to my name. I truly get it and commend them for taking that leap, but it was a lot easier than dealing with the Lebanese Civil War. In my eyes, I would be grateful that I escaped that hell hole and arrived in the land of opportunities.

One can say she had no guidance, but for those who know, you get guidance by intending to get guidance. When a human has no desire or intention for guidance, the person isn't going to receive it. Even without the internet, the person would still receive all the guidance they needed. So, her heart wasn't in the right place. Where was it? It was in the material world. Money. That was her number one top priority. Money. I get it. But where's the faith? She prayed 5 times a day but had no faith that God would provide tomorrow's needs. Her faith was so weak that she would curse God day and night. She would growl at me, "damn your God! Damn your lord! Damn the skies! Damn your religion!" It would terrify me. It would send chills up and down my spine. It would make the hairs on my arms stand. I would think to myself, "what a freaking hypocrite my mother is." I would ask her, "why do you curse God but also do your salaat (Islamic prayer)?" To which she had no reply except for, "shut the hell up before I get the belt and whoop your behind." She hated me for calling her out on all her BS. Sure, I paid the price for it with belt marks on my body, but I didn't care. I wanted to speak the truth regardless of the consequences.

I didn't know where the nearest foster home was, so I was stuck at 62nd street and Bergenline Avenue in West New York, NJ. My life was so miserable all I could do was look out the window at the busy main street, Bergenline Ave, and space out while looking at the bustling traffic. I would escape my reality that way. I had no drugs or alcohol to escape. All I had was my imagination.

I was in a very dark place from early childhood. Unfortunately for me, my very own mother did what was forbidden in Islam, the very religion she claimed to be so devoted to. She went to tarot card readers and witch doctors. She looked into my destiny and wanted to "steal it." So, she hexed me. I remember clearly the day she brought this little booklet tucked in hosiery material and pinned to my shirt sleeve. She told me it was for good luck, but I later discovered it was a hex she had attached to me.

I ended up fracturing my arm 5 times. I was always lost and confused, and in poor health. The spell was meant to make me not see my life purpose.

This can't be all there is, God. Every day, I'd ask, "is it, God?" Please God. Till one day in my adulthood, when the suffering continued, I pondered on God Himself. Wondering what it was like to be Him. My mind started thinking, and I realized, "damn, God has to see all that (evil, violence, murders, rapes, etc.), and I'm over here complaining about my life?" I started to feel sorry for God. I started thinking. "Wow, my life isn't actually that bad compared to God's." Somehow, it made it feel better, the pain, that is. Can you imagine the loneliness of a broken human being with no family and the only genuine friend he ever had who passed away at 15? A human filled with misery was feeling sorry for God? God heals through thoughts and words. He helped me put my life in perspective to God's life.

I kept pushing through life. Kept waking up and living and handling what came my way. What choice did I have? I can't commit suicide. I can't fight back or contact the police or child services (I didn't even know they existed). I was forced to keep living. Besides being forbidden, I didn't commit suicide because I feared I would survive and be in a much worse state than before the attempt. Also, a part of me was scared of death. I didn't have anyone I could go to and get advice from, so I had to talk to myself, console myself, and be my own parent. I had to talk to myself in a motherly and gentle way.

I can't tell you I remember when the clenching of my jaw started. It could have been around 5 years old. It was so spasmed that whenever my mouth was closed, it would feel like my jaw was constantly moving in a clockwise movement, then counterclockwise. My muscles would keep doing this even though the muscles were exhausted from the continuous movement. For the longest, I didn't know it was my jaw being affected. I thought this movement was coming from inside my head. That's how lost and confused I was! My jaw never rested, and the clenching made me even more pissed and angry. I wanted to destroy everything around me!

For those who have experienced TMJ or TMD, you know what I'm talking about. Chances are you didn't have it chronically. Meaning you had it for some time, and it went away via therapy or on its own. My situation was chronic. It was day and night. Twenty-four hours a day, 365 days a year. Every single day of my life. My jaw is still clenched to this day. That's 38 years of jaw-clenching! Not a second passed without my awareness of the tightness, movement, and pain; It drove me insane. It affected my speech because I could never open and close my mouth with proper speed or opening. Therefore, I'd trip over my words a lot.

It's a miracle that after dealing with this for nearly 40 years, I can still be loving, caring, and cheerful - let alone everything else I've mentioned in this book. Take it from me, not many would even get out of bed. If you don't have a healthy positive mindset, it tends to break you down mentally and emotionally because nothing can be done to stop it, and it's occurring in your head in a place where you chew and speak. It's a part of your self-image. The pain, that is.

Had I known the power of the word as a child, I would have avoided the whole traumatic hell that I went through. Words make up our feelings. I didn't know that back then. I would have known that being afraid due to continuous abuse and punishment was causing me to be in fear and creating more scenarios to be fearful of. Sally caused me to remain fearful, and Neuman allowed it to continue for decades. She got a high off of that. She thrived off negative energy like in the movie "Monsters, Inc." To see me in a broken, crying state, laying on the floor, made her feel superior and worthy. In her sick twisted mind, she thought she was doing the right thing.

Neuman would chalk it off to her being crazy. He would give her a pass. "You know your mother. She has no mind. She doesn't mean it. You think a real mother would hurt you?" And I would facepalm myself. My relationship with Neuman was complicated. While I resented him for not stepping in to protect me from the abuse, I also had positive feelings towards him as he was the better parent of the two. Unlike Sally, who would often cause drama with her yelling and cussing, Neuman was more stable and well-liked by others. As a result, I naturally gravitated toward him and preferred spending time with him. It stayed like that for just over 4 decades. Until one day, it was apparent to me. He really didn't like me. He just wanted to keep me around as a resource. He shot down many of my business ideas because he wanted to be seen by the family as the alpha and the successful one.

I remember bringing him to my warehouse where I operated my multi-million dollar business. I showed him the equipment I bought to process orders accurately and efficiently and the custom software I designed with a programmer to process orders paperless with 100% accuracy. He did not react - no emotion. I could feel his jealousy. Imagine not being proud of your son for his success, even after all he went through. If that were my son, Hunter, I would've been so proud of him, and I would have gone to his company's website and purchased $1,000 worth of products to support him, and then I would tell him to keep the products so he can sell them.

11

VICTIM OF DARK FORCES

I'm not the one to shy from saying or writing about things that are not deemed scientific or at least common knowledge. What I'm about to discuss is not foreign to many people. I'm talking about black magic, voodoo, tarot card readers, psychics, and that sort of stuff. As the Bible states, "and the word was God." Words are powerful beyond belief. Unfortunately, some people use their words and intentions for evil via black magic, voodoo, hoodoo, etc. Not all magic and voodoo are bad, but people purposely misuse them for evil.

Sally had already known through the Quran that Allah prohibits Muslims from going to tarot card readers, psychics, and witch doctors. She wanted to know what her fate was. She is a very materialistic woman. She had readings done on me when I was around 5 years old. When she learned my fate, she went to a witch doctor and wrote spells in a tiny booklet and always had it pinned to my shirt.

I was tortured as a child. I had a really bad ear infection that dissolved one of my hearing bones and completely disintegrated my ear drum and would continuously (for over a decade) discharge a disgusting yellow and smelly substance that would leak out while standing, seated, or lying down. I had tremendous pain and wishy-washy sounds and pressure all day long for many years.

I had severe asthma and allergies. I fractured the same arm 5 times. I couldn't go to most shops because the dust would kill me. My eyes would swell up, my nose would start dripping, and I'd sneeze non-stop. My eyes would tear up and swell up like balloons.

It's funny how the decades of health issues and my agony could be summed up so simply. It's too bad I can't upload my memories for you to download and experience what I went through. Even having allergies, Sally would smoke cigarettes all day inside our apartment. Neuman would have to paint the walls more than the average non-smoker would. He'd paint them crispy white, and the walls would become a dingy yellow within a few months. He, too, would smoke inside the house. I've had doctors tell me that my ear issues and allergies stem from the fact that my mother smoked while pregnant with me and continued to do so throughout my entire stay with her until the end of the age of 17, when I went away for college.

I'd still come back on some weekends and holidays and experience the smoke, but at least it wasn't all day every day. I picked up the smoking habit in college because I thought it was normal since my parents both smoked. I felt like I was meant to smoke like them. Lucky for me, I was able to quit even though I was smoking 2-3 packs of Marlboro reds every day 3 years after I picked up the bad habit.

I got lots of colds and flu. It was suspiciously frequent. All that was happening seemed bizarre and really unlucky. I was in agony all day due to my health and being physically, emotionally, and mentally abused at home and bullied consistently outside by many kids and disrespected by adults too. I was living in hell without the flames. But I felt like the flames were inside me due to all of this. I would look at other happy kids; their moms were cool and loving towards them, and I'd wonder how come? Is this my fault? Did I do something to deserve all of this? How come I don't have 1 true friend besides my one cousin who was disabled and had to use crutches to walk? (I named my son after him, who also had a walking disability - who also has a heart of gold like my cousin).

Many spells were done on me, such as confusion, death, isolation, humiliation, pain, and indecisiveness, amongst a few others. Sally's logic was that she could steal whatever my fate was by breaking me down and having me discarded (dead). I don't think Islam approves of any of this (sarcasm).

She ended up paying with her health for all of this. Yes, she, too, had ear trouble and required surgery. She got one of her kidneys stolen in Lebanon during a procedure that had nothing to do with her kidneys. She later developed a tumor on her one remaining kidney and had to get operated on. She's now living in constant agony and fear, worried about her last kidney failing or needing another surgery.

She broke down my psyche. I was so embarrassed to face myself. "Look what I've become." I felt degraded. I felt like a prostitute being violated and thrown to the curb like a candy wrapper. I started developing nice guy syndrome because I was tapped out. I didn't want any more confrontations, as I was

49

already overwhelmed. Little did I know, being nice caused me more pain than I was trying to avoid. And the nice guy syndrome was perpetuated by the teachings of Islam, which encourages you to treat everyone nicely. But that's BS. But I do see Allah's test. I'm sure He intended to see if I'd persevere and continue having love (God) in my heart after all the abuse and mistreatment. I did. I was hanging on to him for dear life, like a person hanging off a cliff with one hand only.

How do I know she went to tarot card readers? Well, she actually took me a few times. But at that time, I didn't know what exactly was going on. It wasn't till decades later that I found out the details.

She wasn't the only one who's done black magic on me. A cousin of mine once "gifted" me a prayer laminated on a 3 x 2" paper. I put it in my wallet and forgot about it. Years later, I was organizing my wallet (yes, I know that's a long time), and I looked at it again and put it back in the wallet as I thought it was some protection prayer.

While studying Islam closely, I came across the topic of black magic and jinns. One of the Muslim sheikhs said that the way people do black magic with these so-called prayers is they throw in a particular letter randomly into the prayer, and the prayer is meant to look Arabic, but if you pay close attention, it's not Arabic or any of the languages using a similar script. And the letter they toss into the prayer is called "Ain" in Arabic, which is the first letter in the name "Ali." When I learned this, I remembered the prayer my cousin gave me and started to read it as I picked up Arabic one summer in Lebanon during summer vacation. Lo and behold! This bastard had given me a curse/hex! I was fuming! I never saw him again because, for sure, I would have beaten him into a bloody pulp.

I prayed to God to please not let me see that douchebag again because I would turn his flesh into minced meat with my bare hands. The agony he caused me was HELL. And if that wasn't enough, Zina and her mother were casting spells on me too. My health deteriorated so much that I developed Fibromyalgia. This horrific condition leaves you with wide-spread body pain, muscle stiffness, and spasms, brain fog, memory impairment, judgment impairment, extreme chronic fatigue, anxiety, depression, insomnia, inability to walk for months, inability to speak or form coherent sentences, back-aches, migraines, and more. My memory was so terrible I couldn't carry on a conversation because I would forget what I just said and ask the person, "wait, what did I just say?" I didn't know at the time that I was being attacked by the woman I thought was my other half. Unfortunately for me, she had unhealed childhood trauma and needed control of everyone, including myself and our children. The spells she cast were to keep me thinking of her, staying at home, being mind controlled, illusions, confusion, death, isolation and who knows what else. It worked for nearly 2 decades.

12

WITCHCRAFT UNCOVERED

*L*ooking back on those days, I realize now that they all thought they could get away with their cruel and abusive behavior and that I'd never find out. But I knew deep down that I couldn't compromise my ethics, manners, and morals, even when it seemed nobody else cared about such things. Despite the difficulties, I delved deep into Islam, and God led me to explore other faiths and philosophies, which helped me to see the truth of what had been done to me. It was when I began to truly acknowledge Christ and reflect on his teachings that God started to protect me from the spells of these people. Their tactics stopped working, and it began to backfire on them. My health, which had been plagued by fibromyalgia, improved tremendously. In fact, I'm now the healthiest I've ever been, with a great athletic physique that I achieved at the age of 42. But it wasn't just my physical health that improved. My decision-making ability returned with greater force, and I could converse and joke with others better. All of this is because I was finally able to escape the grip of my narcissistic abusers.

It pained me so much that my mother would abuse and have spells done on me. It's so sad that your own family would want to sacrifice you. There was no remorse. No love. No compassion. No feeling. No warmth. She and Zina were vicious animals.

I couldn't believe my mother would betray me. I couldn't believe the woman I married and treated like gold would backstab me the way she did. These women broke me down and took my self-esteem and confidence away. They left me for dead and would still kick me even when I was already down.

How could my own mother do this to me? Despite doing every chore she asked of me, going to the store daily for cigarettes and groceries, and folding the laundry, I still couldn't understand why she treated me so poorly. Her behavior shattered my confidence and made it difficult to trust anyone, leading to numerous fistfights and dark days that only worsened with time. I treated Zina better than her own parents treated her, and she told me so. Gave her lots of useful advice and helped her navigate many difficult times. I taught her how to think outside the box. I showed her how to look at the world differently than anyone else would. She always made it seem like everything was perfectly fine between us. Still, deep down, she was envious of me and could not stand that I got more attention than her without even trying, while she had to practically do jumping jacks for anyone to look her way. She wanted my life.

She couldn't believe I chose to be with her because I could be with prettier women. I always told her she was beautiful, but she didn't believe me and always accused me of cheating on her despite being home most of the time, save for the 5-10 minutes I went to the post office to drop off packages which she packed herself. This, I found to be a red flag. The fact that I was home the whole time and being accused of cheating while she was out supposedly doing things for our disabled son's school and medical needs - only God and her know the real truth. The cheating projections speak volumes.

She would spend a lot of time in the bathroom. My best guess is that she was texting other men and having phone conversations with them because she'd turn on the faucet for prolonged periods. She'd also spend a long time in her car in the driveway, texting away. Sometimes she'd be brutally feisty with me for no reason, which is a sign of cheating. That marriage opened my eyes.

When I moved to my apartment after I left Zina, I was friendly with the neighbors. I would make small talk and push the button for their floor in the elevator, something I learned from some of the other neighbors. What good did that do? They end up becoming full of themselves. "Oh, Chris pushed the elevator button for me and talked to me. I must be better than him." That's what I can read from their faces and attitudes. Screw that. I don't even give most people eye contact or acknowledgment anymore. I walk into the elevator and won't even acknowledge the person already there. Some might say, "but Chris, you're overthinking this." No, trust me, I'm not. As I physically, mentally, and emotionally evolved during the 12 months I've been here, people took notice and became intimidated and less friendly toward me. So I pulled back all of my energy. Even the concierge started acting funny toward me. One of them started becoming passive-aggressive toward me. To which I eventually lashed out at him. I let him know that I'm not one to play with. I told him I better not catch him giving me passive aggressiveness, and he better always show me respect. I humiliated him. After that, he started calling me "sir", treating me respectfully, and asking me how my day was going.

I'm grateful for my stay here in this building because there are over 200 apartments, giving me a large sample of people to engage with. I saw people for who they were. I erroneously thought people in a higher tax bracket were more "human." Boy, was I wrong. Many people in the higher tax bracket have lots of envy and are always comparing themselves to others. They think they are vastly wealthy, like Elon Musk or Jeff Bezos. There's a guy here who drives a Rolls Royce. He wonders why I get a lot of attention from all the neighbors and he doesn't. In the summer, while we were at the pool, he had to give everyone watermelon and food just for them to be friends with him.Meanwhile, I didn't have to do anything but sunbathe. He always calls my name when he sees me in the lobby and comes over to talk. He wants to know how I attract people. So he talks to me. He tries to get me to put him on a pedestal by telling me about his finances and properties, how he doesn't like it here, and wants to move to Long Island to a much better place. Knowing he was showing off, I asked, "how long will the commute be?" He said, "an hour and a half." And I said, "ouch! No way, that's not worth it. I'd rather have my time." And I can tell on his face that that upset him. He tried to get me to be jealous of his possessions, and I shot him down with that response. I had him rethinking his whole plan. His face said it all.

One guy from concierge in my building was initially outgoing and hyper, but he noticed that people would gravitate towards me for no apparent reason. This made him uncomfortable as he wanted to be popular too. I, on the other hand, do not crave attention or validation through small talk. The concierge began to emulate my reserved demeanor, thinking that's what attracted people to me, but he missed the point. It's my energy that draws people in - my knowledge, creativity, boldness, morals, heart, individuality, and scars all contribute to the unique aura that people are drawn to.

Nowadays, I walk from my apartment to the parking garage faster without making eye contact with most people. I just look elsewhere. Why? As I said, people start to resent me after a while. I'm tired of the bullshit. People just want validation. Once I give it to them, they act like they just orgasmed. And you know how it goes when a person orgasms. "The money for the cab is on the table." So, I no longer give people any validation. Is it petty of me? Depends on who you ask. I'm not like this with everyone. Just the people from this demographic. It's hilarious how some people act like they're wealthy when apartments in this building rent for $2300 a month, which is the average going rate in the area, including run-down homes.

The people that work at the Chipotle I frequent seem more highly vibrational than those who live in my building. I've gone to this one location for nearly a year, 5-7 times a week. They've always been consistent and never switched up on me. (Of course, they get used to you because they see you daily, but that's normal). They're always in a happier mood and are happy to see me, and they talk to me every time I go there with no jealousy. They even give me 50% off about 3 days a week.

Whoever hires at that Chipotle location knows how to pick the right people. So, I say that to say that I don't avoid all people - just the egotistical and materialistic ones who think they're better than everyone because they earn more than the average.

FORCED TO KEEP MY MOUTH CLOSED

*P*art of my health woes was the inability to breathe through my nose. I had enlarged adenoids, but I didn't know till I was 20 years old. The only way I could breathe was to keep my mouth open and breathe that way. As you can imagine, with my severe allergies, breathing through my mouth caused me to have strong asthma attacks.

My mother didn't like how I was breathing. That's how much this lady couldn't stand me. She was CONSTANTLY on my ass about keeping my mouth closed. She would make a fist and uppercut my jaw shut. I would hear my teeth bang against each other, which would hurt. She was relentless with this. She would not let a single minute slip by with my mouth open. I didn't know how to shut my mouth properly. I had my top teeth resting directly on my bottom teeth, which I found out 37 years later, causes/accentuates bruxism. This resulted in severe bruxism. I would unknowingly clench my jaw tight because of this bad habit. I also didn't know that one should rest his/her tongue on the roof of the mouth and keep the lips together only - not the top and bottom teeth. I didn't know till I was almost 43 that I was supposed to keep my back teeth from touching.

My mother would never let it go. Every single day it was the same crap about keeping my mouth closed. I would tell her I couldn't breathe through my nose. She saw how big my adenoids were when the surgeon removed them. Did she think to apologize and say, "I'm sorry dear, I should've believed you? I shouldn't have been so hard on you?" No. Her ego would never allow it. Just imagine you're sitting at the dinner table, and as soon as she catches a glimpse of me, "CLOSE YOUR MOUTH!" Like a raging nazi bitch. Tens of times a day! For over a decade straight!

You have no idea what it was like to have your jaw locked shut, and your muscles spasmed up while your jaw made constant circular and vibrating motions all day. The clenching of my teeth or bruxism resulted in speech problems. The school wasn't aware I was clenching, but they put me in speech therapy. I felt like I was a captive. Imagine flexing a muscle for 43 years!!

I'm writing this chapter at a local Starbucks and holding back tears. Whenever I think I'm immune to my story, I shed more tears. But this isn't going to be a complete sob story. I'm going to tell you how I conquered all of this. One day, I looked in the mirror, beat my chest like an 800 lb gorilla, and said assertively, "THANK YOU!" I strongly beat my chest quickly two times and said aggressively, "IT ONLY MADE US STRONGER!" Us being the different versions of me.

I would recall other events and keep looking in the mirror like a warrior, beating my chest and repeating, "THANK YOU!

IT ONLY MADE US STRONGER!" My eyes would get slightly watery, and I would hold back the tears until, FINALLY, I overcame the trauma. I rationalized that what I went through was beneficial and for my own good. Once I saw it that way, I conquered the ugly past.

14

PEOPLE PLEASING

*B*ecause my mother would take her love away from me, I developed a habit of people-pleasing. I did this subconsciously. I erroneously thought if I did what people wanted (for the most part), they'd like me. Nothing could be further from the truth. To make matters worse, I was a devout Muslim, and that meant I had to be nice to people. So, it was a double whammy. It was hell! An abusive mother, an a-hole brother, fake bullying friends, a neglectful father, and bruxism, and I'm out in the world getting crapped on by people due to my niceness. I didn't care though. I wanted to keep it 100% authentic with God. I kept treating people with respect.

I had lots of love in me even though my mother and father never showed me love. I doubt they knew how to love. And they didn't love themselves, so how can they love me? But I didn't know all this back then. I felt like a loser. I lost all my confidence. I was embarrassed. I would pray no one ever found out what was happening in my life because it was so sad and pathetic.

I had to be strong as a little boy. After the beatings and berating, I would sit alone in a corner and cry until I had no more tears left. I had nobody to talk to. No therapist. No one at school. No friends. No family members. I just had to sit there and take it. Day in, day out, day in, day out, day in, day out. Despite my being an adult, she struck me because she was a coward who knew I would never retaliate.

So many times, I just wanted to go full ape on her. But I was reminded of Allah. I didn't care that it wasn't cool to hit a woman. I cared that God didn't approve. If God had approved while man didn't, I would have steamrolled her. So, I kept my cool and kept my hands to myself. I developed a habit of always overextending myself. I would do the most to appease my parents, and they both looked at me with disgust - not appreciation.

Neuman never complimented me. After being released from the hospital in 2020 with a fractured arm, sprained shoulder, and bruised hip, I started working out a few months later - in March 2021. My arm and shoulder haven't healed yet. It probably healed less than 5% in a span of four months. I started doing burpees to get out of my depression and gain some energy. I was completely depleted and unmotivated due to the immense stress my covert narcissistic ex-wife brought.

I started doing the burpees with an unhealed arm and shoulder. Every time I pushed up, it was a major struggle to get up, and I feared that my arm would snap. Every time I put pressure on it, I'd get sharp stabbing pains, but I'd push through. Believe it or not, 4-5 months after the injuries, the pain was still as intense as the day I injured myself. The reason is I left the hospital untreated. Being that I was the sole income provider, I *had* to work. And I needed my arm so I couldn't wear a cast or sling.

I kept doing the burpees every single day, 6 days a week. As of this writing, it's August 5, 2022, and I've been doing them every single morning without fail because they got me out of my depression. Suddenly things started to become easier because I was getting stronger. I had more energy. More motivation. More drive. This was a problem for Neuman and Zina because I was self-improving. They didn't want me to get better. It seemed like there was some sort of incentive for the two to see my health go south. They'd both stay quiet when I boast about my improved mood. No, "wow, that's awesome. I'm glad you finally feel better after 40 years of hell!" That was a major red flag for me. I didn't appreciate it, and it made me scrutinize both of them from then on. They never checked on me regarding my injuries. Days, weeks, and months passed, and no one inquired about how I felt. I found this to be a major red flag as well.

Six months after starting my home workout consisting of burpees and core, I started weightlifting full body twice a week. That means I was and still do double workouts on 2 days of the week. After 6 months of weightlifting, the changes in my body became very noticeable, and I was getting compliments from strangers and even police officers. But Neuman and Zina never once said, "I see your progress! Keep going!"

Meanwhile, I was their rock and support. They would come to me with their problems and expect me to hear them out and give them advice (Zina a lot more than Neuman). They wouldn't even say thank you.

People often wonder where I got my superhuman strength and patience from. They don't understand what I've been through. They think I was born that way. I was weak-minded as a boy, and I would quit easily. My mind gradually strengthened over time. The more obstacles and setbacks that came my way, the more lessons I learned and the more resilient I got. But the obstacles kept coming for over 42 years non-stop! As you can imagine, one day, I had an aha! moment and learned how to cope with all my problems.

When my son, Hunter, 15 at the time, had major back surgery to correct his 80-degree curve (scoliosis). It was mandatory. If not, he would die soon, as the spine would crush his internal organs from the curving. It was a life-changing experience indeed. This event was like the final exam of my life. How would I respond? I was practical about it. I asked the questions and did my research. The hospital he had the surgery at is well respected - Columbia-Presbyterian in Washington Heights, New York City. His surgeon had over a thousand successful surgeries under his belt. This put things into perspective. I also rationalized that he'd be under anesthesia and have morphine once he was out.

The day before his surgery, I got two calls out of the blue. One from my mother and one from my sister, Hannah, whom I hadn't spoken to in years. They called, pretending to care about Hunter's well-being. They never once checked on him in all the 15 years he's been on this Earth. He's disabled. Heartless right? Anyways, I spoke to my mother, and she was prying to see what my emotional state was like. Hannah did the same. And I gave both the same reply, "don't you worry about him. He's going to be just fine. He's got the best surgeon and is in one of the best hospitals. I'm just glad my son's not freaking out."

Do you reckon either of them called after the surgery? The day of? The day after? The week after? The month after? A call? A text? Something? NOTHING!? That's right. Nothing. Apparently, they called me, hoping to catch me in a very sad and depressed mood filled with pessimism and hurt. But when they got the opposite, they put their tails between their legs and returned home to their pathetic lives. I did so much for my mother; I just wanted her to love me. But she never did. It was sad. I didn't know she didn't love me, so I let her keep my money. I was so desperate for love. Nobody loved me - at least, it wasn't unconditional love. It was temporary. Just for the moment because I did something for them. This ended up causing me to overextend myself to everyone, and it got me into situations I didn't want to be in.

I became a nice guy. Neuman didn't know any better. He was a nice guy too, but nowhere near the extent that I was. That's where I learned it from - but it also came as a coping mechanism from all the child abuse and bullying and being obedient to Islam's teachings (the faith urges its followers to be nice to others). I saw him like that and figured what I was doing was noble. He was a doormat. So was I for some time. Until one day, I said enough is enough. Eff everybody. I pulled all my energy back and started matching people's energy.

Nowadays, I'm happier than I've ever been. I'm truly joyous and at peace after 43 years of war. Unfortunately, hurt people and narcissists can spot me from a mile away, and they always seek me out and start chatting me up in public. They see me as a shoulder to cry on (the hurt people). The narcissists want my energy which is draining. They also want to control me to siphon all of my energy. These two groups of people LOVE to give me their sob stories. In my mind, I'm like, "seriously? You'll tell a stranger you just met your problems?" I cut them off immediately. "Hey, I gotta run to a meeting! Talk to you some other time!" That's hogwash, and I'll never talk to them again!

Why? Never allow people to do this to you because they'll ruin your joy. As they tell you their problems, you're going to feel and imagine what they went through, and the next thing you know, you're not joyous anymore. You feel drained. They feel energized. That's why. Get rid of these people.

I attract attention wherever I go. Sometimes I like to go to Starbucks and work from there, and I get these random strangers who start talking to me and dumping their drama on me. I put an end to that. I always have my headphones on whenever I'm at Starbucks. I can spot healthy-minded people. A large percentage of the American population has a lot of unhealed traumas from their past. They also have lots of inse-curities.

As a young boy of 5 years old, it was already my 2nd year of being abused by my mother, so I was already hurt when I went to kindergarten. Because of that, I had a terrible attitude. I started a lot of fights and cursed out a lot of people. I mooned the principal, further solidifying my 'crazy bastard' reputation. Oddly, my hurt from home gained me some popularity in school. My so-called "friends" still bullied me, but if anyone started a problem with me, they'd defend me, which is why I stuck with them. I felt like the bullying just came with the program.

I can remember my grammar school days vividly. I'd stand in the line outside at 8 am, and fight #1 starts! Between then and lunch, I'd get scolded by my teacher at least 5 times. Get thrown in the corner or made to take my seat to the hallway and sit there quietly. Once lunch came, I'd head to the cafeteria, eat and go to the playground for an inevitable fight #2. Depending on how fight #1 and #2 went, I may or may not get sent to the principal's office. And finally, after school, fight #3. The building we lived in was 2 streets away from the school. I'd walk home and face my mother. Already exhausted and depleted from school, the snarky comments start when I enter the apartment. "You loser. Look at you. You're pathetic; you can't breathe right and are useless. Close your mouth. You'll never become anything."

When the person you believe will protect you and guide you the right way tells you these things repeatedly, you start to believe them. I was like, "wait a minute, maybe mom is right. Maybe I'll never become anything. Maybe I *am* a loser. Look at my life; I am living like a loser now."

She'd make fun of my looks, and Milton would copy her, making it twice the fun (sarcasm). She'd say I look Jewish in an insulting way because, at that time, Israel had just invaded her home country of Lebanon. I was the black sheep. Mother would only be nice to me when she needed me to run an errand for her. She never cared how many times she hurt my feelings. She had zero cares in the world regarding how I felt and what she was doing to me and my psyche. She was so controlling. I used to tell her she was manly (masculine) and that it was disgusting, and I don't know what Neuman sees in her being so manly. She wanted me to sit or stand completely still without an expression on my face. That was her idea of a perfect son.

Milton was favored highly. He was a brat. Mother deemed him to be the golden child and I the black sheep. Why? Because she knew I had a good heart and was strong enough to handle her bullshit. He was so envious of me that everyone knew it and he even admitted it to everyone, including me

As the kids say, "I wanted all the smoke." Everyone knew that about me. They would purposely trigger me to get a reaction out of me, and sometimes I'd go bonkers, and they'd laugh hysterically about it. I eventually stopped allowing people to do that to me but only after years of going through that. I got into so many fights over my mother. That's what used to bother me. At home, I'm getting beat up by her. At school, I'm beating and getting beat up because of her. I would tell her, "I can't believe I defend you when the kids make fun of you." She would give me no reply to that. Deep down, she knew I had a point.

I always provided the sole income for the household. I wanted my ex-wife to concentrate on our children's upbringing. I provided a stable home for us. We were living comfortably, and we weren't lacking anything unless you're one of those people who only think you're successful once you can buy a Lamborghini. In my eyes, I was successful. I could've bought several Lamborghinis at one point but decided to drive my minivan instead.

Although all of this was conducive to my children's development, it was never enough for Zina. When I met her, she would tell me she didn't care about money and that if she did, she would've accepted a marriage offer from someone whose father is filthy rich. I don't know what the real reason is. Perhaps she didn't find him physically attractive. And perhaps she felt like she wouldn't be able to manipulate him. Narcissists have their eyes set on their targets, usually an empath with a good heart.

When a woman is a stay-at-home mom, her mind wanders off sometimes. These days, we have Instagram, where people flaunt their lifestyles to make the average person feel like they're not as cool or worthy as them. Zina wasn't happy; we had a single-family home on a 100x100' lot, 3 cars, 3 refrigerators full of food, savings, and businesses. We got Amazon packages every single day. We ate steaks and other expensive meats almost every day. We went on vacations, although less often than I'd like - not due to lack of money but just because of work. Still, this wasn't enough for her. Whenever she'd mention that person's father (who asked to marry her), I could see her eyes light up because he was rich (he was friends with her father). He had a lot of dollars. Unfortunately, people value dollars over people. After I left her, my good energy left with me. My vibe left too. My good luck left as well. The hyper and outside-the-box intellectual conversations are gone too. My generosity left. That listening, caring ear left as well. The valuable advice I used to give her was gone. The rescuing - gone.

After I left her, she realized she had messed up and that I truly am one of a kind. I have no reservations about that. I know who I am, and people should know who they are too. It's not arrogance or being conceited; it's knowing your worth and what you have to offer to this world. Never let anyone shortchange you. When I left her, she begged me to remain as friends, to which I told her, "you think I'm stupid? That's all I was to you this whole time. You never considered me as your lover." She said, "please, can you at least continue advising me?

You give really good advice." I told her, "heck no. I don't want anything to do with you." She said, "but please can you come to the house once a week and have sex?" To which I replied, "everything goes with me." I strongly suspect she cheated on me most of our marriage due to numerous red flags. One time I unexpectedly started making "love" to her when I came home early from work, and she already had some new matching lingerie underneath her clothes. It was around noon, and I usually came home around 5 pm. She never wore lingerie until we were about to have sex. She'd go to the bathroom and change into them. Oddly enough, she never wore that set of lingerie ever again. Hmmm...suspicious? Yeah, I think so too.

Nevertheless, I'm sure I was the best she ever had. Then why did she cheat? She was damaged goods. When I met her, she had just been divorced a month prior. She never healed. She had unresolved childhood trauma. And we had a disabled boy. While I was busy fighting off the ghetto crowds in New York City, she went looking for attention from other men. It is what it is. I'm not upset about it anymore because she wasn't the ideal partner. During our marriage, I asked God, "is this my life forever (with her)? Such a sad existence." Thankfully a few years later, God separated us and gave me a new life. One that's far more appealing. I know for a fact that I was the best she ever had, otherwise, why would she beg me to go to the house and have sex with her once a week when she was fooling around? If I was her best, then why would she cheat, you might ask. Well, as good as something is, people get bored. You can find a 10 out of 10 woman whose boyfriend or husband is tired of banging her.

Can money buy you respect, loyalty, love, and care? I gave

her everything. My soul included. Although I'm happy we ended up getting divorced, a part of me is still appalled at her behavior and infidelity.

I worked at Neuman's store in Manhattan, New York, for 9 years where I operated my own hat business inside the store while running his business simultaneously.

Guess where a lot of our customers came from? The ghettos. It was a constant struggle dealing with many people coming into the shop. Very rude, confrontational, and disrespectful. You had to set your ego aside to deal with this crowd. There's no amount of money that 99.9% of the people will accept to work that position, and that's not even an exaggeration! Of all the family members, I was the one person who could handle the manager/cashier position. I handled it so well, and I made a lot of friends and connections from all over the country and the world. There were always a few groups of people outside selling their wares. Some would sell CDs, others, fake designer handbags; It was the counterfeit zone. Some were selling drugs.

I met people from all over the world and saw the common fabric in all people. Gang members of the Blood gang would jump inside the store if they heard any commotion and ask me if I was alright. They were ready to pounce on the other person for me without my request. I could connect with anyone; they'd appreciate me and show me love and gratitude.

There was once an incident with one of the Blood gang members. I wasn't there. Milton told one of them to get out of the store in a rude way for having ice cream in their hand. They would have walked out of the store if he had asked them respectfully. I know because this was a daily occurrence for me.

The gang member didn't appreciate Milton's tonality and demeanor, so he fought him. I was in the South Bronx at that time. I had just opened my sneaker and hat shop a few months prior. When Neuman spotted the fight, he pulled the two apart. He stepped outside the store momentarily, and as he was walking back in, the gang member swung his fist from behind and landed a clean punch right under Neuman's left eye. He broke his socket, and my dad fell on the floor; he got knocked out. My friend called me and notified me. I was furious! That S.O.B.! Not the gang member, but Milton! I rushed to the hospital to check up on him. I was so upset. I wanted to go and beat the crap out of him. This moron wouldn't let us work like we were supposed to. He constantly added more stress to me. I kept telling Neuman, "tell him to stay home and give him $500/week. It's better than him coming to the store and causing problems. Besides, he wasn't doing a damn thing to help us. Employees were quitting left and right because of this asswipe. Did Neuman listen to my sound advice? No. But in 2009, after I left due to this idiot, Neuman finally told him he was not allowed back in the store. I was already gone, though. Too little, too late.

15

TORTURED BY FIBROMYALGIA

*I*n 2008, I started developing fibromyalgia. It's a debilitating condition that left me in constant chronic widespread pain, shooting pains, muscle spasms, brain fog, memory loss, indecisiveness, inability to carry on a conversation, anxiety, depression, chronic fatigue, and much more. I had referred pain all over my body. It took me many years to realize the pain was coming from the bottom of my ribs, thinking it was all in my back. My back and ribs were constantly in pain, as if a heavy weight was pulling down on my shoulders while I dragged it through the mud. The agony only worsened over time until the muscles in my lower leg finally spasmed to the point where I could no longer walk properly. Despite seeking medical help, doctors could not offer a remedy for my condition, leaving me to suffer from the unrelenting agony of fibromyalgia from 2008 to 2020. It was a living nightmare, and I often felt hopeless, resigned to a lifetime of pain. The thought of it worsening with age was unbearable.

There weren't many doctors who claimed to treat fibromyalgia. I found a doctor in North Jersey who made that claim. He tried everything under the sun. I was on 9 different medications at one point! And I had a severe reaction in 2020 when he added the 9th medication. I wasn't sleeping enough for a few days and started hallucinating one night. He said I was his worst patient and advised me to quit working and just stay in bed. Unfortunately, that wasn't an option for me. I had two children, a wife, a mortgage, and bills up the wazoo. I continued pushing through my days relentlessly when no one else dared to. It was like having a barbell with four 45lb plates on each side right on top of my shoulders and traps. It was my life's hardest struggle, and I felt completely hopeless and defeated. I only saw the symptoms get worse and worse. I never imagined I'd heal. I thought it was going to get progressively worse and worse.

I was on 9 different medications. The final medication he added to my regimen sent me to the ER. I got a bad reaction. My doctor screwed up. He didn't realize I couldn't mix all these medications. I started hallucinating. I was taken to the hospital. About an hour before I was taken to the hospital, I opened the front door of the house I used to live in with Zina. There he was! It was my business' landlord. He was in his company's Ford F650 work truck. I remember seeing the company logo decal on the front door. I looked inside the passenger window, and there he was. He was in the driver seat, his head extending towards me through the passenger window, waving at me. "What the heck was he doing here?" I thought. It turned out it wasn't him, and I was hallucinating. It looked so real! His truck fit in the parking spot perfectly. It didn't seem out of place; it didn't overlap anything in the scenery and wasn't semi-translucent. It was as real as real can get. I was flabbergasted. How in the heck is this even possible? The mind is a marvel, I tell you.

I was kept in a psych ward. No one told me what was going on. Whenever I'd ask the guards when I was leaving, they'd ignore me. I started heating up inside me. I started freaking out. I felt like I was held captive, and the guards ignoring me made it feel like a nightmare that would never end. Hours passed, and still no explanations. My body was overheating. No matter how much ice water I drank, my insides were on fire. I was starting to feel claustrophobic. Still not quite out of my hallucinations, I made a run for it.

Yes, you read that right. I was in my hospital gown and those thick socks. I could barely get any traction with those socks, so I couldn't break records with my running speed. One guard stood in my way, grabbed me in a wrestling way, picked me up, and slammed me hard on one side of my body. I hit the rock-solid ground floor (hard tile over the ground floor concrete). The impact made my soul jump out of my body. It was the most pain I had ever felt, and to make matters worse, I wasn't 100% in my right mind and was full of fear. I thought for sure my hip and arm were broken. I laid there on the floor, moaning in agony. I had never felt so violated and alone in my life. I stayed down for a minute, and as I was moaning, I slowly got up. I started limping like a soldier who had just got shot in his leg. My whole arm was in unbelievably sharp pain with every step I took. My hip was throbbing in pain. I would take one step, limp profoundly, moan, moan again, and walk towards my room, moving at a snail's pace. Hoping the guard or anyone else doesn't continue attacking me. I had never felt so alone and defeated in my life. Neuman wasn't there. My ex-wife never bothered to visit me. My shoulder felt like it was going to pop, and my humerus bone felt like it had a sharp knife inside, stabbing me every time I moved my arm or took a step. I could barely get on my bed. I had to roll into it without the aid of my right arm and right hip. There were about 3 or 4 guards (who were dressed like state troopers) and about 3 hospital staff members. They all looked at me in horror and surprise. I can read their thoughts. They were thinking, "how in the WORLD did this guy get up and walk to his room? Anyone else would have needed a stretcher and taken for x-rays." They never cared to take x-rays! I walked to my room as quickly as possible to protect myself from being attacked further. I figured if I was in the room with the door closed, the guard(s) couldn't do me any harm.

There was one guard who I made a connection with. We would talk, and he would tell me that I was very philosophical and wise and ask me what happened to me that made me end up there. While others wouldn't tell me how long I was there for, he told me, "don't tell anyone I told you this, but you're supposed to leave tomorrow." He was right. Except, they sent me to a behavioral center for observations for a week. I pray to God that that guard is blessed forever because he gave me hope. He was ex-military.

When I got to the behavior center, the man who was receiving me took one look at me and said, "why would they send *you* here? You look just fine." The reason he said that is because almost everyone that was in there was mentally screwed. I'm not going to lie. I was a bit on edge because I didn't know what to expect from the other patients. I feared one of them attacking me. I couldn't defend myself with only

76

one good arm. The place sucked. I wasn't allowed to use my cell phone. They gave me one pillow that was 1/8th the thickness of a regular pillow. Personnel would come by the room every 30 minutes to check on me, including overnight. They'd open the door, making a loud squeaking noise and shining a bright flashlight at me. It was hard to get more than 3 hours of sleep each night. I stayed there for about a week. The food was atrocious; they served rubbery boiled chicken with zero flavor. Everything was inedible. I ended up drinking a lot of milk to get enough calories because the food portions were not enough for a grown man. They were hardly serving me 1200 calories for the day.

What did we all do there? Nothing! You would think they would teach us something, but they didn't. One of the exercises they gave us was a list of caffeinated beverages asking us to put them in order from highest to lowest in caffeine concentration. "What the heck," I thought. When I got out, I told Neuman and Zina about this exercise, and they were shocked. They thought they'd be giving me actual help. It was just essentially a holding cell. Each morning I had to go to the staff station, get my medication, and then check my blood pressure. Apart from that, there was no care. I had and still have trouble sleeping, so I take three benadryl pills and three 10mg melatonin pills to sleep. That sounds like overkill, but that's what I've been doing for about 3 years now, and I've had zero adverse side effects - hopefully, nothing bad comes about in the future. They wouldn't give me anything to sleep at the behavior center. I pleaded with them to give me just 1 benadryl, but they denied it, saying they could only give it to me if I had allergies.

This was the lowest point in all of my life. Neuman stopped

by a couple of times for about an hour at the first hospital, where I tried to escape but wasn't allowed at the behavioral center. Zina never bothered to visit or call. That was the biggest wake-up call for me. She made me feel guilty that I had hallucinations when it wasn't even my fault - the doctor made a mistake. I was in the hospital thinking I was in the wrong because that's how she made me feel. And because of that, I didn't think it was a red flag that she didn't come and visit me. The first hospital was a 10-minute car drive. I felt abandoned. Clearly, I was with someone who didn't truly love me. That was the beginning of the end of our marriage. It occurred to me that if I stayed with her and ended up in a hospital for other health reasons, she would not support me but would probably look for a new husband.

When I left the first hospital, Zina (and Neuman) assumed I had lost my mind and was gone for good. I say that because she wasn't concerned about my injuries when I returned from the hospital and had zero compassion or empathy. Days, weeks, and even months passed, and she never asked if I was feeling better. That was a major red flag. Another major and even bigger one is that Neuman didn't care either. They both looked guilty. They'd remain quiet whenever I'd mention my injuries and pray I stop talking about it. That really pained me. I couldn't believe them. These are the two people I counted on. The two people I *thought* were genuinely for me. People I helped tremendously throughout the years. I had already cut off my mother and siblings, so I didn't have much family left. Never would have thought these two would treat me that way in a million years.

Even though Zina showed no empathy when I arrived

home, she craved my sex. She was extremely passionate during intercourse. A part of me felt like she slept with someone else while I was away and was disappointed by that other man. Who is that someone? I guess it's speculation and one I will never know. When I talked to my psychiatrist, he prescribed Wellbutrin to help me with ADHD, focus, and memory. I started gaining my focus and memory and was recalling the red flags, and that's when she set out to get me off Wellbutrin. My daughter was dorming at NYU. She had my daughter call me and tell me that Wellbutrin is no good. My world came crashing down on me. I couldn't believe what was happening. This confirmed that I had been cheated on and lied to during this marriage.

What I found extremely odd is when I returned home from the behavior center, I was still helping Neuman get his supplies for his business. He would call me and ask me to please place orders for such and such, and I would do it, even though I didn't want to. When I finally left Zina months down the road, he stopped asking me to help him get his supplies. Instead, he went behind my back and started calling Zina to do it for him.

Hmmm, But why? He never called to ask me how I was holding up after leaving Zina. I was broken and all alone. He never bothered to come see me at the hotel I was staying at. I might be wrong, but I suspect something was going on between Neuman and Zina. He would visit her daily at different times and talk to her on the phone for prolonged periods. Mind you, they have been secretly talking way before I even had the hallucination - when there was no sign of me going to have one. The only other logical explanation was that he was upset that I left her and was trying to reassure her that she would be alright so long as he was alive. But that doesn't explain why he was secretly talking to her without my knowing and it doesn't explain why he started going to her for the supplies once I left her. It would make sense if he stopped talking to me altogether, but that wasn't the case.

Why go to her to get your supplies when I was the one who found these suppliers for you three years ago? He couldn't turn a profit with his old suppliers when he first started his business and was looking to quit the business. I took the initiative to track down other suppliers and negotiate better prices on his behalf. I used my credit cards to buy him his supplies and was happy to help him.

I was certainly in a better state of mind when I left Zina than when I came home from the behavior center. So, there was no doubt that I would reliably get his supplies. That's a major red flag for me. And it's not like he completely stopped talking to me after I left Zina either. It's very suspicious and I'm not surprised.

He was always jealous of me. Whenever I'd innovate or come up with a great idea, rather than acknowledging my creativity, he would act like he came up with the idea and downplay me. He was especially jealous when I bought my first house in 2005. It was a newly constructed house and looked stunning, while his house looked like something from the 1980s. There he was, looking at me with my then peaceful wife in a brand-new house and a brilliant and beautiful daughter. He was fuming. He wanted what was mine. He was married to a complaining hag who never really conversed with him properly. He saw Zina as much more desirable because she wasn't combative and spoke Spanish like him. Unfortunately for him, he was looking at a mirage. She wasn't peaceful, and she wasn't classy. She loved the drama just like his wife did. The only difference is Zina contained herself better. And she was damaged goods racking up miles while I was at work with God knows who. She always needed male attention and validation.

As of this writing, it's been nearly 1 ½ years, and she's still trying to get me to go back to her. She's done everything she could to force me back with her. She's called the suicide hotline numerous times on me. She's called the police on me. She's stolen my money. She's even opened a 2nd life insurance policy without my authorization, withheld some of my credit cards, maxed them without paying a cent, and took my credit score from 820 to 450. She has tried to devastate me. The worst she's done is to convince my children not to speak to me. As of this writing, it's been nearly 7 months since I've spoken to them. I call and text every single day, but I never get a response except one time about 2 weeks ago in January 2023. My daughter replied to one of my texts with, "your wife's a bitch." She didn't elaborate. I've been trying to reach her, but it's been unsuccessful.

Neuman and Zina didn't always behave unconcerned towards me. It was new. It made me wonder what happened when I was alone in the hospital. I was in that psych ward with a fractured arm, messed up shoulder, and hip. Boiling from my insides. All alone with a cold hospital staff and guards wondering if this was my fate for the rest of my life.

The way they interact with each other has changed as well. The two used to innocently and happily talk in Spanish to each other when we first got married, but now they're pretty awkward and quiet around each other in front of me and no longer speak in Spanish to each other. You do the math. You make the conclusion. I could have chalked this up and said people change, but I found out they've been secretly talking on the phone to each other without my knowing. I am curious to know how long it has been going on. I remember I once said something about Neuman to her. It was something small. I complained about how he handled something, and she lashed out at me when she'd agreed with me in the past.

These are some of the red flags that she was unfaithful to me. There would be days when she'd get out of character. She would lash out at me for literally no reason. It was continuous. I would tell her to shut the hell up and stop acting like that towards me. I suspected something was up and even told her her behavior was suspicious. Once I said that she immediately went back to "normal." She didn't want me to pry into what was going on. People behave this way when they cheat. They do this prior to cheating or after to justify their actions. Some people do it in hopes that their partner will leave them.

At my lowest point, I was suffering tremendously from fibromyalgia, and financially, I wasn't where I once was after Hurricane Sandy destroyed my e-commerce business in 2012. After being married for 19 years, she suggested she join a gym and get a male trainer. This is after I already suspected her of infidelity. What was even more eye-opening was that she suddenly wanted to get an IUD (intrauterine device) as a contraceptive. Additionally, she'd drop off our son at school exactly one block down from the house and wouldn't return home for at least 1 ½ -2 hours. All that was left was for me to catch her screwing another man in our bed. I was done with her. She erroneously thought I loved her so much I would put up with her. I think she's very dumb because she should have known better. If I cut my mother off, who gave me birth, surely, I'd cut off a nasty promiscuous woman. What's hilarious is that when I left her, she begged me to go to the house and sleep with her once a week. I declined immediately. I guess she assumed that I would take the deal. No, I have my dignity and standards. As of writing this, I have been celibate for a little over a year.

I'm very used to it now. I don't even crave sex anymore, and I look at my semen as liquid gold. I think to myself, "the next woman I sleep with has to be well worth my energy." I never realized how depleted one gets from ejaculating and how much creativity, determination, and discipline are lost. If I were to ever have a girlfriend again, she has to be worth my time and energy. I'm a straight male. I'm not bisexual or gay. I love women A LOT, but so many are not worth my investment. So many women, not all, are delusional and immature. They have a false sense of confidence simply because men give them lots of validation. They're not confident because of their knowledge or skills. I feel like getting with an immature woman of legal age is just as disgusting as getting with an underage girl. In my mind, it's illegal. So, until the right woman comes along, I'm perfectly good on my own. I mean that. I have a great routine that's fulfilling and peaceful. And my days go by very fast, so I'm having a good time. I'm never bored, and I never feel lonely. Sure, it was different when I first left Zina, but I adapted and created a nice routine for myself. This is just one story of my journey through hell. The fact that I still love and smile after all I've gone through is a miracle. I praise the heavenly Father, the Holy Son, and the Holy Spirit for shining light on my hidden enemies.

Four months before this happened, I started a gratitude meditation whereby I would run down a list of people and things I was grateful for each morning. It was the 2nd thing I did each morning - the first being relieving myself in the bathroom, brushing my teeth, and washing my face. Neuman was on that list, and so was Zina. I felt gratitude in my heart for them. But the Creator could no longer watch me be grateful for these backstabbers. So, the light was shining on my betrayers. Everything was revealed to me. During my gratitude, I was grateful for my health despite dealing with severe fibromyalgia. Around the same time my enemies were revealed to me, I started to heal tremendously from fibromyalgia. Everything came together all at once. I thank God for protecting my heart against this betrayal. It was the one betrayal God wouldn't allow me to shed one tear for. Had he not shielded my heart, I would have surely died from a broken heart. All praises are due to Jesus Christ, the Mighty Loving God.

I hold men accountable just like I do with women. If they are not on my level, I don't befriend them. I hardly give people my phone number. I avoid narcissists like the plague. Besides, so many men compete with me - it's vomit-inducing.

This is just one example of men competing with me and needing to prove themselves. There's this guy who lives in my building. He's got a wife and kids and drives a $300,000 car. Whenever he sees me, he flags me down. I'm not interested in small talk anymore, but I don't want to be rude. It's as if he's talking to me while tip-toeing. He starts raving about his finances, what he has, and is about to get this and that. The last interaction was funny to me. He said he didn't like the building we're in, which is ridiculous. It's a nice building. He said he didn't like the way the garage door opened. He wanted to live on Long Island. He was trying to flex about the big house he wanted to buy. Without intending to hurt his feelings, I asked him, "that's nice. How long is the commute going to be?" He said, "about an hour and a half." I made a face that said, "ouch." I told him that was too much and that I'd rather have those 3 hours to do other things. His energy plummeted. He was trying to get me to put him on a pedestal, and God gave me the right response. I didn't mean to bring down his spirits.

I was stating the truth. Why does he do that with me? Because he notices that others are drawn to me, and I'm not even wearing designer clothes. I wear Levi's jeans and $150 boots. When I work out, I wear knock-off Chuck Taylors that cost me $25. So, it pisses him off that I get attention without having to spend so much and without having to give people things. The funny thing is, I don't care for the attention. Why? Because a lot of people are phony. I've dealt with tens of thousands of people, so I have a large sample of people to deduce that.

UNCONDITIONAL LOVE

*L*ife was very hard. Just imagine all the violence, the mental abuse, the emotional abuse, the crying, the tears, the headaches, the moaning, the begging, the hopelessness, the victim mindset, the neglect, the people pleasing, the desperation for human connection, the sorrow, the abandonment, the disrespect, the humiliation, the pain, the degradation, the school fights, the fear, the confusion, the mental impairment, and all the suffering; that was my life every day beginning at 4 years old till I was 42 years old.

How did I deal with all of this? I mean, it was like an evil prank by the universe. I started to believe this and accepted it as my truth and reality. Every day I'd pinch my arm and leg real hard to see if it was real. I would cry up to the heavens, "Allah, pleeease, help me! Pleeeeeaaaaaseee," as I wept and wept. My cries were that of someone who fell to the bottom of a 400-foot well. But Allah would never reply. Since I was my own parent, I tried looking at the bright side. I would gain great happiness and satisfaction from riding my bicycle and going to the town pool, where my ear infection progressively worsened. I would go outside and play and have lots of fun. But when I got home with a grin, mother didn't like that. She told me to stop laughing and smiling and that I was doing too much. I'm causing a ruckus. She'd ask me, "what are you laughing at, you loser? Where's your job, wife, and house? Huh? You're 9 years old. You're supposed to be a man already, and you should be taking care of your siblings because you're the oldest. Such and such is married. What are you doing with your life? Riding a bicycle? You're a laughingstock. Look at you. You don't even know how to breathe right!"

I don't know how someone can be that cruel to a child or even an adult. My self-image was in the gutter. I was this violated, raped soul. I saw myself as the biggest laughingstock I knew, a loser, as mom said, and no good. Not enough. Not worthy of love. Not worthy of authentic friendships. I was ashamed of my situation. I was embarrassed by her. Even though I was my own parent, I couldn't teach myself how to escape this mess. I didn't want any of my friends to come to our apartment because I knew she would humiliate me by either lashing out at me or just by the way she's aggressive and in a pissy mood all the time. I didn't want my friends to see that. I also didn't want them to know I was being abused. None of my "friends" had any idea. I tried my best to be strong and pretend it wasn't happening. I never told the school. I kept it inside because I worried about what would happen to me. She wasn't the ideal mother, but at least she was familiar.

I didn't want to end up with strange people. If I could go back in time, I would have definitely ratted her out and taken my chances in a foster home. That was one of life's major lessons for me. To never put up with people's shit. To stand up for myself. Never be a doormat for anyone. Never tolerate disrespect, even from your parents.

I know I've healed because, in the past, the mere thought of them would trigger me, but now my emotions stay neutral without any effort. Recognizing that we are all interconnected as one consciousness, I choose to extend love to myself and them. It's the love that says, "it's ok, you're just immature imbeciles. I'll love you from afar. I'm praying for you. I hope God (Jesus Christ) guides you out of your evil ways." I love fire because it makes food taste much better and provides heat, but I love it from afar. I'm not going to sit by a lake of fire. My parents are like fire, except they don't make food taste better, but they heat up my internal temperature from their stress-inducing ways.

Throughout my life, I have always had this feeling or vibe within me, which is the feeling of unconditional love. This feeling got me through everything. I'd always positively look at things because of it. How? I would always say, "yes, this or that happened, but we still feel great. We still got the pool, the bike, and a bunch of other things" I was carefree, which added to the overall positive feeling. Essentially, the feeling would console me whenever I suffered or cried. Now that I think back, tears roll down my eyes because I now know God was within me, helping me get through the abuse and trauma. It's so funny to me now. I would lament and cry to the heavens, "God, where are you?" And God was within me all along. The Quran didn't state that fact, but it nudged me towards the Bible, and the Bible says that. The Quran didn't explicitly say

God was within, but it says God is closer to us than our jugular vein.

Furthermore, it said that Allah blew something of His spirit into Adam and that we're all descendants of Adam. We must have that "something of His spirit," too. Which essentially says God is within man. However, Muslims don't put it this way, but that's how I interpret it - with no disrespect to Islam or the Muslims.

It wasn't until I learned about Christianity that I understood God is love. I realized that the Holy Spirit resides within me because of Christianity. When I discovered who Jesus Christ was, He took control of my life. His guidance, support, and assurance brought me peace. I had prayed to God my whole life, starting with the Muslim salaat at 12 years old and fasting at 7. It only made sense to me that something created us. At 37, after struggling, I shifted my focus to the afterlife and read the Quran 30+ times in Arabic and English. Once, I came across a verse in the Quran that encourages the believer to seek out The Bible. Having familiarized myself with the Shi'ite and Sunni hadiths (traditions and sayings of Prophet Muhammad (PBUH)), I decided to peek over at the Christians and see what they were doing over there.

I learned about the Holy Trinity, which finally made sense, so I became a Christian. I had already been checking out the Buddhists and became a Buddhist. I did the same with Judaism, Hinduism, Baha'ism, Zoroastrianism, and Animism. Oh, and I was still a Muslim. So, I unintentionally became an omnist. I've understood everything perfectly. So much so I can show how they're all correct and compatible with each other. I can also show that atheists are correct too. I can even show how

Satanists are correct as well. You're probably thinking, "oh, he's one of those religious nuts." And you'd be wrong. I'm bigger on spirituality than religion. However, I recognize the wisdom within each theology and philosophy, like stoicism and Buddhism. I would say I'm a spiritualist more than a religious person by far.

My strong love and curiosity about God led me to other religions and philosophies. When I used to refer to Him/Her/It as Allah, I was blind to many things. Although I still consider myself a Muslim, as I recite the Shahada (the Muslim testimony that there is only one God and Muhammad is God's messenger), Islam only taught me so much. But I'll tell you from experience, if you adhere to the laws of Allah, Jesus Christ will guide you. He will show you more, and it'll be from several sources.

Once I got the overall picture. I understood that Allah, The Father, and Yahweh were all the unseen God within us all and that Jesus Christ represents the physical manifestation of God but that Jesus Christ is also The Father, the unseen. The two (unseen and manifest) are the same. Everything is God. Show me where God is NOT. He/She/It is even in hell and makes up hell. Glory be to God!

That might sound blasphemous to some, I understand. There's nothing *but* God. If we all understood this, there would be world peace. People would help each other out because they'd know they're helping themselves, not just the other person in front of them. They're helping the same Being within them that is also "located" in another human. There is no real separation. God is the location. God is the here-ness of here. The where-ness of where. God is Distance, and God is Journey, and God is Destination, and God is The Departure. God is three hundred and sixty degrees of perfection, which also contains imperfection. To exclude God from imperfection is to limit God. God has no limits. God can create a reality where God can't lift the heaviest rock, yet this is just a subset of the infinite realities where God can or cannot control that reality, depending on God's will - yet God will still prevail.

Jesus Christ represents man, which means all men are gods as stated in the Bible, Psalms 82:6 "I have said, Ye *are* gods; and all of you *are* children of the Most High." - King James Version. Although I respect all faiths and consider myself an omnist, the story of Jesus Christ is the most alluring. Once understood, you realize who you are and the power you hold because you are unconditional love.

What got me into the different religions was that I hit rock bottom one day and prayed to Allah. One night, I got up at 2 am and started praying in the Islamic way (The Night Prayer or Salaatul Layl) for 4 ½ hours straight. These weren't prayers asking Allah for anything. These were recitations of certain chapters of the Quran, along with praises to Allah. I did this because I read that Prophet Muhammad (PBUH) prayed for 4-5 hours. I wanted to emulate him. I figured if I hit rock bottom here on Earth, the least I could do was shoot to be up there in heaven with Prophet Muhammad (PBUH).

Furthermore, Muslims are required to do 5 daily prayers. However, I was doing more than that. I prayed 10-15 times, plus the night prayer, which is done before the morning prayer. I watched sermons from Shi'ite sheiks as well as Sunni sheiks for hours. I would listen to Sufis and Salafis. If we're talking about someone going to the gym, as an analogy, I was that guy that was in the gym for 6-8 hours a day. I was relentless with it.

All I could think about all day was Allah (SWT), Prophet Muhammad (PBUH), his companions and the 12 Shi'ite Imams. I wasn't only reading and watching but also taking everything I learned into practice. I didn't do this to appear religious in front of people. That wasn't it at all. I was in a rut and wanted to ensure I didn't lose my afterlife too!

The divine entities - Allah, The Father, Jesus Christ, The Holy Spirit, and Yahweh - witnessed my unwavering devotion and, eventually, guided me towards a different spiritual path. While exploring other options, I discovered Buddhism, which instantly captivated me with its peaceful and wise philosophy. The guidance and wisdom offered by the Buddhist community proved to be a healing therapy for me during a time of great distress that lasted for over three and a half decades. They taught me meditation, breathing, and healing techniques, which helped me to connect with God, albeit unconsciously. My encounters with them also sparked my interest in Jesus Christ, whom they hold in high esteem. Although Buddha is not a deity, it pains me to think that he may not have realized his divinity. The misconceptions surrounding Buddhism often lead people to believe that Buddhists worship Buddha, which is not true, as Buddhism is not a religion.

I saw Judaism as similar to Islam; they had similar dietary restrictions and prayed often, and both gods were not playing around. I accepted Judaism. And so on and so on. Ultimately, I understood that God was extending His hand to different tribes and nations differently. And God made it so that if you really wanted to get to know Him, you'd have to explore them all. Because think about it, if you add up all the different holy scriptures (the Torah, the Bible, the Quran, the Vedas, etc.), that's just way too much reading for one religion only. So God split it up. You see, in Buddhism, it doesn't matter if you know you're a god or not because, in the end, you are living in peace, love, and harmony. That's what the Father wants for us. He doesn't want us to be anxious and depressed. He wants us to relax and be happy. He wants us to put ourselves and God first.

One day, seeing us all having God as our main focus and foundation would be a great sight. Focusing on God means you follow the scriptures, but it also means focusing on yourself. It is said, "know thyself, and you will know God." The spirit of God is within all of us. It's what gives us life and movement.

I have an innate knowledge that my life was scripted. I was meant to undergo harsh treatment from everyone. I was meant to be an outcast. The black sheep of my family. The one that people bullied because he was different from the other kids. I can say without a doubt that all of my childhood problems stemmed from feeling fear. I was always anxious and scared of what was to come next. I learned from the Buddhists and the Christians in my 30s that whatever you feel is what you'll attract. In other words, by feeling fearful, I attracted more experiences that further instilled fear in me. And the cycle repeats until the feeling is given up.

I stopped watching the news when Donald Trump was elected in 2016. I stopped checking for them online as well. I stopped discussing politics with everyone. I can't tell you how much fear the news instills in us. It will leave you scared of everyone and hate everyone. In his book, "As a Man Thinketh," James Allen's main theme is that whatever you think about all day, that's what you'll see in your world.

Without knowing it, getting off the media was one of the

greatest things I did. At first, I was a bit hesitant as I thought I might be out of the loop with regard to my peers. But I said, screw it; I don't care. Enough is enough. I have to try something different. I'm telling you, I didn't miss a thing. When Covid-19 started, I didn't need the news. Everyone was the news.

I realized that other people's problems aren't mine. As a super empath, I feel deeply. I was born hyper-sensitive. I can't shut it off. I reasoned that I couldn't possibly care for everyone's problems, so why would I absorb these news stories? Why should I give some events attention but neglect everyone else? That's not fair! I wanted to be fair! No attention for anyone - that was the verdict. Why should I give a crap about what's happening in Russia or Ukraine? Does anyone give a damn about me? Nope. There's literally no one in both countries that care about me or any other American.

Zina would pile a bunch of burdens on me as part of her emotional abuse campaign against me. She would create problems out of thin air. She'd raise hypothetical negative scenarios to get a reaction out of me. She loved seeing me feel sad as I empathized with what she told me. I didn't suspect she was doing this to me on purpose until one day, out of nowhere, videos regarding narcissism flooded my social media feeds. I was 42 years old at the time. Instagram, Tiktok, & Youtube showed me numerous narcissism videos day in and day out. It caught my curiosity. I said to myself, "this is odd. Why am I getting all these videos on narcissism all of a sudden? Why not check this out?" And I'm telling you, God orchestrated it. God was trying to wake me up to the abuse, which I had no idea was happening. I started learning more and more about narcissism, and the things I learned described her to the letter.

I thought this might be just a coincidence, so I decided to track her for the next few months. I wanted to see if she was doing it intentionally. Lo and behold, she was attacking me. She did it covertly. She wore an Islamic veil (hijab) and portrayed herself as a respectable, pious, and innocent person. But she wasn't. In fact, she was rude and disrespectful at times to me, and I didn't say much because compared to my situation with my mother, I figured it wasn't a big deal, and besides, she could be stressed out because of our son, who is wheelchair-bound. But it wasn't because of our son that she was disrespectful. I suspect infidelity as I once caught her looking at someone with lustful eyes in front of me. She was smiling at him, and her eyes looked like they would pop out of her sockets. I called her by her name, and she ignored me while continuing to look at another guy. She did this during Hunter's back surgery recovery in Columbia Presbyterian Hospital. It was in the hospital courtyard. It looked like the guy worked there. That was the final nail in the coffin for me. The manipulation, emotional abuse, the brazen act of lusting after someone in front of me, the disrespect, I said, "skank, I'm gone!" I stopped talking to her two months after that. I blocked her phone number, changed my phone number, and blocked her on all my socials. She started a smear campaign against me as retaliation. She talked to anyone who would listen. She tarnished my reputation amongst the community here in New Jersey and Lebanon. I'll discuss that further in a bit. I want to first describe her behavior towards me.

She would dump all types of stories on me daily - she was addicted to drama. She had to tell me all the negative things going on in each of her 5 siblings' lives, along with her parents, uncles, aunts, and grandparents, in Lebanon, South America, etc. She was like a news channel pumping out negative stories every day. One day I had enough. I told her, "I don't care! You need to STOP immediately! I don't want to hear about any of this crap anymore!" I told her I knew what she was doing to me and that she was the lowest human being I'd ever encountered. I told her I had lost all respect and trust for her. And that she is inhumane and a criminal. I told her that she should be in jail. And I'm not exaggerating about that. It was like I was under her hypnotic spell, and suddenly, the penny dropped and I realized I was her prisoner. It was like Adam and Eve when they were in paradise naked and never thought anything of it, and then one day, suddenly, they realized they were naked. It was that type of realization.

You have to be one bitter soul to do that to someone who stood by you for 20 years and cared when your parents didn't care. I'll never understand some people. I understand if a person doesn't like the person, but why do something so evil to them when they never caused you harm but instead protected and cared for you financially? I was heartbroken. I felt betrayed like never before. I felt like my core manhood was shattered and violated. She was close to me and knew more about me than anyone else. We slept in the same bed and had regular sex. I'll never understand.

She was always in competition with me. She couldn't stand that I naturally got attention from strangers, and no one batted an eye for her. She was so desperate for attention, especially male attention. She was not the person I thought I had married. I married her because I wanted a religious woman with pure intentions. What I got was a secret enemy and a shameless brat.

After I figured out what she was doing and considered the numerous red flags over the years, I decided to leave her. It was a difficult decision to make because we had two children. I was mentally drained from the abuse at that time. Packing a few things in a suitcase and leaving was an incredibly major mission for me due to the brain fog, fatigue, and widespread aches from the lingering fibromyalgia.

To make matters worse, I'd be leaving my then 15-year-old son, who can't walk and relies on a wheelchair. I was faced with the toughest decision of my life. Do I choose my son, or do I choose myself (my health)? I chose myself. I knew if I didn't choose myself, I couldn't call myself a man anymore, and knew I'd wind up dead.

The way I rationalized it is this way. Aside from his condition, I told myself that Hunter had had a decent life. He's always had his own room. I took him on several vacations. Got him lots of Nintendo games. Took him out to eat weekly. Took him on long drives. He had everything. Anything he wanted, I got it for him. Amazon was delivering packages every day. I figured it was time for him to encounter a tough situation. Part of growing up is dealing with life's problems. As a 15-year-old, it was tough that his parents were getting a divorce, but it was time for him and my daughter to learn how to deal with life's problems. I told myself, "I went through a lot more trauma than that. They can handle a divorce." This can sound a bit cruel; however, it's the truth.

I became emotionally mature and strong from all the abuse. I learned how to control my temper and my reactions. These tough life experiences made my foundation as solid as bedrock. One day, I found myself as the captain of my emotional ship. I became fully aware at all times and directed my emotions as I pleased. The worst news can be imparted to me, and I'll stand there like an unmovable mountain, absorbing the blow gracefully without a flinch. There is a strength within man that's truly remarkable.

Along my journey called life, it was sorrow after sorrow after sorrow. Things got progressively worse and harder. I kept developing my strength with each unfortunate event. One day, I decided never to complain to anyone again, including myself. That catapulted my strength into a new league of its own.

Today, I tell my followers on social media to pray and ask God to give them their life's worst calamity ASAP; any problem after that will be much easier to deal with.

17

THE SUPER STORM

O ne of the worst days of my life was October 22, 2012. It was Zina's birthday. That is the day Hurricane Sandy, or Superstorm Sandy wreaked havoc on Northern New Jersey and New York City. At that point, it's been 3 years since my e-commerce cap business launched. I was so proud of my business as I built it from the ground up on my domain, CraniumFitteds.com. After working in the family business for 9 years in Manhattan, New York, I decided I'd had enough of Milton and his shenanigans and decided to go my own way. Milton was evil to the core. I wanted to bury him alive. He made my life a living hell in that store. As if it wasn't bad enough dealing with thugs and angry mobs all day, I had to deal with his immaturity and jealousy.

I often complained to my parents about him, and they did nothing. They prayed I would resolve the issue on my own. They had no willpower to raise children and discipline them. Despite our employees walking off the job due to Milton's behavior and attitude and despite the fighting with the customers, Neuman never put his foot down and said something.

My friend helped me create an open commerce website on my domain for $200. Remember, getting traffic to your domain is a mighty feat. In August 2009, I launched the website and started promoting it on Twitter. I was relentless. Three months had passed, and I still hadn't gotten a single sale. I felt defeated and started pondering whether or not to throw in the towel.

I kept going and going until finally, I broke a sale! I was just about to give up. I was so happy and excited, and I couldn't believe it! In December 2009, the website sold over $20K in products which was amazing. Had it stayed like that, I would have been more than satisfied. It did. The following year, revenue was approximately $250K. And in 2011, the business spiked hard, with revenue totaling $5M. In 2012, I was on pace to do $8M+ but along came Hurricane Sandy to rain on my parade, no pun intended. I did end up with $5M in sales in 2012, which was great.

The storm came out of nowhere. We barely got a 1 to 2 day notice. Something told me to prepare. I told my guys the Friday before, "We won't process any orders come Monday. We will move all the products from lower to higher shelves and get everything off the floor." Along came Monday, and only 2 out of 10 guys showed up. The storm had already begun; the winds were picking up. The roof was howling and moving. As my 2 guys and I worked as quickly as possible, I only moved electronics from the floor, not the merchandise, as planned, as I didn't want to risk getting injured in the building. We had to get out fast.

We did the best we could and got out in a flash. I looked down the street, and it was flooded. I got concerned because the storm hadn't officially begun yet, and already the street was flooded. That night I went to sleep only to wake up to a text message from my employee, Sean, "my girl's house (in Little Ferry, NJ, where the warehouse was located) got 8 feet of water." I said, "WHAT?!" He said, "the berm nearby broke, and the water came rushing in. The town has 5 to 8 feet of water."

(Tears roll down my eyes as I write this). My baby! My precious baby. The 16 hour work days, 7 days a week, flashed before my eyes. I was wondering what the warehouse looked like. I waited all day for the storm to cease so I could go and check on the warehouse. That night, Neuman drove me out there, and the streets were so flooded it was impossible to drive through to get to the warehouse. He took a risk and drove slowly until we arrived. I unlocked the door and walked inside the offices; everything was all over the floor. Products inside the warehouse floated to the front office (traveling 100 ft). I looked at the watermarks on the wall. We got about 8 inches of water, which was odd. My next-door neighbor got 4 feet, and we share a 100' wall. Nevertheless, those 8 inches devastated my entire business.

I lost my server, which was an utter disaster. It was supposed to be uploading backups every night, but the programmer said he never got an alert regarding a payment issue which caused the backups to halt. The server had all of the inventory and locations of all products within the warehouse. We had 10,000 sq/ft of product on a 5-tier shelving system. We had to manually add everything to the new server, which took 10 days to complete. When I walked into the warehouse, I was shocked and disappointed. With the floor still wet, everything on the bottom shelves got destroyed. Just like that, I lost 20% of my inventory. Customers were becoming impatient, "what happened to the website? When will it be back up?" My amazing team did their best to clean up and organize the inventory. In 10 days, the website was up and running. That first day, we got a healthy amount of sales. However, it didn't last. A lot of customers had products from the lower shelves in their shopping carts. And when it was time to check out, their product was no longer available due to water damage.

I wanted to do the right thing. I declared that I would not sell damaged caps to my customers, as that's not the moral thing to do. They're paying for a new cap, not some cap that was swimming in raw sewage. I didn't want that bad karma on me, and I didn't want to tarnish my company's stellar reputation. Unfortunately, our sales kept declining. The loss was too great. I couldn't replenish the damaged caps with new ones in time and had no financial means to support such a big product restock. I kept promoting the website. I kept bringing in new styles, but sales kept slipping no matter what I tried. The website lost its momentum completely. We went from a few hundred orders daily to just 30, and that number kept dropping.

The first day at work after the storm, my guys walked in. I remember Sean looking at me with sympathy. He said, "I don't know how you're doing it, how you're just standing there emotionless. I would have fallen to my knees and cried!" Had it been my first calamity or even 10th, I would have fallen to my knees and cried. I took it on the chin and kept walking.

Truth be told, years later, I had to cry. I had to let it out. I didn't know I was in so much pain. Even writing this, I cried. I cried when I reviewed the book for errors. I cried when I proofread it again. The business was supposed to be my ticket to retirement. I was excited about possibly passing it down to my kids so they don't have to worry about money. And just like that, the universe said, "come over here!" Before the storm, I felt so secure. Money was coming in regularly, and it was the least of my concerns. I never, at that time, thought I'd ever worry about money again.

I understand today that I wasn't ready for that kind of success just yet. And God didn't want Zina to benefit from my success. I truly believe that because it happened exactly on her 30th birthday. Call it coincidence if you want, but the way things panned out regarding her malicious intentions, it was clear to me that The Creator wanted to make sure she didn't reap my rewards. Once it was clear that the business was heading in the wrong direction, I tried starting a few businesses, and none got off the ground. I tried another e-commerce business, but it was much harder to rank on Google, especially for the products I wanted to sell.

Although I had a bachelor's degree from Rutgers University, I didn't know much. Most people think that once they graduate from college, they know everything to know, but that's not true. After failed business attempts, I gave real estate a shot. I hung around real estate investors, agents, and industry workers.

I'm grateful I decided to look into real estate because it forced me to start buying and reading books. This is another reason the storm hit. It was meant to elevate me and ultimately free me. Until then, I hadn't read any books since my college days (9 years prior), which was mostly literature books. I became intrigued and started reading 1 to 3 books a week on all sorts of topics: real estate, business, marketing, sales, advertising, personal development, psychology, and more. And I logged in several hours a day learning off YouTube. I set my mind on learning as much as I could. After all, Prophet Muhammad's cousin, Imam Ali Ibn Abu Talib, the 1st Imam in Shi'ite Islam (and 4th caliph in Sunni Islam), stressed that one should always seek and obtain knowledge and wisdom. And the mysterious prophet of Islam is Khidr (or Khizr), which means wisdom, sage, and green (represents love). My birth name was given after Khidr (Khizr). I looked up to these men and decided to follow their advice.

I didn't bother going to clubs and bars or hanging out with friends at night. Instead, I read till my eyes closed shut. I watched so many YouTube videos. My jaw was clenched, which caused me lots of tension and stress. Learning is strenuous. Not to mention, some of the things I was learning were disturbing and really taxed my brain.

I learned to stay humble somewhere in my mid-teens - early 20's. This meant that every time I accrued a new skill set, I balanced myself, and it was as if I didn't have that skill to others. I had to constantly balance myself while learning to avoid becoming an egotistical maniac. After all, according to Shi'ites, I was leaning on the advice of Prophet Muhammad and Imam Ali ibn Abu Talib, who was Muhammad's successor after he passed away. Sunnis say Abu Bakr was the successor, and that's been the quarrel between the two groups.

Because the advice came from godly men, I had to take God's advice on behavior. I heard it over and over again, "be humble! Or I'll take it all away from you!" It was my intuition speaking to me. "You better not dare be arrogant!" I complied. I kept balancing myself after every epiphany. Because of this balance, many people are stunned at the number of things I know because I don't act like it. I'm not a showoff.

Although my online business was dying, my mind was growing. I had two employees picking and packing orders and uploading products while I took pictures of the new products at home and did real estate. I learned a great deal that I would give up that business to know what I know due to all those books and YouTube videos. In other words, I became more than that old business. And had it not been for the destruction of that business, I would have never worked on myself and gained great freedom and power. That's why you must always be thankful, even for the "bad" things.

I learned the power of emotions. I understood why my life was in shambles most of my life. It was fear! It started when I was a toddler. I remember vividly crying when I was 3 to 4 years old, so my mother would come and feed me. I knew I was 3 to 4 years old because we were living in the first apartment in West New York, Jersey. We lived there for approximately 2 years. I recall it took her a long time to come over. And I was freaking out. Finally, she came, and she got mad at me for overreacting. She was gone for a while. She was outside of the apartment. Who knows what she was doing. What she did to me had me in a constant state of fear. I didn't know back then that I was feeling fear, creating new life experiences that invoked more fear in me. And the vicious cycle started and didn't let up until I was in my late 30s when I learned that our emotions produce reality. Because I was in fear, the other kids could tell, so they would bully me and make fun of me. I had anxiety all of my life until approximately March 2022.

My mother was supposed to protect me and keep me safe. Neuman was also supposed to protect me, as that is one of the men's duties. But I was treated like a rag doll; I wasn't looked at as a full human being, and my feelings weren't considered. It didn't matter that I was fearful as long as it wasn't her (my mother). She didn't care. After all, she blamed me for getting pregnant with me. It took decades of trying to get over all of this. I eventually did it at the age of 42. I did a lot of healing after I left Zina. I started recalling all the abuse, the betrayals, the backstabbing, the gossip, the finessing, the insults, and harsh criticism I received from numerous people, and I let the emotions rise in me. I started healing in the hotel room I stayed at for a week after leaving her. I had a perfect suite because it created another sound barrier between me (in the bedroom) and the front door.

I'm not ashamed to admit I let it all out. I was really bawling! I wailed at the recollections. I would ask while tears came down my eyes, "how could they do that to me?" I asked that question when I'd think of my mother, ex, and anyone else who abused or bullied me. After hours of doing this, I thought I had emptied everything out of me. Wrong. This process lasted months. As I wrote this book 9-10 months later, I still shed tears as I recall past hurts. Thankfully, it's nowhere near the level of sadness and pain. I've healed from Sally and Zina. It's just certain little things left that are still trapped that I forgot about.

When I was healing my inner child, I told him, "I'm so proud of you, little man. You did it. It's because of you that we are who we are today. I appreciate you so much for staying strong and not committing suicide, little guy. I know, I know. It was terrible. The world forgot about us, but God didn't. You are a prime example of a faithful servant of the Lord" And to my teenage self, "you did the best you could, buddy. It wasn't your fault. You're a true warrior. You had to put up with way more than anyone should ever have to. I'm proud of you for not killing yourself. It's because of you we became who we are today. Thank you for praying to God regularly. Thank you." And to my young man phase and man phase, I told them, "Thank you! Thank you for focusing on learning and for remembering God constantly. Thank you for spending every free hour you had to educate yourself on various subjects and topics. It's because of you guys that we're here now. Here's a pat on your back. Rejoice! We made it! We made it out alive, stronger than 99.9% of the population! We lived to tell our story and help others in the process. We (different versions of me) took control of our emotions and, therefore, our reality because of your hard work and resilience. I am forever grateful for you two and little me. Remember, guys, I am you. So just because you didn't live a nice life then, you have it now. So, enjoy it."

18

THE RED FLAGS

I grew up without proper guidance, lost in ignorance. At home, there was no emphasis on the importance of reading and writing, leaving me confused and struggling in the third grade. It wasn't until I realized the power of communication through written language that I began to appreciate the value of literacy. However, I still struggled to find engaging material in school and believed all books were uninteresting. It wasn't until my literature course at Rutgers University that I discovered talented authors who wrote in plain language, captivating me to read their books in one sitting.

I'm convinced that my life is a testimony. Those who watched me grow up as a child until now don't believe their eyes. I came from ignorance and poor manners. I was a mere peasant. Confused. Didn't know how to carry myself. Didn't know how to talk. Couldn't hear that well. Yet, my teachers were baffled because they could see I was not slow. They'd tell my parents, "he's so bright! But I don't know why he's like this.

He hardly pays attention, yet he understands everything." They didn't know I had ADHD and autism. I was so confused! I had no idea where or what I was doing most of the time. I barely had any knowledge, wisdom, or even common sense then.

In addition to ADHD and autism, I had ear problems that left me feeling like I was under water. Kids would laugh at me and say, "damn, you're so lost!" And they were right. I was in a whirlwind. I didn't know where I was or the point of everything. I couldn't follow along with people's conversations because I lacked focus. I was incredibly frustrated and stressed dealing with all these things all alone, with almost everyone against me. I didn't know what I did to deserve this. I thought I was being punished by God/Spirit/Universe/Yahweh/Christ/Allah.

In grammar school, I didn't know I had options. I didn't know that I could have talked to a counselor. Had I known, it would have been a lot of help, as I'm sure they would have taught me to change my mindset, which would have altered my frequency and gotten me out of that hellhole. But that wasn't written in the stars for me. I was meant to undergo unbelievable trials and tribulations.

And if that wasn't enough, I was dealing with a bad back and an arm that kept fracturing every year. I broke my arm 5 times in 6 years, starting in kindergarten. When I wore my first cast, my kindergarten teacher treated me aggressively. She'd nudge and yell at me to walk faster whenever the class went outside the school. I protested that walking faster hurt my arm (from the increased vibration from walking on pavement). She had zero patience: didn't care, and was known to be a lunatic. Her name is Mrs. Marks. And, of course, lucky me, I got her as my first teacher.

I fractured my arm once more when I was 40 years old for the 6th time. And my back pain persisted until today. Along my spine, there are two vertebrae that hurt to the touch. No matter what I do, I feel the muscles around these two points very achy and in pain. It's hard to sit up and stand as back muscles are constantly engaged that shouldn't be contracting to maintain posture - they are not made to hold that much weight. Unfortunately, I was born with a weak core. Because of this, my back takes on way too much of the load. My back constantly feels like it needs to be cracked, even after being cracked.

I started doing Schroth therapy for my core in March 2021 and have been doing the exercises 6 days a week, but that tightness in the back never goes away. In addition to the therapy, I started doing core exercises. While the therapy and core exercises provided some relief, my spasms persisted. As early as age 5, I would request my mother to massage my back in those areas several times a day. The relief was so profound that I often fell asleep during the massage.

She would keep rubbing my back, and I'd tell her to keep going when she stopped. It made me feel super relaxed, and I'd fall asleep. Today, I use a handheld massager with an attachment made so I can reach my back, and after I'm done, I feel like my head's in the clouds. I live in constant burning pain. And to make matters worse, I have a condition called kyphosis which is the curving of the spine (hunchback). I work so hard to maintain a good posture every day.

One day I saw a reflection of myself, and I didn't like how my head and neck looked. I decided right then and there to work on my posture. Of all the things I've done: quit cigarettes, quit alcohol, skydive, jump off a building in Las Vegas, and remove 4 wisdom teeth at once, correcting my posture was probably the most difficult thing I ever had to do. Since I already had back pain, the additional pain and discomfort from standing straight were overbearing. The pain was over-whelming and exhausting. And only 5 minutes had passed. I thought surely I'd get used to it by tomorrow. Tomorrow came, and still, it wasn't easy. I was in agony and was conscious of my posture all waking hours. I kept constantly correcting my posture. And it just felt like I would collapse from the tightness, aches, and pain. Weeks had passed, and I still hadn't gotten used to it. The sensations didn't subside. I was still struggling the same. Several months passed until I realized I was holding my posture without consciously doing it. I kept monitoring myself the following days and weeks, and months until, one day, I stopped obsessing over it. I would randomly check my posture throughout the day to ensure I wasn't slipping back (no pun intended). With the improved posture, though, I always feel like my back has to get cracked, even more so now.

If correcting my posture was the hardest thing to do, then doing burpees with a fractured arm was a close 2nd. To treat my depression, I tried doing intense exercises that would increase my heart rate. The home I lived in then was at the bottom of a very steep hill. I'd sprint up the hill as hard as I could. I felt like I would fall back on the hill if I didn't lean in at a 30-degree angle. I'll tell you, it was an effective way to get the heart rate up. However, it wasn't sustainable due to the inten-sity of the workout, and the weather would interfere via rain, snow, extreme cold, and extreme heat. I remembered burpees from Brazilian Jiu Jitsu, where I trained for about a year until some new guy tore my ACL by holding on to my ankle and bumping into a punching bag hanging from the ceiling, falling and twisting my leg, never letting go of it. All I heard was the sound of a plastic cup being crushed violently under an armpit. That sound was my knee being obliterated. I walked it off. No aids. I continued to walk around, although I was limping profoundly. I limped my way into healing, which took a while. I was doing real estate sales at the time, and I was limping into my broker's office and clients' homes. I had no choice. I was the sole income provider, back to the burpees. They were perfect because I could do them at home, and they raised my heart rate pretty well. I did 3 sets of 10 reps. I noticed the tension in my body was gone from exerting myself through the exercise, which made me feel really good!

I couldn't believe the difference it made for my depression. I was hooked. The next day, I dropped into my first repetition, and as I was coming up, I felt the soreness in my chest. My intuition told me to keep going. After a couple more repetitions, the soreness faded, and I went to complete the 3 sets. Again, I felt incredible. I was gaining energy. For example, regular chores started to become effortless. I was hooked even more. Despite the sharp, stabbing pains in my shoulder and humerus bone, I kept going. I would do them very slowly to avoid injuring my arm any further. I often felt like it was about to pop or break, but I kept doing them anyway. I was slowly getting out of the pits of hell, aka mental rock bottom. It was at this time I stopped complaining to everyone, including myself. I didn't know it then, but I was pulling myself out of the darkest time a human can ever go through. I was dragging myself out of stagnation. I was fighting hard and relentlessly, and I wouldn't stop. 6 days a week, 1 day off, said my intuition, to which I obliged. I kept going. No pain, no gain. My chest was getting bigger, and I was getting compliments which got me further hooked. I don't need compliments today, but it was welcomed back then as I was an unhealed version.

In chapter 14, I discussed my hospital visit in 2020 and how I hurt my shoulder, fractured my arm, and bruised my hip. When I returned from the hospital the next day, I shoveled a 100x100' lot with 6" of snow alone at night. The house had a 4-car driveway on a moderate incline. Since the house is situated on a corner, I was responsible for two 100' sidewalks. I kept pushing through the pain. My hip felt fractured - my buttocks were in great pain. My arm was fractured, and my shoulder stabbed me with sharp pain. I felt so abandoned. That night, I felt all alone. I was cold. I looked into the heavens and wondered why I was going through all this. It was very lonely and painful. Zina didn't bother to visit me in the hospital. And she didn't even bother to come outside and help like she used to. She would at least clean the snow from the top of the cars, and I would clean whatever fell on the floor. But this time, she abandoned me, knowing I was doing it all with a fractured arm and a messed up shoulder and hip.

The snowblower's auger was messed up. I had to do it all manually in pain. I felt so humiliated because she knew my arm and hip were injured. I saw her behavior as a red flag, and she kept accumulating more red flags over time until I had enough and left her one day.

The amount of manipulation that was going on was unreal. It turns out she's a master manipulator. She was clever. Unfortunately, she used her smarts for evil. She had no belief in God. She's made it clear before. "If there was a God, then he's playing a game with us," she would say. Unfortunately, I didn't see that as a major red flag back then. Had that happened today, it would be the beginning of the end of the relationship because a woman that doesn't believe in God isn't aligned with my way of understanding and living. And, of course, with her beliefs, there was no guilt regarding sin.

I felt stripped naked. How did this happen? I was loving, I provided, I advised, I taught, I entertained... I did all sorts of good things. This is my payback? Why? I'm so confused. My thoughts fade as I wait for the answers to my question. I wait for the universe to say something. I wait and wait like a dog waiting for its owner. Nothing. I don't get the answer to why she did that. All I get is, "we (the universe) saw everything. Justice will be served. Forgive them and pray for them." This is the thought that comes to mind as communication from Source. It took me a while, but I forgave her and others and prayed for them. I later realized that praying for them was in my best interest because I was putting great energy into the universe, and that would all return to me.

Never, in a million years, did I think my wife would envy me. I thought we were on the same team. I thought she'd be proud to have someone like me to call her husband. Instead, she would downplay all of my accomplishments. Never celebrated me. Never said, "I'm proud of you for accomplishing (that thing)." I never felt loved by her. She was married before me and got divorced within a month! She claims her first husband was gay. I doubt it now. He's a medical doctor, and my best guess is he saw that she was mentally unstable.

She's a compulsive liar and a manipulator. She wasn't ready for a new relationship with me back then. My parents are so ignorant that they didn't know that someone must heal before moving on to someone new. I asked my mother about her and if she recommended I marry her even though she had just been divorced a month ago. Trusting my mother, I followed her advice and married her. I have no one to blame but myself. Why in the *hell* would I listen to my mother? She's only got a 5th-grade education, and she just got done abusing me for 20+ years. Sometimes, I think back to my young adolescent self and tell him, "dude, what in the world were you thinking, bro?" To which he replies, "I don't even know, man!"

Zina was still hurt from her first marriage. I didn't know it back then, but she made a commitment to herself never to commit to anyone again.

After our 2nd child was born and diagnosed with Spinal Muscular Atrophy (SMA), things started to get blurry and confusing for me. I can feel the lack of love towards me, but I would think it's because she's worried about our son. I gave her many passes with this in mind. I gave her the benefit of the doubt. When she had an attitude, I would forgive her and think, "she's just under a lot of stress. Let's not dwell on it."

The reality is she exhibited many, many red flags. I mean MANY. I kept sweeping them under the rug because I figured her parents were conservative Muslims, and she would never do anything to shame her parents. Boy, was I wrong!

Another thing I wasn't fully aware of was Zina's issues growing up with her parents. She had abandonment issues. Her father was never around. And at one point, neither was her mother. They were both working on their business. I knew this when we met but didn't know the implications. Abandonment issues in females cause them to crave attention from many men when they're adults. She was an attention seeker as a child. How do I know this? Because she told me she used to abnormally cry a lot. And I mean non-stop as an infant and a fully grown toddler. She wasn't considered pretty by her parents and uncles, and aunts. Whenever they'd visit their house, they would neglect her and instead play with one of her sisters. She decided to make up for that lack of attention while married to me. She'd talk to men in a high-pitched girly voice and give them strong eye contact, whether it was the landscaper, the sprinkler guy, the plumber, the physical therapist, the doctor, the nurse, or whoever. She'd have my brothers' contact stored in her phone, but it was a problem if I had her sisters' contacts, who were all across the Atlantic Ocean.

These days, I tell people to find out as much as they can from their partners before committing to them. You want to learn about their upbringing and whether or not there was some abuse or neglect. You need to scope them out and figure out if they've healed from their childhood wounds because it can make or break the relationship. I also suggest to friends never entertain someone who's just come out of a relationship.

As someone who left his wife of 20 years, I can confirm that it's unwise and unhealthy to pursue a new relationship anytime soon. As of this writing, it's been 10 months since I left her, and I'm just starting to feel like I'm ready to meet and date new women. Why did it take so long? So many betrayals. I'm embarrassed to write about them.

Unintentionally, I started healing all my pain after leaving Zina, not just the breakup. As stated, I was healing from my mother and other family members. I was healing from all the bullying I had experienced throughout my life and all the humiliating memories. I cried and cried for many days, weeks, and months. Every time I would think, "surely, this is it, I cried it all out." However, each time I cried another day after.

I can't stress how important it is to heal this way. I didn't realize how much pain I was holding inside me. I thought the things that happened 30+ years ago were all forgotten by my system (body). But no. That wasn't the case at all. I kept bringing up painful memories, then the emotions would stir up to the surface, and my pain would turn into relieving wailing. As a man, we're taught we shouldn't cry. I agree to a certain point. I believe men shouldn't cry in public or in front of their women, but it's perfectly fine to do so privately. I never told anyone that I healed in this way. I'm being vulnerable in this book in hopes of helping those in need of help.

After a breakup, many people catch a rebound and try to keep coasting through their lives. But the problem is, they are still hurt. These people are meeting innocent bystanders and projecting their pain and insecurities onto the poor individual. Case in point. Zina wasn't healed after her first failed marriage and therefore projected a lot of toxicity onto me.

Besides her grave manipulation tactics, one of the projections that made me seriously consider a divorce was her constantly accusing me of cheating. I found this to be very odd because, at the time I was being accused of this, I was working from home. It was impossible for me to cheat. I couldn't help but think that she was the one who was cheating, especially since she was angry with me for no reason and for the fact that

I couldn't get in touch with her sometimes for hours, to which she'd say, "my phone is acting up."

Leaving her was the hardest decision of my life. Here I am faced with a tough choice. We have a daughter who's a freshman at NYU, and we have a 15-year-old with special needs who is bound to a wheelchair. Do I leave, or do I stay for my children's sake? I already gave her many chances and even threatened to leave her. Each time I packed my luggage to leave her, she'd talk me out of it. She's a smooth talker, and I'll give her that. That was a grave mistake on my part. If a man ever threatens to leave, he should follow through and leave no matter how much the woman begs him not to. She needs to know you're serious, and if you don't follow through, she'll do whatever she wants in front of you and behind your back because she assumes you'll never leave her like all the other times you threatened to leave.

The last time I packed my bag was the last. She was out of the house, so I was able to go around and get all of my essentials without her knowing. When she returned, I was shocked because I thought I had more time. I preferred to leave without any commotion for the sake of our son. Nevertheless, I proceeded with my plan. I told her I was leaving her, and she started fake-crying. I can tell they weren't real tears. I felt like she was spitting in my face with those fake tears, insulting my intelligence. How dare she insult my intelligence! She grabbed my wrists and buckled her knees to anchor me in my place. It didn't matter because I kept pushing towards the exit with her dragging along. Physically, I was at my weakest point ever. It took great courage to decide to leave. It took tremendous inner strength to escape her grip and to walk away from my crying son, who was begging me, "please, dad, stay. Don't go. Pleeeease!" I can't describe how I felt looking at him and walking away. It was extremely painful. I recalled when Neuman would walk away as my mother beat me. I rationalized with myself, "ok, but he (my son) isn't being physically abused, and he's never been scolded or spanked." That was my thought process amid my escape. But now, I realize that I did abuse him, mentally and emotionally - by leaving. What choice did I have? I could stay there and die a slow, agonizing death through emotional and mental abuse by Zina, or I could roll the dice and start a fresh new life. I chose fresh.

Before I could get out, which was very hard because of all her weight on me and the fact that I was suffering from fibromyalgia symptoms then, she did the unthinkable. She got our son involved. I was surprised she did this. I never thought in a million years she'd do that. I thought she'd want to protect him from what's happening. So, she told our son, "look, you're father's leaving us, tell him not to!" And he starts crying and begging me to stay. It was a traumatic experience. The day is still vivid in my mind. I'm sure he will never forget that day, either. It pained me to see such a sweet boy seated in his wheel-chair, trying to protect his mother and trying to fix her problem from his chair. Poor kid. As a super empath, I felt his pain completely, but I had a difficult choice. Do I choose Hunter and his sister, Felicity, or do I choose me?

The answer was clear this time. I choose me. I choose me; the heck with everyone else. I was tired. It's been 42 years of non-stop struggling, pain, and heartache. It ends today; I'm done. People are going to freaking respect me from here on out. I don't tolerate bullshit from anyone anymore. That was my attitude and still is. Once I chose myself, things started to improve vastly. The universe or God rewarded me for standing my ground and not being a pushover. I am always ready to defend myself now. First, I'll try cutting my aggressor with my words. If that doesn't work, we're fighting! Yes, physically. I'm ready for whatever. I always walk with some protection on me as well and I always have a weapon in the car; I'm not tolerating any disrespect from anyone.

After I left, the kids were swayed not to interact with me. They were fed many lies about me. It's been 9 months since I've seen my two kids. It's been hard but having dealt with so much in my past, I could withstand this attack against me. I didn't cave in and run back to her to see my children. I kept choosing myself. She wasn't happy with that, so she and her family started a smear campaign against me. Spreading gossip about me to whoever would listen. I was upset, but my intuition told me not to worry and that it will all catch up with them. They spread so much gossip about me that people started to doubt what was said about me, especially because some of these people have had positive interactions with me. Eventually, people started to see them for who they were, and everything backfired on them. The way I beat their smear campaign was to get on TikTok (@TheChrisJosh) and make helpful videos, so others don't fall into the same traps that I did. Many people who heard the lies against me watched my TikTok videos and were scratching their heads, "is this the same person?" More and more people found out about my TikToks and saw Zina and her family as evil liars.

On the other hand, I never once said something ill about her or her family, even though I had lots to say. My intuition warned me to stay put and not say anything. My intuition is my guiding system. It helps me navigate through life. It is what helps me overcome the limits caused by ADHD and autism. I didn't always listen to my intuition, but after learning many lessons, I only listen to *it* from now on. The breakup and time away from my children have been something to overcome. Initially, I thought my life was falling apart, but it turns out I was being gifted a great new life.

I decided to cut all ties with Zina since she's a narcissist, and that's the best way to handle a narcissist. I went completely no contact. I knew she was getting updates about me from certain "family" members and "friends," so I cut them all off, too, except for Neuman. He and I share a warehouse space, and we only communicate regarding that.

I figured since my life was caving in, I might as well cut off the entire past and start all over again with new friends - now that I know what red flags to look for in people. Besides, I had changed so much. The people of my past had an old image of me. I no longer wanted to associate myself with stagnant people or those who are still the same people they were 20-30 years ago. I decided I want high-caliber, trustworthy people in my life, and I will not settle for anything less. I will never again settle for anyone who doesn't match my energy or reciprocate. If I have just one friend like this, it's more than enough. After the separation, I fell in love with being on my own and enjoying my company without anyone nagging me or complaining. I got rid of my co-dependence on feeling good or worthy. All I need to feel good is myself. And I know my worth now. No one can ever tell me who I am except me. This divorce seemed to be a curse initially, but it became a great lesson and catalyst for a much fuller and happier life.

I didn't always look at the positives, but I'm glad I was into positivity during the breakup. And I'm glad I already had cut off my mother and some other toxic people in the past. This made handling the breakup so much easier. All I had to say to myself was, "well, if I cut off my own mother, surely cutting off Zina will be relatively easy." And I was right. Besides, I was wronged on many levels, making it a no-brainer to leave her for good. She was always projecting onto me her insecurities and what she was doing.

To say I was a perfect husband, I'd be exaggerating. I made some mistakes, but I was a great husband. I provided our family with a house and everything we needed. I supported her and uplifted her. I boosted her confidence while she was destroying mine. I gave her lots of great advice. I taught her different ways of thinking. I transformed her. But that doesn't mean anything if the person doesn't appreciate it. She was and is ignorant. She didn't know it then, but she had a very good life.

The fact is, when someone has unresolved childhood traumas, they will sabotage their relationships. They'll see the extraordinary as ordinary because they don't appreciate the effort. Even worse, some will look at their partner in an envious way. She was envious of me. She hated that I was intelligent, strong, positive, happy, and lucky.

The fact of the matter is she's not strong enough to handle the light. Light is energy. When you hold the light, you are holding great energy, which is vibrating very high. Not many can withstand the power. I can handle the light because of the adversities I dealt with all my life. She didn't walk the dark caves with me, where mother would violate me when I was 4 years old till I left for college and even when I'd come back for the weekends. She didn't experience all the bullying from fake friends and harsh treatment from adults. She doesn't know she wouldn't be able to walk a day in my shoes. And it's not just her. All of my family members were envious.

For the same reason, they could see that I was different and God's hand was on my life. They didn't like that. They, too, thought, "why him and not me? What makes him so special?" In short, it's me because God/Spirit/Universe is who I think about literally all day long - unless I'm conversing with someone. In addition, I dedicated lots of time to reading different scriptures, abstaining from the unlawful, and putting in the work by praying way more than required. In addition, I would never cheat people. I would always, and still do, make sure it's a win-win situation for everyone I encounter. God favored me because, despite the hell that I went through, I still shine my light everywhere I go. I still show people unconditional love - even when I'm down and out. When I lost my children, house, and Zina, I didn't run to social media to cry about it as some men do. I ran to social media to enlighten others instead. I buried my tears in front of the public. No one knew what was happening until later when I healed. That's when I let my followers know that I was in the middle of a divorce.

They say, "why him and not me," because I'm raw - I use profanity sparingly. I don't go around putting up a false image. I keep it real. I'm vulnerable. And when you're like that, people tend to look down on you. In their eyes, I was evil for whatever reason. I'm the one who did for others with no expectations of anything in return to make God happy. As long as God was happy, I was happy. Hence, that is why I was always happy. It was because I was always making God happy. In turn, he made sure I continued to stay happy. And I've been in this divine loop since I was a child. I never say, "ok, I've done enough for God. Let me take a break." No. I never think like that! I keep going and going like the Energizer bunny.

Where do I get my morals from? I got them mostly from Prophet Muhammad, PBUH, and the 12 imams of Shi'ite Islam. They were balanced men. Their masculine and feminine energies are perfectly balanced. Imam Ali Ibn Abu Talib, the 1st Imam in Shi'ite Islam, would go around the villages at night with his face covered and feed the needy men, women, and children. No one knew it was him until he died because the kids waited and waited on him, but he never showed up again. Imam Ali was accused of not performing his 5 daily prayers, yet he was murdered while prostrating to Allah during prayer or salaat. His assailant struck him in the head while Imam Ali's forehead was on the ground in prayer. When the people asked how he died, it became apparent that the rumors about him never praying were lies. Other Shi'ite Imams would go to the slave market and buy slaves just to free them. These are the only men and Prophet Muhammad (PBUH) I had to look up to until I learned of the Buddha and Jesus Christ.

Because I was so curious about God, I stepped out of the religion I was born into, Islam (Shi'ite). I learned about Yahweh, The Father, Jesus Christ, The Holy Spirit, Buddha, Krishna, etc. Learning all the different religions and philosophies made my prayers more effective. Although I don't subscribe to Islam exclusively, I still follow the morals, and I don't drink alcohol or eat pork. I don't eat them because I tried them both. Alcohol has many cons, like hangovers, looking stupid, dehydration, excessive calories, and hunger. Besides, alcohol can make one angry and be in a low vibration. Pork is too high in calories. Also, pigs are smart. They're the 5th most intelligent animals - more intelligent than dogs.

Becoming an omnist, family members thought I was seeking attention from others like "look at me! I practice all these faiths!" That's nonsense. I became an omnist by being led by my intuition and The Creator. I became an omnist because of my hunger and thirst for God.

I didn't set out to be the first omnist in my family. I simply stumbled on all of this without planning it. I didn't wake up one day and say I will look at the rest of the sects in Islam and then Buddhism, Christianity, Judaism, and the rest. It didn't happen like that. I was very skeptical most of the way. In fact, I was lost more than ever. But even when I doubted God at times and didn't understand what all these religions meant during my becoming an omnist, I stuck to my morals. I felt like that was the right way to live. And I kept Source/Yahweh/Allah/Christ in mind 24/7. Eventually, as I progressed, a light bulb went off in my mind, and it all made sense. I arrived at the truth! But before I claim to be an omnist, I claim to be a spiritualist. Many people are into spirituality or religion, and I'm into both.

Never before have I had such clarity. I wished to share this with everyone, but after talking to Neuman and Zina about it, I quickly realized most people won't be receptive and are hell-bent on their ways. It didn't matter if I brought forth verses from the Quran to prove my point; they thought the devil possessed me. I realized that most people claim to follow a particular religion but don't look into the scriptures. They take the pastor's/sheikh's word for it. And without looking into the scriptures, how could they think that what I was saying was nonsense or wrong? That's like an F student telling the A student he's wrong when the A student is the one who actually read the text.

Nevertheless, I didn't push my ideologies on them. I decided long ago that I was not here to preach or "wake" people up. I feel as though the person should want it. If a person sets his or her intentions on seeking the truth, they will be led to their awakening. Think of it as attractive marketing vs. spamming. I create the content, and if someone looks for it, they'll find it, as opposed to me sending an email out to everyone, including those swimming in alcoholism.

Rather than devote my time and energy to preaching to others, I continued gaining more knowledge, giving me more power. The more knowledge I gained, the more in tune I became with the universe. Life became effortless. Things seem to always go in my favor now. As they say, don't fix it if it ain't broke. I learned that I have to always stay true to myself, no matter what.

Now that I'm nearly 43 years old at the time of writing this, I look back at the younger me. The younger me was scared, worried, embarrassed, insecure, lonely, confused, in pain, depressed, ignorant beyond imagination, lacked etiquette and basic consideration, unruly, combative, and stubborn. I look back at all of that, and it's truly shocking and jaw-dropping when I realize how far I've come and evolved. I'm sure if I were to visit my grammar school teachers, they'd be in complete disbelief that it's truly me. The analogy I use for my life from the day I was born until today is as if a single-cell organism evolved to Christ's consciousness in just over 40 years - a stellar and remarkable journey!

I always questioned why I had to undergo such excruciating pain and torture. Since there's a God, why am I going through this? Why would he do this to me? I didn't get the answer till yesterday, 8/22/22. It came through my intuition. It said, "You didn't experience love from family and others because you wanted to experience yourself, love / God. You wanted to experience your own love. That's what you were born for." Tears rolled down my face, and it made perfect sense. The Buddhists say that the universe is experiencing itself. And here I am, the universe, experiencing itself.

My intuition kept nudging me to write this book to give others hope. That they can overcome anything with God in their hearts and minds, I can't tell you how much I've cried until this point while writing this book. The tears brought resolve as I recollected what I was going to write. I had no idea how much stuff I had bottled up inside me for all these years. Remembering the events in detail and formulating your opinions on them while letting your emotions out through tears truly brings closure and comfort. If you're a guy, don't cry in front of anyone, especially your woman. Do it in private. If you're a woman, the healing process is the same. I urge you to also cry in private so that your healing work is uninterrupted. This way you can heal as quick as possible. If someone's there with you, them consoling you will get you off track. Let God console you.

I've lived in my current apartment of over 200 residents for 10 months. I moved here after I left Zina, and the neighbors have seen my progress in real-time. It seems like I shed more and more trauma each time they see me, and in turn, I'm vibing high, and it's noticeable. When I first arrived here, I was pissed. I'm pretty certain people thought I was a killer. I was ready for any confrontation. I hadn't been this ready for a battle, ever. As mentioned previously, I shied away from confrontation about halfway through college.

After a failed marriage, I was tired of putting up with anyone's bullshit lies and manipulation tactics. I recalled how people disrespected me because they could tell I wasn't ready to defend myself. But that all changed. I was like that because I was appeasing Allah. I was treating people like Prophet Muhammad, and his Ahlul Bayt (People of the House) did (the people of the house consist of 14 people: Prophet Muhammad, his daughter Fatima El Zahraa and the 12 imams). But all it ever got me was assholes and douchebags. I had enough! I put the gloves on and was ready for anything. Nowadays, people can sense that immediately, so no one disrespects me anymore. On the contrary, I've never received more respect than now.

19

KICKED WHILE ON THE FLOOR

$\mathcal{J}$n Islam, it is said that to reach heaven, everyone must pass through hell. Let me tell you, hell is not under the surface with a blazing inferno. It's Earth with lots of pressure, heartache, betrayals, and losses. I must be honest; I don't know how I survived. There were just too many things going on at the same time. How on Earth could I survive all of that without killing myself? How did I survive the voodoo and black magic attacks?

Unbeknownst to me, Zina had put several spells on me: death, isolation, binding, love, financial losses, and more. This resulted in me always being attached to her and thinking about her all day. I always thought that it wasn't normal. I developed severe fibromyalgia. I lost my multi-million dollar business on Zina's 30th birthday, and every business after that failed. I lost a lot of money. I was isolated. Zina would check my call logs, call my friends, and spread lies about me to ruin my relationships.

I can't believe someone can be so cruel. I had a choice. I can cry about it, or I can move forward. I did both. I cried to heal while at the same time working on new projects and creating content for my social media account. When I left Zina, I decided to maintain my routine and not break it because of the separation. I continued my workouts without skipping a single day. I also continued on my calorie-restricted diet. That was the best way to go about things. Giving up on the gym and diet gives her the satisfaction of telling others, "see? He's nothing without me." I proved her wrong.

When a calamity ensues, do not stop your life. Continue doing what you were doing and add something like a passion or a hobby. Think of ways to add value to the world instead of laying on your couch all day sobbing and ruminating. When I left her, I felt like I had lost everything: a wife, children, and home. Fast forward 10 months later, I wouldn't have it any other way - of course, I yearn for my 2 beautiful children. Maybe one day, they'll come to their senses and finally respond to their father's calls and texts.

I realized, once again, things happened for me, not against me. God saw everything. He saw how kind and loving I was to that woman. And He saw what an ungrateful brat she was. And He saw all the ill that she did behind my back. And He heard all the nasty gossip. That's why He put an end to the relationship. He saved me. She would complain about everything, including the house.

I tell you, I would have had a heart attack if God didn't remove me from that relationship. She put a death spell on me because a fortune teller told her and her mother that I'd be successful and famous one day. My mother also got the same info from a different fortune teller and placed hexes and spells on me from when I was just 5 years old - that's when she attached a spell to my shirt sleeve saying it was the Quran, but it wasn't. In their puny peanut brains, they thought the success would be stolen from me and given to them by killing me off.

The two had zero remorse and zero empathy towards me. Being who I am, I couldn't fathom people being *that* cruel. But then again, people get murdered every minute of the day, and someone's doing the murdering. Imagine you see two men fighting, one getting rocked with a wild right hook. The man plunders to the floor. You think, "OK, the fight's over!" But to your surprise, the man who laid the other guy out is now kicking the man while he's dazed and confused. I'm sure you and others would protest; some would even run toward them and break them apart.

I was that man on the ground. My mother and ex saw me dazed and confused, laying on the floor in poor health due to their abuse and black magic, yet they continued abusing me with no regard for my life. They kept adding more and more spell work. The success I mentioned earlier was prophesied as material wealth and fame. They did all the horrible things to me for some material wealth and fame. But they don't understand that they don't have the capacity for either, as my mother has a 5th-grade education and never improved herself, and Zina never cracked open a book after going to a less-known state college. What would they be famous for exactly? Zina couldn't even be famous for a sex tape!

That's the thing they don't understand. People are usually famous for giving some value that many appreciate. Material wealth in the hands of an ignorant person is like water in a person's hands. Yeah, you got the water, but for how long? They would blow it immediately if large sums of money came into their lives.

Had they just shown me genuine love, I planned on taking my loved ones with me to the top. Not anymore. I'm going to the top with God only. And I plan to give my money away to the unfortunate. After dealing with such grotesque people, I noticed nearly everyone is opportunistic. They want to come by with smiles when they can see God's blessings over my life. However, when I was struggling, they were making fun of me behind my back. Sadly, I won't even take my children to the top with me. I want them to earn everything. When I update my will with all the blessings, 99% of it goes to people in need - not charity organizations and not "family."

After leaving Zina, I was all alone in one of my darkest hours. Neuman was the one person I was banking on asking me, "hey, how are you holding up?". Days passed, and I didn't hear from him. Weeks passed. I was surprised. MONTHS passed, and still, nothing. I found his behavior odd. I live one town over, and he never bothered to visit. Yet, he connected deeply with Zina and would visit her daily instead of me. I finally understood; I have no family, and Neuman betrayed me. You would never think your parents would abandon you and hurt you on such a level. I have no doubts that Neuman had an extraordinary relationship with Zina.

Was Neuman all bad? No. But he is a narcissist. He is a MASTER manipulator. His choice of weapon is silence. His kids are fighting? Silence. His wife is berating him? Silence. His second eldest son is acting like a brat? Silence. Anything can happen, and he just stands there, not saying a single word. Again, it's not because he's lame. In fact, he's crafty and smart.

Unfortunately, he uses his "gifts" to manipulate others. In my situation, he was playing on both sides of the field. He'd act like he's on my side and cares about me - yet takes any info I give him and tells everything to Zina. I only communicate with him regarding the warehouse space we share and to ask about my children, and it's done via texting. He was the last person from the family with whom I maintained a relationship. That never sat well with me because I knew he was updating Zina, mother, and siblings about me. I cut off all mutual friends between Neuman, Sally, Zina, and siblings.

Neuman wasn't all that bad. He's helped me, of course. The thing is, I helped him a lot too. I took him out of bankruptcy twice and gave him many years where he didn't have to worry about money. After his 2nd bankruptcy, he came to me for help to start a new business. I put all his business purchases on my credit cards and got him a vehicle in my name. I sourced his materials because he was overpaying elsewhere and not making a profit. I made profits possible for him. For him to treat me that way is unforgettable. I've forgiven him and the rest but will never forget what they did or the lessons learned.

Neuman has many friends; you'll never hear anyone complain about him. To others, he was a great friend. To me, he was an absent father who didn't know how to raise a child. A man who was jealous when he saw his son in his new home with his wife. He wanted my life. So, he went after it. He and her were secretly talking to each other without my knowing. He never taught me anything - not even how to shave. Never gave me the sex talk. Heck, I got hard hearing in both ears and spoke loudly without knowing it for many years. He couldn't even tell me, "son, lower your voice a bit. I know you can't hear that well, but I don't want you to look foolish." Do you know when I noticed this behavior? At the age of 42! Yes. How? I was calling the doctor's office to make an appointment. And every month, it was the same response. The lady on the other side of the call would be noticeably irate. Something told me to speak lower and softer next time. I did just that, and suddenly the entire staff was receptive and went out of their way to help me and were pleased to talk to me.

Do you know why he didn't guide me? Because he's a narcissist. He wants to appear as the best male and leader of the family. He doesn't want anyone else to be respected and successful. Hell, he socializes so much that he has a lot of social skills. But does he share that valuable information with me? Never! He barely even talked to me. He wants me and everyone else to look up to him. Imagine. How sad is that? A 60-year-old man wants his 42-year-old son to look up to him like a complete fool in front of everyone. Did he not know I was representing him out there in society?

I started to see him for who he was when he didn't give a rat's ass about my shoulder, arm, and hip injuries. The ultimate confirmation was when I had lost 50 pounds and got shredded while putting on muscle. Did he say, "you've made an impressive transformation?" Absolutely not. Again, silence.

I maintained a mobile number for about 15 years. I loved that number. Here's why. I didn't know who Nikola Tesla was when I got that number. It had the 3 Tesla numbers. When I learned about Tesla's 3,6,9 principle about 9 years later, I was taken aback slightly that my phone number consisted of those numbers. You don't know how hard it was for me to shut that line off. At that point, I said to myself, "I might as well cut off everyone from the past and start a new life altogether." I did this because I was a different person 10, 20 years ago. I'm nowhere near the same person anymore. And honestly, people will see the old you no matter what, so I figured it's best to start over with the lessons and experiences I gained to form new strong relationships.

The new me demands respect. Otherwise, there is no discussion. There is no interaction. Respect first, then they can get my attention. Around 2015, I worked in real estate sales and at a Keller Williams brokerage. I was friends with the office manager, and we would talk. One thing stuck with me. I'll never forget it. She said they interviewed 39 other people for her position. She was very professional and was very well put together. She was very sharp and had great body language. It dawned on me that by interviewing enough people, one can land a top-notch employee and asset to the company. I started applying that concept to friendships. Now the word friend has different levels for me. What people call a friend, I call an acquaintance. What people call a best friend, I call a friend. I didn't have to really interview many people for the acquaintances, although there *are* standards and boundaries they must respect. But to find a good friend, I needed to interview 40 people.

I realized there weren't that many high-caliber people in terms of percentage relative to the overall population. I, unfortunately, experienced a lot of low-quality, hateful, jealous, and envious people throughout my life of 42 years. I encountered so many that I gave up on there being good people out there. As a result of this and my past dealings with my abusive mother and neglectful father, I also had major trust issues. I looked at people in a negative light and viewed them as connivers, liars, and cheats. People turned me off. I thought everyone was the same. I didn't realize back then that my attitude attracted these people.

One day it occurred to me that people are good with some and not so welcoming to others, and that was something I never understood in the past. I thought it was luck or because the two individuals spoke the same language or had some other commonality. But really, it was because of their attitudes and beliefs. The average person didn't get physically, mentally, and emotionally abused daily by the woman that was supposed to protect them. They weren't betrayed continuously by family and "friends." Their outlook on people wasn't as gloomy and doomed as my outlook.

So, to be realistic as to who I call my friend, I adopted the "interview 40 people for the position" rule. Meaning I wasn't surprised if I met 10 new people and all of them weren't deemed to be called my friends because there were 30 more people I had to go through. As a result, my outlook on people is more hopeful and positive. Rather than saying to myself, "everyone's an asshole," now I say, "there are lots of good people I can meet and be friends with. They're scattered all over the place. I just have to talk to enough people."

After leaving Zina, I looked hard at myself and said, "Enough. I won't shy away from confrontation anymore and won't allow anyone to disrespect me either." Seven months before leaving my ex-wife, I started a home workout. I also started dieting. I worked out 6 days a week and only took Sundays off. In 1 ½ years, I never once skipped a workout. I never once took a cheat meal or cheat day on my diet.

As a result, I developed a great physique. One time, I had a cop press me hard regarding what my chest routine was like. He kept asking what I was doing to get my chest developed the way I did. And when I told him to be consistent, he scoffed and said, "I've been working out for 10 years, and don't look like that!" That was such a great moment for me. Not because the cop wasn't developing, of course not, but because it boosted my confidence. And it wasn't just one cop. His partner was also very impressed. I think getting a compliment like that from a police officer is meaningful.

I was enthusiastic about my physical transformation. I was losing weight and gaining muscle. Here's where I really started to question Neuman and Zina. People noticed and complimented me, but these two would never even acknowledge my progress and transformation. It was as if nothing had changed about me. It was a telltale sign that there was some jealous energy. Neuman saw what I went through in the prior years. He knew what a mental toll everything took on me. How much pain I was in and how lethargic and drained I always felt due to my battle with fibromyalgia - to the point where going to the supermarket was a major mission. You would think he'd be excited that his son is pushing past the pain and transforming his life. But no. I was taken aback. It was clear to me then why he was always quiet with me.

I always wondered why Neuman was social with everyone except me. I thought it was because he was just tired. That wasn't it. He wanted to purposely make me feel unwanted.

Here's what is interesting. I've weight trained on and off since I was 12 when I joined the high school football team, and we trained the summer between 8th grade and 9th. While married to Zina, I attempted to get 6 pack abs. There was a time when I went to the gym and dieted for 2 years straight, and I couldn't get rid of the belly fat, or love handles. She always puts her two cents on what's healthy and what's not. I told her I needed to stay within a calorie range, so she would cook dinners and tell me their calorie contents. I don't think she was counting the calories correctly because I never was able to reach my fitness goals and gave up because I thought without steroids, you couldn't achieve a nice physique,

The fact that Zina didn't compliment me raised a red flag because no one else saw me go through the brutal punches of fibromyalgia as she did. She saw me get "manhandled" by the condition. She knew how much it affected my ability to function. Of all people, I thought surely my wife would be happy. But no. She didn't say anything. Did she think a compliment would make me arrogant? Did she think other women would take notice? It's possible that she had these thoughts. But it's clear now that the two wanted to assert their dominance over me; what these two didn't understand was that I was showing them authentic love based on the assumption that they deserved it - not because I was desperate for their approval. I just had tons and tons and tons of love within me, and I wanted to bless them because I thought they genuinely cared for me. "The lie detector determined that was a lie" (use Maury Povich voice).

I felt bad for Zina because she was always running to doctor appointments for our son. So, I did things to try to cheer her up and show her love because her family never taught her anything about love. Therein lies the problem. When I showed her authentic love, she thought it was insincere. She thought I was doing it to manipulate her. But she's obviously not thinking straight because I was the same loving person for the 20 years we were together. Some people are so mentally gone they can't think straight for themselves. But she's a narcissist. She thinks everyone must think like her. Her loss! I was the only person who stood by her, listening to her complaining, and did things for her without expecting anything in return. She's learning the hard way now. She's finding out no one has time to listen to her bullshit. No one will do anything for her unless she gives something up for them - like her body.

As for my "father," I suspected something was going on between him and her, and it still was. And it would make sense that transforming myself and my body would threaten Neuman's ego because he's afraid of how she views me versus him.

As mentioned, Neuman never asked me how my arm was doing. But several months later, he hurt his arm and back. A part of me said, "don't ask him how he's feeling. He didn't ask me how I was feeling. An eye for an eye," but my nature couldn't carry out that plan. So, I would ask him daily, "how's your arm and back? Are you getting better? I ordered you a heating pad. When you come to the house, I'll give it to you."

He must have shown up within a day or two. When I went to my man cave to get the heat pad for him, he was standing near Zina. As I handed it to him, Zina or his wife (at this point, I might as well call it like it is) immediately commented, "oh, for his back?" in a low, depressed tone. Hmmmm. How would she know this? Neuman hadn't come to the house since he injured himself. If they talked on the phone, how come she never told me, "I was talking to your dad today, and he told me he injured his arm and back." Major red flag.

Surprisingly, I'm writing this about him, and I have zero emotions. God truly saved me from this heartbreak that my own father caused me. I'm unsure if I need to let the emotions out because I have zero emotions when I think of his betrayal. I don't get upset or anything like that. Usually, when I need to heal from a person or situation, the thought of that person causes me to be angry, sad, and emotional.

I used to take the bus from West New York, NJ, to Washington Heights, NY, multiple times a week to visit him. I would call him every day. I was rooting for him. I was glad he was my father at the time because my mother was so crazy. I felt like our bond was special. Unfortunately, it wasn't - not to him. I don't know when he started screwing up, but one day I noticed how they talked to each other was completely different than how they used to. Much different tonality. I'm very aware, so I noticed this shift.

20

THOUGHTS OF OFFING MYSELF

$\mathcal{I}$t was an extremely long, lonely, and heartbreaking life. I had no hope. I had God in my heart but wasn't seeing things improve. My suicidal thoughts started as early as 9 years old. The thought would cross my mind as much as sex would cross the mind of a teenage boy. I can't tell you how many times I got real close to going for it. I kept these thoughts and feelings to myself, although I often told my mother I wished I was never born. She didn't think much of it. The reality was that I was plotting on myself.

I would let my mind wander for hours. I would think, "what's the best way to commit suicide without the possibility of a failed one?" Besides it being forbidden by God, I often worried that if I used a gun, for example, maybe the gun would backfire or worse, the wound wouldn't take me out and instead leave me in a vegetative state. I often said, "screw it, let's do it." But then I'd remember God. I DID NOT WANT TO GO TO HELL!

Imagine living a life of hell only to wind up in hell. No, thank you. Although I never saw God, I still believed in Him because I knew something created all this. There was too much intelligence and order for there not to be a higher power at work. I thought about jumping off the George Washington Bridge many times. I thought about jumping off a high-rise building. I thought about poisoning myself. I thought about hanging myself - this option seemed most likely to succeed. I thought about suicide by cops. I thought about stabbing my lungs and heart. I thought about driving 150 mph on the opposite side of the highway right into an oncoming vehicle. I thought about drowning. I can't say I ever thought about burning myself alive, though - that's too painful. I did think about overdosing on prescription pills and hard drugs. I thought about joining the military and going to war to get shot up.

I can't tell you what a dark place I was in. I can't believe my own mother had zero empathy for me. I saw her for what she really was, a demon. No, I won't say she's an animal because I've seen plenty of animals care for their offspring and defend them against predators. She cannot be an animal - those are higher beings who have love for their offspring. They are not in competition with their babies. They're not jealous of them. They want to nurture and protect them and get them ready for nature.

A demon is only concerned with money and power over others. A demon wants to live as a tyrant. It doesn't know how to compromise and wants to impose its will on others through force or manipulation. Whenever a demon spots me, they get enraged. I should mention my mother and others weren't actual demons but that a demon possessed them.

This light I carried from birth. It's why I'm always happy, positive, and smiling even if I'm not "rich" by my mother's standards and society's. And even when abused. This light and my attitude irritated the hell out of my mother and father and siblings and "friends" and "family." You get the point.

It bothered my mother that I could still smile and laugh despite my health issues and her beatings. She didn't know what else she could do to me. She tried so many things, and still, I overcame them with the feeling of love that flooded my veins. She could never be happy. She was always thinking about the family's financial situation and how her friends' husbands were advancing in America, and Neuman lagged behind. This infuriated her. I told her, "mom, at least we have a roof over our heads, and we have food in the fridge. She would say, "you're so dumb. Get the hell out of my face, you idiot! You don't understand anything." And then, "you're just like him! You're a loser just like your father." And I would look down all sad and say nothing.

She's such a hypocrite because while she said things like this to me in private, when she was on the phone with her sisters and friends (she was literally on the phone all day nonstop), she would boast about the things I did, and how bright I was. That is the classic textbook definition of a narcissist. She needed so much attention, and it was comical. She was on the phone literally from the minute she woke up, which was 10 am, till about 1:30 am. As you can imagine, back then, there were no Airpods. I went to Radio Shack and discovered a phone that came with a headset so she could talk to them hands-free. She was happy with me for a day or two and praised me to her friends for the discovery, but then she reverted to her old ways. Remember, the phone is hands-free, which meant I was getting whipped while she was on the phone with her sisters. Had I known that, I would have never told her about it.

Did any of her sisters say anything to her regarding her abusing me? I had one aunt who sometimes told her, "but why do you keep hitting him? That's not right." God bless her heart. That was literally the most anyone ever intervened for me.

The way I learned to heal my past hurts is to recall them and reflect deeply on what happened. If it's sad, I let the tears roll. It's the best way to detox from these past hurts. Whenever I go through the healing process, the next time I recall that memory, it doesn't have as much of an emotional impact on me anymore. In life, we hold a lot of baggage. It's our job to let go of everything and to face our shadows. It's normal for someone to want to forget unfortunate events. Unfortunately, that doesn't work. You might think it's out of your system, but it's not. Until you experience the emotions and let everything out, it's still there, hindering you from achieving your greatest joy.

Part of the healing process is to figure out what exact detail(s) hurt you from the encounter or event. Get specific. There may be several things. For example, if your lover cheated on you, ask yourself what exactly about the cheating hurts? In my case, I found that it was because I thought she was my property, and it was violated and stolen. But the truth is, she's not my property, and I can't control what she does. Once I understood that, I finally healed from that situation. So be sure to ask yourself what exactly triggers you, and don't be too general.

Refer to the end of the book to find the appendix, entitled, "The Shadow Self Workbook." There you will find questions and information to help you dive deep into your traumas of your past and help you get over them. You can also view and print the workbook at **http://ChrisJosh.com/pages/work book** I also highly recommend you get my free eBook, entitled, "How To Become Your Higher Self," at **http://ChrisJosh.com/pages/free-e-book** All you have to do is enter your name and email addres, then click on submit and you'll receive an email with the download link. The eBook in conjunction with this book will help you transform into the most healed and happiest version of yourself. You will attract great abundance, including wealth, health, love, joy, and peace.

All the hurt of the past prevents you and millions of people from being joyous. For example, many people are disappointed when they find out their baby will be a girl. Many men unconsciously neglect their daughters and don't give them the attention they need. This causes a feeling of abandonment for the girl. She learns to accept it as a fact. She tries not to let it affect her so much. She tries her best to forget about it. However, this deep hurt of abandonment plays a crucial role in the girl's life, especially when she hits puberty. Because of the abandonment wound, she starts to seek a lot of male attention and validation. Many women shake their behind on the internet, desperate for attention, comments, and likes. It's incredible how the neglect of a father, one person, can cause a woman to seek exponentially more validation from multiple men.

This abandonment wound in women often causes them to leave their marriages or relationships. This has been a major issue in the United States. It has become common knowledge that most, not all, but a very high percentage of women cheat. Of course, many men cheat, but the estimate is that about 57% of men cheat (men can't find sex as readily as women do), while 85% or more of women cheat. This makes sense since girls are often frowned upon and thus get abandoned. Again, in the United States, many men are extremely skeptical of relationships for fear of getting cheated on. As a country, this is detrimental because it's threatening the American family. This can have profound effects on human development as well as many citizens having to pay higher taxes to support the children who don't have a father in their lives.

In my opinion, awareness must be spread regarding this matter. We need to educate these men that they are responsible for their daughters. They can't just go to work, come home and sit on the box while drinking a six-pack. That's unacceptable. Effort is required to be a parent. We need a nationwide campaign to raise awareness regarding daughter abandonment by one or both parents. That campaign should guide the father (and mother) on how much time and attention they should give their daughters. I don't claim to be an expert in that area, so I'll leave that up to the child psychologists to provide that information.

If you're a man, spend as much time with your daughter(s) as possible and show them that you truly love them. Females are different from males. They're different mainly because they are emotional, while men are logical. So, as the father, you think logically that she's fine because she has a roof over her head, food on the table, clothes, and electronics, but that's not enough. That's just the basic necessities of life today. You must pour into your daughters (and sons) and teach them about God and who Jesus Christ is. Teach them God is love and that they are unconditionally loved, which makes them gods. Lift their spirits. Educate them. The daughter is the flower of the world. She has very little logic. She needs a man to lead her, protect her, and help her expand her consciousness.

If you love your sons so much, remember that it's the woman who is raising them. If her father didn't teach her much and her husband didn't either, what do you think she'll be able to teach your sons? We need to start the healing process for these women and the planet. If we heal our women, trust will be regained between men and women. However, men need to work on themselves too. Too many men are concerned with sex all day and only view women as sex objects when they should be viewed as humans. Many women deeply hurt by childhood psychological issues will not want to be respected by men; they actually find it repulsive. In fact, that's a turn-off for them. We need to change that by elevating our women so that they can see clearly what's right and wrong for them.

The fact of the matter is most women are unaware that they have childhood trauma that's causing them to be promiscuous. Men have to balance their lives. They can't be entangled with social media, cars, beer, sports, and the couch and not put any effort into themselves and their families. It's not easy being a man. I get it. Men have to go out and work, pay the bills, work out, and protect, and now I'm asking them to do all this? If men want to see their sons married to great women, they need to solve this problem because their sons won't find a woman who's slept with less than 50 men (and we all know you have to multiply that number by 3). Remember, there are consequences for everything you do *and* don't do. I'm only talking about the promiscuous women, not the many decent women out there.

I experienced abandonment issues. On top of the physical, mental, and emotional abuse I received from my mother, I felt the vacuum created by my absent father. I can feel the emptiness in the home and my mind. The abandonment feeling was amplified because whenever my mother abused me, I would wish he was there to stop her. I had no one. He was my only friend, or so I thought. Because of this, I was people-pleasing. I did this unconsciously. I would go above and beyond for others in hopes they don't leave or shun me out of their lives and accept me. As a young boy, I didn't know I was people-pleasing, but I was.

One day around 1990, I was playing video games at the local independent video rental shop. At the time, I was working for tips bagging groceries at a supermarket on the same street. The supermarket was located between the video place and our apartment. I used to get many quarters as tips and would spend some of it at the arcade (I couldn't spend too much because I had to hand over the money to my mother). I remember my cousin and mutual "friend" came into the video store, and I was desperate for them to like me, so I handed them some quarters and happily told them to go ahead and play. They both looked at each other and made a face that said, "he's a stupid fool, but let's take his money." They didn't have to say it. I can practically read people's faces and minds. I developed strong emotional intelligence at a young age due to the traumas I endured.

The abandonment issue and the Islamic teachings of being nice to others turned me into a textbook Mr. Nice Guy. And boy, oh boy, let me tell you. People do not like nice guys!! I was flabbergasted. I was courteous and friendly to people, but they weren't responding positively. I thought I was trapped in a nightmare. I tried being nicer, to no avail. The thing is, I was genuinely nice because that's how I wanted people to treat me. It wasn't till I left my wife that I finally said, "to hell with everybody!" And I stopped caring about people's opinions and whether they liked me. I could give two shits.

I no longer have the abandonment issue. I no longer have codependency, either. I left Zina 11 months ago, and I've been living in a 1 bedroom luxury apartment by myself, with an amazing view of the New York City skyline - it's absolutely breathtaking from the 20th floor. I decided to rent a luxury apartment because I wanted to pamper myself through the divorce. I wanted to have a local vacation and heal. It was the best decision of my life. Living here got rid of my social anxiety since there are over 200 apartments here. I'm friends with many of my neighbors, and we chat every now and then. It helped me get comfortable talking to people again. I used to be quiet and awkward. When I was in my relationship, I could hardly speak due to the emotional abuse she inflicted on me. As you can imagine, I had zero confidence in my cognitive abilities, and because of that, I avoided people and conversations at all costs. I would speak a sentence and forget what I just said and, as a result, could not carry on the conversation. When I was with Zina, I would ask her, "wait, what did I just say?" I really couldn't do that with strangers.

I have an incredible view of the New York City skyline with 6-foot windows spanning from wall to wall. My apartment is satisfyingly quiet. No interruptions from an ungrateful hag. No more listening to all of her negative news regarding her 4 sisters, 1 brother, and the rest of her family - not to mention she felt the need to update me on every tragedy that occurred in Lebanon and other countries around the world. Towards the end of our relationship, I once told her, "listen to me; I don't give a *damn* about what's going on in those countries or your family. I have enough on my plate here with our disabled son and bills. Don't you dare ever mention that bullshit to me again!"

I want to give men some good advice. Before committing to a woman, find out everything about her upbringing. Don't turn it into an interrogation. Let the questions come about naturally - don't make it so obvious. You want to find out what her parents and siblings were like. Did any of them oppress her? Did one or both of her parents neglect her? Was her mother a liar and a manipulator? Did her aunts, uncles, and grandparents love them? Does she complain about how her father was never home? Did she grow up with a single mother? If the answer is yes to any of these, you need to understand that she might have a big void that needs to be filled by many men. She may "behave" at the beginning of your relationship, but you'll soon discover she craves male attention. And it runs deeper than attention. She will cheat on you repeatedly, and you won't even know about it until one day after she's slept with dozens of guys. You'll notice she's become cold and unloving.

Another major thing to consider for men is to check the relationship between their girlfriend/wife and her mother. Be discreet about it. Don't seem judgmental in front of her mother and family; take notice of her mother's behavior. Is she manipulative? Does she stretch the truth? Does she tell a lot of white lies? Does she try to justify her lying? If so, chances are, her daughter will be the same - not always, but a great chance. In my case, Zina was attached to her mother since her father traveled a lot. She learned all her manipulative ways from her mother. And I suspect her mother became that way because she married her husband at the age of 14 while her husband was 28. Zina resented this and thought of her father as a pedophile.

Another piece of advice I would give men is to *make sure* she genuinely loves you. If she doesn't, she will leave you when times get hard. Sometimes a woman will "leave you" and still sleep in the same bed with you, so don't assume that just because she's still living with you, she hasn't mentally checked out of the relationship. Remember, some women need a pushover as their main guy who will do whatever she asks and provide her with food, shelter, clothes, etc.

Another reason why it's so important to make sure she loves you is because if you end up in the hospital for a week, she'll never make an effort to call or visit. She might call you every 3 days to tell you she was busy. Someone who loves you will rearrange her whole life and schedule to see you every day. Most men are unaware of how important it is that the woman he's with loves him for who he is and not be interested in him for what material things he has to offer alone. Don't get me wrong, a man with a woman who loves him should buy her material things every now and then, but it shouldn't be the glue to the relationship; love and attraction should be.

I would also gauge her importance on money. If her eyes open wider for a split second whenever a rich person is on tv or she hears someone say a large sum of money, then understand she's a gold digger. Ok, so why's this important? It's important because A) she doesn't love you for you, and B) the minute someone with a lot of money asks her out, she will go with him without thinking twice about it. Understand that many women don't value men unless they are wealthy. Many are looking to hustle men and take whatever they can from them. If you're a wealthy man and don't mind, that's your choice, but don't go on social media venting how your chick is a gold digger and left you when you lost your empire.

2 1

DIVINE INTERVENTION

*G*od saved me.

One day it started. The videos kept showing up on my feed on all social media platforms. Videos about narcissism. There were countless content creators making videos on this topic. Until this point, I've only heard of the word once, about 20 years prior. I only knew that it had a negative connotation. I didn't know all the details, signs, or even what it meant. After scrolling past 10+ consecutive videos regarding narcissism, my intuition told me to stop scrolling and pay attention.

A light bulb went off in my head as I watched a couple of videos. "Wait a minute." This sounded awfully familiar. They were describing Zina word for word; I was dumbstruck. Is this for real, or is this just a mere coincidence? I kept learning more and more. Then, I devised a plan to observe her for a few months and document things that fit the description. I kept seeing the red flags. I couldn't believe it; It was like a movie.

Suddenly, the veil was removed, and I was shocked at my discovery. I was betrayed in the worst way!

It finally made sense. Why my physical and mental health was suffering, she was attacking me emotionally without me realizing it. Sneaky miserable turd.

When I say "hurt people hurt people," understand that your happiness irritates the HECK out of them. She told me she was so happy I came into her life and that she was so depressed (regarding her first divorce). She said I helped her take her mind off things. How did she repay, though?

When it came to physical attractiveness, she wasn't anywhere near my ideal woman. I married her mainly because I wanted a good woman who has God as the center of her universe so she can raise our children in the same way. She completely took me for granted.

Some people will never be satisfied with what they have. I was a God-sent to her, and she completely mistreated her blessing. She normalized my good character and started focusing her attention elsewhere while simultaneously using covert manipulation tactics to cause me great emotional distress. She knew *exactly* what she was doing! She intended to get me to commit suicide. Why isn't this illegal? There needs to be more awareness regarding emotional abuse because it's just as painful, if not more, than physical pain. And what makes emotional abuse pain so bad is that it lingers daily, whereas physical pain subsides and heals.

Emotional damage is as real, if not more real, than a fractured arm. I know because I fractured one of my arms 6 times and dealt with severe emotional damage, so I can talk about both from experience.

When I stated it's more real than a fractured arm, I mean it's criminally wrong! There are so many people in mental prisons right now who have no idea they're being controlled like a puppet by the woman they "love" or that close family member. Why did Zina do this? There were a few reasons. Number one, she didn't want me to fly away from her hands and leave her. Very insecure. That was a great fear she had. Another reason is that she resented that I was creative, more intelligent, and happier than her. I also received more attention than her. I honestly didn't care for the attention. Coincidentally, my mother hated me for the same reasons. They absolutely hated the fact that I was always happy. They didn't think I deserved it since I wasn't a billionaire. These two and many others don't understand how I'm happy. The new people think I had an easy life, and that's why. Laughing out loud. If only they knew my sorrows. If they only knew that I now go by the name Chris, I don't want to use the name my mother picked for me and instead pay homage to the Lord and Savior, Jesus Christ. The name my mother gave me reminds me of her and other family members. I don't even want to keep my last name because of Neuman. I've already picked out a new last name, Josh, and will file a legal name change request soon - I'm just waiting for the divorce to be settled. I chose Chris Josh in honor of Jesus Christ. Chris for Christ and Josh short for Joshua which means Jesus. "So the last shall be first and the first last."

Here's sound advice: NEVER enter a relationship with someone who just got out of one. It's impossible for a human being to heal from that pain in such a short time. It takes a good year, minimum if you're really working on yourself relentlessly to heal. Again, hurt people hurt people. So they'll act like they've forgotten their ex and the past, but in reality, they haven't, and you will be on the receiving end of abuse. They'll be hurt inside, and you'll be normal or even happy, and they won't like that. So, your person will downplay and break you down verbally by criticizing you excessively and reminding you of past failures. Your person will do this, so you're miserable, just like them! I say this from personal experience.

I didn't always understand that Zina was jealous of me. I thought it would be in her best interest if I was the best version of myself. She proved me wrong after Hurricane Sandy struck my e-commerce business. That was when I got into real estate sales and dabbled in real estate wholesale investing. I didn't have to crack open any books in my previous business. I just read blogs on topics about marketing and advertising and try to look for new web technology to improve the website's customer experience. With real estate, however, you really have no choice but to read books.

At the beginning of my real estate journey, I was so deflated. Everything that I worked for got destroyed by that storm just like that! I put so much heart into that business. I spent 16 hours on it, 7 days a week. I was wearing many hats but could do it because I loved what I did. After it got destroyed, my heart broke into millions of pieces. It was as if the rug was pulled from under me. I wanted to set my children up financially. I didn't want them to have to worry about what they were going to do for money.

It was an incredible experience. In 2012, business was expanding rapidly, and the number of employees kept growing. Every time I hired a new person, we'd need to add another team member to help us. Then one day, I was thinking of ways to ensure customers got the correct item and size. So, I contacted a local software engineer, who built me a warehouse management system from scratch. I devised a step-by-step action plan to get the order into the system from the website and into handheld mobile computers, giving us the product's location, size, image, and title. I also created the entire workflow, including the most optimal way to lay out the shelves and products in the warehouse to get more done in less time. After implementing that system, we never shipped a single order with the wrong product or size, and the hats had 10 different sizes!

The number of employees was getting to be too much. I started thinking of ways to be more efficient to get more done with fewer employees. I got an automatic conveyor system that brought in all the orders to the packing stations and then made their way down to the automatic tape machine and then to the shipping department. I estimated that this setup saved me from hiring an additional 10 people. Now I know some people would scoff at that because that means there are fewer jobs for people. However, having too many people is counterproductive, and hardly anyone will take accountability for anything and shrug and say, "I don't know."

All of this was great, but the truth is, knowing what I know today, I was going to lose the business and any money I had anyways because I didn't have the necessary tools. I had a multi-million dollar business, but the truth is, I didn't have a multi-million dollar understanding.

People don't want me to be happy. Whenever they see me happy, they try to do something to upset me. These days, I recognize when someone is doing that, and I immediately walk away and never deal with that person again - I don't care how much they try to talk to me again. I no longer give people the benefit of the doubt when it comes to that. I'd rather sift through these types of people, get rid of them, and continue searching for authentic people who want to see me win and be happy.

These days I don't give too much energy to people in general unless they give me energy, and I know they're genuine people. Additionally, even though I'm happy and feel good, I don't show it to people. They can tell from my face that I feel good, but I'm not smiling as much. I used to think I was spreading positivity and encouraging others to be happy, but it always had the opposite effect - making them do evil things towards me.

If that wasn't enough, being happy draws a lot of insecure people, especially men. They feel the need to one-up me. So, upon meeting me for the first time, they start to tell me about their net worth and all this other stuff to impress me so I can think, "jeez, he's got a much better life than me." And honestly, they want me to tell them that. They want me to be wowed and drool over their stories. I know what they're doing. Not only do I *not* validate them, but I excuse myself immediately. I don't deal with competitive people. Competition should be reserved for business and sports. I'll be damned if I allow someone lame into my space so he can constantly try to one-up me and make me get out of my character. Those people are no longer welcome. I admit, growing up, I put up with that - no more!

Comparing myself in 2022 to 2012, I've transformed into different versions of myself a few times. My last transformation started in March 2021 when I started doing my mini workout, which consisted of burpees and ab exercises. I did that until September of 2021 when I added my major workout, consisting of weight training. I do both workouts to this day.

The transformation started to become apparent by December 2021. I still had a lot to work on. I was still at an undesired weight. I still had cognitive issues from dealing with Zina's emotional abuse. My face wasn't glowing, and my skin wasn't clear. I didn't have a 6 pack. I didn't have a good memory. I still had brain fog; I was indecisive. I was scared to speak with people because I lacked the confidence that I would be able to focus on what the person was saying since I was having severe focus and memory issues. This focus and memory issue prevented me from having normal fluid conversations. I always hesitated, said the wrong thing, or was awkward.

As I got into 2022, things started to improve a lot. By May 2022, my focus was back. Also, I saw a few of my abs. I was a lot more decisive, and I was able to have normal conversations. I kept working on myself in every way possible - physically, spiritually, mentally, and emotionally. I didn't let the divorce get to me. I swore to myself in October 2021 that I would not miss a single workout, and I stuck by my word till this day, September 8, 2022. I continued lifting weights, and I stuck to my diet. Today, I have the best body I've ever had - bar none. I achieved my dream body without performance-enhancing drugs, steroids, or any illegal or legal fat-burning substances. Heck, I didn't even take any creatine. It was all hard work and discipline, both with my workouts and diet.

That is how I transmuted the pain of divorce. I had a choice. Do I lay down and cry all day on the couch or do I chalk up the loss and move forward? I chose the latter. Rather than complaining to others about my marital problems, I started a TikTok account and made content that adds value to others and helps them avoid many of the mistakes I made. Knowing how the universe works, I knew this was the best route to take. By adding value to others, the universe would reciprocate and add value to my life. I also knew the universe would be happy to see me take the higher road and would reward me even more for that.

Throughout my life, I gradually learned how to transmute negative situations into positive productivity. For decades, whenever a major disappointment would befall me, I would be immobilized and could not function. I couldn't stop thinking about it, and it would be very hard to get over it. I would be stuck in life. Later in life, I started looking at transmutation as if someone was passing me the baton, and I was running towards something productive and positive. I won't take it where it was intended, which is a lower vibration.

I learned to use the back stabbings and betrayals as fuel. For instance, when I did pull-ups and felt I needed an extra boost, I'd recall one of the many betrayals and push out a few extra reps because of the recollection.

When my son, Hunter, was about to have back surgery to correct his scoliosis curve, I realized there was no point in discussing it with anyone. There was no point in complaining. At that point, I swore never to complain to anyone, including myself, ever again. My "family" was intimidated because I wasn't complaining about my son's surgery. I figured there was nothing anyone could do for him; it was just a burden on others. There's nothing to gain. Neuman was visibly bothered by the fact that I wasn't talking to him about it.

I finally had enough of complaining. What allowed me to stop complaining was to stop saying 'no' to what was happening, accept everything, and not be bothered. I started to wonder if the stuff happening was for my own good. So many unfortunate things occurred in my life that I got tired of complaining once and for all! No matter how sad my story was, I stopped feeling sorry for myself. I promised myself that I would strive for excellence, no matter how much adversity I faced. Even when life knocked me down, I believed I could always rise stronger. With each setback, I refused to give up or give in. Instead, I dusted myself off and forged ahead, determined to make progress. As time passed, my resilience grew stronger, and the time it took to bounce back from disappointment became shorter. Now, I am unbreakable, and no one can ever bring me down again. These days if anyone does or says something annoying, I brush right past it, while in the past, I would have ruminated on the issue for a day or more.

I discovered a potent superpower when I stopped complaining. By adopting the "no complaining" attitude, I freed up all of my mental resources and could focus on the present and the task at hand. Rather than moping around feeling sorry for myself, I suddenly felt unbreakable. Nothing could touch me anymore. I was immune to complaining. Because I wasn't complaining, life stopped presenting me with scenarios that would cause me to complain. This turned me into a tall rigid structure that can withstand all of mother nature's elements. By not complaining, I freed up emotional space to allow happiness and joy to arise within me. You can't be happy and complain at the same time. And while you may not complain outwardly, you are still complaining on a subconscious level.

Complaining keeps you in a stagnant position. You keep ruminating about the injustices and how things could have been different. In a way, you are trying to change what already happened or is happening. This never allows you to be creative or come up with money-making ideas or just ideas in general. When something unfortunate happens today, I say, "whatever." I trust that things will work out in my favor. I realized that there are lots of lessons to be learned through "unfortunate" events and, therefore, shouldn't take them for granted but should take full advantage of them.

No one likes a complainer, and neither do you. You really don't like to hear yourself complaining about yourself, and you don't know any better. You'll see this is true when you try not to complain for a while. The real you just wants to be happy, peaceful, and joyous. When you complain, you rain on any possibility of joy. Realistically, you feel anger, resentment, hurt, and pain when you complain. You don't feel any of the higher frequencies, such as peace, love, happiness, and joy.

You attract what you think of but, more importantly, what you feel. If you feel like you're in a complaining mood all the time, then guess what? Life will present you with more situations that are worth complaining about. This perpetuates the never-ending cycle of complaining. If you become aware of your self-complaining and make changes so that you start to feel positive emotions, the universe will present you with situations that will inspire peace, love, happiness, and joy.

Complaining to others makes you look weak. You never want to complain to others, especially your woman. Guys, there's nothing worse than complaining to your lady. She's expecting you to be her rock, not the other way around. She needs to feel safe and that you can support her during tough times. If she has a complainer on hand, who can *she* complain to?

When you stop complaining in your mind, you become stronger, and you appear stronger amongst your peers. You will seem to have your shit together. People will see you as a leader - as someone who is resilient and can be counted on. They know that with you, things will be alright. You will appear to be more grounded and mature. You will even be perceived as smarter.

Let's use fire to show how complaining can influence the outcome. Say you come home one day, and your living room is on fire. If you choose to fret and yell and start complaining, you'll waste precious moments that you can use to think of a way to put the fire out. However, since you're stuck in victim mentality mode, you watch the fire spread to other parts of your home. Had you been grounded and present, you would have thought to run, grab the fire extinguisher, and put the fire out. Complaining in everyday life is a lot like the fire scenario. When you're caught up in the complaining mindset, you'll stand by and watch your life crumble before your eyes as you continue complaining about everything. But when you stop complaining, you have mental clarity and can focus much better. You allow space for solutions to enter your mind. You give creativity a chance to flourish and provide you with sound solutions.

When you stop complaining, it positively affects your anxiety and depression levels. You're no longer worried and sad/angry all the time like you used to be. Every time you complain in your mind, you trigger depression and anger. Depression, according to psychologists, is underlying anger. In other words, some things have really pissed you off, but you can do nothing about it except try to suppress your feelings. You can't act out with violence because that will get you in trouble, so you try to diffuse the anger, but it's still there in the form of depression. Recognizing all of this is the key to a great life - one that is based on freedom.

2 2

CRUTCHES OF VALOR

I was difficult to label because I was one of a kind. People seemed to dislike me for simply existing. I could sense their discomfort in their facial expressions as if they were looking at the sun while biting into a sour lemon.

No matter what I tried, I always got the same treatment. I have to say in all of my childhood, I only had one genuine friend, Hunter. Hunter was a couple of years older than me. He had 2 brothers - one older than him and one younger. At that time, I thought asking him what had happened to his legs would be disrespectful. I thought it would be offensive and rude to ask. He walked on elbow crutches. I can still hear him coming down the street as he lunged his crutches ahead of him and slammed them on the ground. He got enough leverage to lift his legs off the ground and swing forward, although his sneakers would drag on the floor most of the time. All you heard was metal clanking and shoes dragging on the concrete. You didn't have to see him; you just heard him coming.

Everyone loved him for his tough spirit. He would fall numerous times a day and always get back up; he always had scabs from the falls. Along with our mutual "friends," we would play baseball behind the local bank's parking lot. It was pretty spacious. I'd say it had a 35-car limit. We'd play with a wiffle bat and a green tennis ball whenever the cars were gone. Whenever Hunter would bat, we'd put our fastest guy as his pinch runner. It worked out pretty well. He was the only one that showed me unconditional love. He loved me as I was. He was very protective over me. When his older brother would bother me, by God, he'd grab one of his crutches and whack him over the head with it! I was taken aback by this level of love. No one ever defended me quite like that. I hung out with him all day. Well, until his mom came home. I was scared of his mom; she was always loud and argumentative. His parents had marital problems. As soon as she arrived, I'd take my stuff and leave. I didn't want to hear her bullshit. I already had enough at home. I would wander off in town somewhere.

My "friends" didn't truly like me. I always felt like they tolerated me around them. They'd always pick on me. I mean even this one kid, Jorge, who was 2-3 years older and twice my height and 75 lbs heavier than me. He felt empowered by being able to bully me without me being able to manhandle him. I had no choice. These kids were close to where my family and I lived. Even though they didn't treat me like one of them, I tolerated them because "home" was a lot worse. Therein lies the problem. After my experience with my mother, I formed relationships with people who weren't for me 100%, and because I always compared those relationships with the one I had with my mother, I'd always view them as good. So, I tolerated relationships when I shouldn't have, but because life with my mother was so bad, I figured these other people were normal.

I didn't know that I was settling. I thought it was normal for people to be like Zina. I thought it was normal for people to do a lot of things. Until one day, I learned that it wasn't normal and that I shouldn't tolerate these types of people. I started setting standards and boundaries. In my relationship with Zina, I tolerated a lot of disrespect. The main reason was our son, who has spinal muscular atrophy (SMA). I would always give her the benefit of the doubt because of the stress caused by the situation. But I was completely wrong about that. I learned that I should have never tolerated any disrespect. That I should have put her in check the very first time. You live, and you learn. As a man, you should never allow a woman to disrespect or order you around, NEVER! I don't care how anyone feels about that!

When you go through child abuse, you don't realize you're developing coping mechanisms and traits like people-pleasing. I didn't learn about this till I was in my late 30's. Once I learned about what was going on, I made adjustments. For one, I stopped giving a crap in general. I stopped giving a crap about people's opinions of me and in general. I stopped seeking and desiring validation from others. Instead, I started doing whatever I wanted to. I realized that I was wise and qualified enough to validate myself.

I stopped people-pleasing. If I don't want to do something, then the answer is no. People need to prove themselves to me, not the other way around. If they want to tag along in my movie, they're welcome, but the sad reality is most end up becoming jealous of me - for the same reasons I was hated on as a young boy. They get jealous that I appear to be happy, put together, and perfect. The reality is I'm just resilient. I don't let life bog me down and get me depressed. I might look like my life is perfect, but we all have our issues. Many people falsely assume I was born with a silver spoon in my mouth, not knowing I went through something their whole lineage (combined) would not have survived. I'm smiling because I'm no longer being abused and bullied. I'm happy because I'm free from attachments to people. They see the light in me because of my strong ties with God.

These days, some people get butt hurt when they see me. Some have a lot more money than me and wonder why I'm confident with less. Some have expensive cars and wonder the same thing. Some are married and wonder how I'm happier than they are while being alone. They don't know that I walked through the furnace for four decades. They didn't see me shriveled up, and all cried out, calling out to God to please stop my pain day after day, night after night. They only see the version of me who's given himself top-notch self-care. They see the emotionally intelligent and stable version of me. They don't know what I went through to be who I am today. It wasn't given to me. There was no silver spoon; I worked as a child and gave my earnings to my mother. There was no real childhood.

People are hardwired to be careful of overly friendly/nice people, especially if they have just met them. Now, suppose these friendly/nice people are intelligent too. In that case, that's a major red flag for most humans because they believe the person is using their intelligence to manipulate them through nice behavior. I have to say, this is sound programming from a biological standpoint. However, it made it difficult for genuine people who wanted to see others win and be happy. I had to learn the hard way. After thousands of encounters with different people, I found out that people do not like nice people, especially women.

I'm not an asshole these days, but I'm not going out of my way for anyone. I will always make sure it's a win-win for everyone, but I'm not putting anyone on a pedestal anymore. And I no longer give people more energy than they give me.

I highly suggest, as a man, you appear to be the guy no one wants any problems with. You need to give off that aura. Never be overzealous to be with anyone. Never get too excited. Be calm and cool - laid back. Be in the present moment. Get out of your head. Understand the other person's crap probably stinks worse than yours. Don't put anyone on a pedestal - not the CEO or the 10 out of 10 gal. You should be the only one on that pedestal. Never give people too much enthusiasm; they will feel emboldened and superior to you.

You must adopt the attitude of "I don't give a rat's ass who likes me." And just be yourself. The right people will stick around because they like the real you. You don't need to kiss anyone's ass to be your friend. It should be a mutual desire. Beware of the fake friend who doesn't cheer you when you are victorious. And beware of the so-called friend who downplays your achievements. These people are not worthy of your acquaintanceship, let alone friendship. Move on.

I urge you to study psychology and all the manipulation tactics, including the dark ones. I can't stress enough how extremely important this is, especially in this era of easily accessible information where people are going to social media to learn dark manipulation tactics to use on you and others. This knowledge can prevent you from ending up with the wrong life partner. Many men and women are in relationships with conniving, manipulative partners who are hungry for control. And if you're an empath, even worse because they will cause you emotional distress and ruin many of your brain's functions.

I was a victim of a narcissist because they love targeting nice guys and empaths. I was treating her nicely because I thought that was what she wanted. I was wrong. Sure, I was nice, but I always had a dark side. I put the lid on my dark side from age 21 to 42. Once I left my wife, I allowed my dark side to float within me and come out whenever necessary. The days of being nice are over. I was being courteous to show God that I was following His teachings. But all I got was a lash back from people. I can't tell you how much they despise nice guys. I'm not ashamed to admit that one day I told God, "I really don't care about being nice to people anymore. If you want to punish me, go ahead, I'm already being punished anyway." He responded, "that's it, my child. Do not overextend yourself any longer. Do not be a nice guy. Do not be a pushover. I need you to be as *BOLD* as a lion, son!"

Neuman is a nice guy though he's balanced it out better. Nevertheless, he has no enemies. He would never object or say something to upset the other person, even if the other person is wrong, for the most part. He'd avoid that person in the future but would never speak his mind. I learned nice behavior from him. One might think that that's the right way to be, but I beg to differ. I can't be fake and pretend I like everyone. When I was about 7 years old, and one of my mother's brothers was traveling back home from Lebanon, my mother would wake

Neuman up at 2 or 3 am and *order* him to pick her brother(s) up. He would say yes to anything.

I give credit where it's due. Neuman wasn't all bad. I did learn to do right by people through him. He showed me that it was better to take the high road. This was one of the very few lessons he ever gave me, indirectly. I can count the lessons on one hand. I also learned patience through him. I learned to be even more patient when Hunter was born and diagnosed with spinal muscular atrophy (SMA). When he could walk up the stairs, I needed to be patient! It takes a kid with normal muscle function to go up the stairs in 10 seconds. However, my son would take more than 5 minutes to climb the stairs. I had to slow down my internal mechanisms and learn to be patient. I often reflected deeply on the staircase while ensuring he didn't fall. I would count my blessings and be grateful for my muscles, legs, and ability to walk.

Unfortunately, Hunter has nice guy syndrome as well. Poor kid. His reason is different from mine. He's nice because he can't defend himself; that's his coping mechanism.

I've had to be strong throughout this divorce process. I had to be strong enough to say 'enough's enough' and walk away from Zina. To accept that my kids won't talk to me. To lose my house. To lose all of my belongings that were in that house. I went through it all alone. I didn't have a parent to talk to. Didn't have a sibling or cousin to talk to either. I didn't have friends to comfort me either. I had one friend who I had known for 20 years. I mentioned the divorce to her, but then I found out she was talking to Zina and giving her information, so I had to cut her off too. Zina would get my call and text logs, then call up my friends and convince them that I was the problem, and hence they would stop communicating with me because they didn't want to get involved in the drama. Zina ruined my relationships by going through my call and text logs and calling everyone. She called up the cell phone carrier and pretended she was me. She gave them my social security # and mother's maiden name to gain access to my account and call/text logs. I've already changed my number twice since the start of the divorce, with two different carriers. She found both numbers. Instead of looking for a job, she spends her entire day stalking me on social media and doing things to ruin me financially and socially. My credit score has dropped about 400 points in the process so far. No one will lend me money or open a new credit card.

She tried to isolate me and have everyone turn against me, hoping I would surrender and take her back. Yeah right! There is no chance! I'd rather jump into a lake of fire and be done with it!!! Everything she did to me only made me stronger. Sure, my kids don't talk to me, but you know what? I learned to deal with it and not let it affect me anymore. It's not that I'm heartless; it's just that I accept things as is. I can only call and text them. If they choose not to answer, I can't force them. I know the kids will come to their senses and come rushing back one day because they will realize that not all fathers treat their kids as I did. However, I don't take it to heart. My kids, especially Hunter, depend on their mother a lot. My son probably thinks, "I should listen to whatever mom says because she's helping me with my doctors and other things."

So many people live with unresolved childhood trauma and insecurities and lack self-esteem. Because of this, they don't feel like they deserve nice treatment. And if they are bitter and hurt, they're going to look at the nice person as cringe and weak - and they're going to be visibly jealous. What's funny is that it takes strength to be nice in a world full of assholes. I know a lot of guys pretend to be nice to get in some girl's pants, but I was/am authentically nice.

It's not easy quitting being a nice empath. Naturally, I feel love within my veins, and it's hard for me not to exude it, but I've been practicing withholding it, and I've been practicing not being excited to talk to others. I've adopted the belief that the current population's collective consciousness doesn't deserve good energy. Perhaps it's their karma; to exist in misery with no one to show them kindness and love.

When you work hard on yourself, it starts to show after a while. Everyone takes notice. It's easy to stand out because most people don't work on themselves. Most don't work out or eat the right amount of food; they don't maintain their hygiene. They don't read, grow, or elevate themselves; their conversations are surface-level and superficial.

I stick out like a sore thumb when someone like me steps on the scene. I encounter a lot of insecure men. I can't tell you how often a man walking with his woman would freak out when he sees me because his woman will see me too. The guys end up clutching their woman by the hip and start rambling about who knows what - to get her attention off of me.

Since I was a young boy, many people have competed with me, and I have NEVER competed with anyone. I'm not even in competition with myself. I just keep pushing forward. I keep looking ahead. I don't look back at my old self to compare. I'm not in competition. I'm simply taking advantage of the opportunities and the time I am given here on Earth. I never let a day go to waste. I always have to be chipping away at something at almost any given time of the day. Since I'm not competitive and I'm always positive, people can't stand that. They think I'm gloating, but I'm not. I'm just enjoying myself.

I learned a lot of lessons as a child. Many older kids would cheat me or steal from me. I learned how to spot those types of people when I got older. I learned so many lessons as a child that I'm now able to recognize certain spirits within people. I can easily identify the spirit of my mother in others. This allows me to filter people like her out of my life quickly. I can also identify Milton's spirit in others; boy, does it come in handy. Same with Neuman's spirit. I can't tell you how many people I've avoided because of the lessons I learned young. I can read faces and energy immediately and adjust my dialogue to shift the energy back higher.

If you're giving energy to any and everybody, then you're losing yourself in the process. What I've learned over the years is that YOU have to be your ideal best friend and your ideal mother, father, brother, sister, and any other family member. Leaving your emotions in someone else's hands is detrimental. One minute they adore you, the next minute, they hate you, then, they adore you again, and hate you. You can never rely on a person to be consistent with their sentiments towards you.

About a month before I left Zina, I started weightlifting in September 2021. Six months prior, I started what I now call my mini workout, which consists of burpees and 4 core exercises. Once Spring '22 came around, and my jacket was no longer needed, suddenly, the people who were friendly got noticeably quiet and hurt when they saw me in a t-shirt. They couldn't tell under my jacket that I was jacked, and because of that, I was worthy of their friendly gestures. After several weeks, most people adapted and started talking to me more. Until summer came along, and it was tank top and shorts weather. Forget about it. I got deafening silence from everyone. They were in their heads, speechless. Even if I walked into Starbucks, I'd hear the entire shop quiet down and become awkward. One obese barista wouldn't even hand me my cup. He'd set it on the counter approx 2 feet away from me. This is the guy who'd put it in my hands with a smile when I was covered in a jacket.

This doesn't only happen to me, but not many emotionally intelligent, jacked and ripped men are writing about it. As a society, I find it comical that we will cheer on a 300 lb man who lost 75 lbs but will show you zero love if every fiber in your shoulders and arms is visible. But isn't that the goal? Don't most of us men aspire to look our best? Shouldn't they view me as inspiration and proof that with consistent effort, it's possible? Imagine if there wasn't a single man in sight that's in great shape. Who would believe it's possible? Not many! That's how I look at things. When I see someone with something admirable, I think, "wow, I never knew that existed," or "now I know I can do that too."

That's the difference between operating from your heart space and operating purely out of ego. You are in touch with the divine when you operate out of love. You're not competitive, and you know that The Creator can provide for all. You don't worry about how that would get done. You just know

God works miracles. Sadly, most people never realize how nearly impossible it is to sustain such a large global human population along with all the animals and insects. It's truly remarkable and a miracle indeed. When a woman is sitting in the park and eating her sandwich, some crumbs fall on the bench and floor - food for the insects and birds. God provides for all in mysterious ways. I understood this at a very young age; that's why I operate from my heart.

I love guiding and teaching others, especially young men and women. I don't remember where I heard this from, but when you teach others, you also learn in the process. You'll learn from the people you're teaching and from the universe - in ways you could never imagine. I've been through one heck of a life, and being a super empath (heyoka empath); it hurts me to know millions of people out there suffer from the same things I did. I'm naturally a warner. I'm naturally someone who stands up for others and is against injustice. I've always been like this.

Get rid of all those filters and masks you put on yourself. Don't try to be like everyone else. Don't be a cookie-cutter type of person. Relax. Drop your guards. Stop overthinking and be your natural, quirky self. It's ok to be different. That's what makes you valuable. Remember what Steve Jobs said, "think differently." The more different you are, the more rare you are, and the more valuable you are. People want rare things. You tell someone Rolex made 500 million watches this year, and the affluent won't want them. But tell them Rolex only made 1 million of them, and watch how they scramble to get one!

Plenty of delusional people think I should be kissing their asses when they have hardly any value to give. Get real, buddy! Don't get me wrong, I respect the sub mediocre man and love him, but some people genuinely get butthurt because I'm not acting like their fan. This is what's wrong with society.

When I'm at a big box store, for example, I'll have a woman that is probably a 3 out of 10 checking me out - someone I'm not physically attracted to at all. Like staring me down really hard. Staring right into my soul. Waiting for me to walk up to her and ask for her number. I cringe and crack up within myself. I laugh because of the audacity. I can't believe this is what society has become. And the stare says, "hey you! Come over here and talk to me!" To which I reply telepathically, "hell no! Stop looking at me!" You might think, "sheesh, Chris is harsh." Well, the truth is I have my preferences, and I'm just not physically attracted to some women. I'm attracted not only to a woman's looks but also to her morals, mind, and soul. I don't find women who look at me aggressively in a sexual way attractive. In fact, I find it creepy. If she's a 10 out of 10, looks-wise but lacks morals, and isn't highly educated, she's a 4 out of 10 in my book. I'd much rather take a 7 out of 10 look-wise with the aforementioned attributes.

I say all of that to say this. We've become a civilization hyper-focused on sex. It's ridiculous. You can't open any social media apps without a woman shaking her behind for attention. Guys are directly messaging hundreds of women in hopes of hooking up with one of them. As a result, practically every woman, attractive and unattractive, gets flooded with messages from men all day long. Sex has gone from something sacred to something you can buy from a gumball machine. Guys are a huge problem in all of this because they're constantly soliciting attention from women and giving women undeserving attention. This increases the demand for women, increasing their value - not for their intellect but for their bodies. This great increase in attention over-inflates women's egos tremendously. False confidence. Which leads to unrealistic demands from their male counterparts.

America is a failed state. I believe shit is hitting the fan currently, and we will eventually grow up collectively and start focusing on improving ourselves and seeking knowledge, including knowledge of self. We need to get God back in the schools and our homes. The men have to focus on things other than sex and women; they need to teach their sons to be real men, lead their wives, teach them, and point them in the right direction.

After studying the different faiths and philosophies, I've finally concluded that the Islamic lifestyle would be perfect for America today. I know that sounds radical, but this is coming from someone who left Islam for a while and didn't consider himself a Muslim at one point - for reasons I do not wish to share. Years later, it hit me; Islam is the solution. For example, marriage is no longer an option for millions of Americans due to the high divorce rate and all of the cheating. In Islam, women are to dress modestly, as well as men, and men and women aren't allowed to hang out or be friends. Adultery is punishable in Islam. We can all agree that the family is the nucleus of a successful nation. If people are no longer getting married, then the foundation of our country has been broken. Islam is the only way to get marriage considered an option again. Do men and women in Islam cheat? Yes, but I'd have to say not nearly as much as American society. Also, if they do cheat, it's because their country doesn't enforce the Islamic adultery law. If it was enforced, cheating would be very scarce.

I propose the Islamic way of life, but I also propose people practice their original faith side by side. It would seem contradictory to those who haven't fully understood the different faiths, but it's not. The Creator is a vast being. Naturally, He has a lot to say. Imagine if He released a book that contained the Bible, the Torah, all other Jewish texts, the Quran, and the Vedas. Can they even publish a book that large? If they can, what percentage of the population would read it from cover to cover, assuming it's been translated into their native language? Exactly, no one! The Creator wants us to seek Him constantly, for He dwells in all things. According to Islam, Allah sent a warner/messenger to every group of people/nation.

I was grateful to have been guided to study the different faiths. It was at a time when I was at rock bottom. I was dealing with severe fibromyalgia symptoms and couldn't socialize, so I stayed home and learned for hours once my work for the day was completed. I love myself for putting in the work. Many people look at me and wonder why I get blessed but don't see all the hard work I put in over the years. It's hard to tell because I make it look effortless, and I don't look like I've struggled a day in my life - that's a great blessing from the Most High.

The good news is you can get this blessing too! It's not reserved for me and a select few. It's available to whoever diligently seeks out the Most High and practices all the teachings down to the letter. It's available to those who can control their sexual desires and not be tempted, especially if they're in a relationship. Available to those with unshakeable faith, pleasant manners, excellent conduct, respect for all life, live in love, constantly pray, and constantly add value to others.

If you're a follower of Christ, then live like Christ. The

common misconception is that no one has to follow the rules in the New Testament because Jesus died for our sins. Do they think He died for nothing? He sought to spread the truth about our Father, who has guided Jesus Christ to a certain way of living - because God knows best.

If BMW made the car, do you think it's wise to treat it the way you think is best or what the manufacturer suggests regarding maintenance? If BMW says you need gasoline, would you put diesel in it? 99 out of 100 would say they'd follow BMW's recommendations. So why don't we follow the One who created us when it comes to our body's maintenance? Not only are God's teachings beneficial to men and women, but by following the laws, one elevates and gets closer to God, meaning they start to form a relationship with God. And over time, as long as the person is consistent and is not intentionally doing wrong or breaking the laws of the Torah, Bible, or Quran, whichever the person follows. The more one is consistent, the more one shows the Creator that they are serious about their relationship with God and honor Him. God is knowledge. Therefore, you must continuously gain knowledge to approach God (think of calculus as x approaches infinity). How can you get to know God without knowledge? The more understanding you have, the more you step into your Godhood because understanding is love, and love is God. To be God, you must be in unconditional love. In Psalms 82:6, Christ says, "I have said, Ye are gods; and all of you are children of the most High."

Many people look at the laws regarding alcohol and scoff. For years people wrote it off like it was a crock of crap. Now, people are starting to wake up and realize that alcohol is dangerous and creates problems rather than solving them. Here are some of the cons of alcohol: being drunk and acting a fool, puking, overeating, dehydration, hangover, lots of calories (beer belly), and possible drunk driving killing yourself or someone else. The worst part is that it makes you angry and irritable. Why would anyone in their right mind choose to drink alcohol? Now, don't get me wrong. I'm not judging because I drank for a couple of years in 2010 and 2011, but if you do drink, you may want to seriously consider quitting - for your own good.

I started drinking in 2010 because my e-commerce business was stressing me out since I was the sole person in every department in the company. I was the buyer, the bookkeeper, the supplies manager, the delivery driver, customer service, packing and shipping, website manager, project manager, product development, and God knows what else. I had to learn a bunch of software. This was at a time when Shopify didn't exist. The website was started using Open Commerce, a free website platform that allowed full customization but didn't have any of the tools and plugins Shopify has.

A silly thought entered my mind with all of these hats I was wearing, along with increased business and difficulty finding competent workers. "Why don't I go to the liquor store tomorrow and buy a couple of beers to relax a little?" It started with a couple of beers. Eventually, I was drinking entire bottles of Ciroc (P Diddy was marketing Ciroc heavily back then). I gained a good 30 lbs easily. I still remember ordering a ridiculous amount of greasy food after getting drunk. Please don't ask me how, but the business was operating normally. Every order went out on time and correctly. Customers were satisfied, and word of mouth spread like wildfire. And business kept soaring while my drinking problem worsened.

In 2011, I said I was done. I quit cold turkey just like that. I haven't had one sip of alcohol since 2011. It was much easier than when I quit cigarettes (which took over 10 attempts to accomplish).

23

___

POPULAR LONER

I believe sex should only occur between two people who genuinely love each other. Casual sex is not what it's cracked up to be. So many men can attest that sleeping around gets boring and feels dead. We live in an era of instant gratification where most people are weak. They're too weak to love. They're too weak to wait for something of high quality. They want to rush everything. They don't want to struggle or work for anything. Many women believe it's ok to sleep around with several men and keep a rotation of 10+ men. And the same is true with the player-type of men. I could fall into the player category if I wanted to, but I choose not to. Now that I'm older and wiser, I can read a person's energy from across the room. If a woman's energy isn't up to par, I'm not investing any time or energy into her. I've found that being in my own energy is a million times better than being with a woman who doesn't have knowledge of self and belief in God.

Whenever I leave my apartment, I'm bound to get several

women check me out and give me choosing signals, including staring into my soul while biting their bottom lip and/or twirling their hair. That sounds really arrogant, I know, but it's a fact. I don't let it get to my head and I'm fully aware I'm no Brad Pitt. However, you have to understand that many women, including men, think and say I look like the actor Jason Statham, from the movie he did with Dwayne "The Rock" Johnson, "Hobbs and Shaw." While he's not every lady's cup of tea, the ones that do find him attractive, obsess over him. And because of this, these same women find me really attractive and give me animalistic energy. Again, I really don't let it get to my head as I know there's more to life. It's kind of a curse actually. When I go to several big box stores and the mall, I get lots of attention - even from married women. They give me all types of choosing signals while their man is around them.

As I previously stated, I can read the energy pretty well. And because of that, I can discern who's who and what's what. Almost 10 out of 10 times, I get a negative reading. I can pick up on the woman's immaturity and recklessness, so I pass up on their offer to talk - meaning I don't walk up to the woman after she shows me some interest. That is because I no longer think sex is worth all the headaches that come with the average woman these days.

These days, I'm in a much better state of mind. I'm whole and complete on my own, and I learned to genuinely love myself, life, and existence. People can read me too. They can tell I'm happy on the inside, and there's a glow about me. This attracts a lot of people - women and men. It attracts similar-minded people, but it also attracts broken people and narcissists. People want to latch on to me so they can:

Copy me.

Try to break me down.

"Steal" my energy.

Dump their problems on me so they can feel better while I feel like crap.

I've gotten really good at recognizing these people. For example, the other day, I was working on this book at a Starbucks, and an older woman randomly started a conversation with me. Not to be rude, I gave her what I thought would be a minute. She was devious. She started the conversation on a high note but then quickly started complaining about some man she was dealing with over 50 years ago. She gave me a look that said, "do you feel sorry for me? Don't you think my story deserves a sorrowful reaction from you? Come on, be sad about my situation."

Meanwhile, I'm thinking to myself what a life this lady must live. To hold that story in her mind for 50 years and complain about it to a complete stranger she had just met. After I realized what she was doing, I told her I had to get back to work, to which she said, "oh, go ahead. I didn't mean to keep you away from your work." Instead of leaving me alone, she continued talking again. I gave her about 15-30 seconds and told her again, and this time I put my headphones on and ignored her. If this happens to you, don't feel bad. You're not a martyr. You're not supposed to listen to people's problems at the cost of your mental and physical health. If she paid me $150 for the hour, I still would not entertain her because that negative energy passed onto me would cost me far more than the $150. So be careful not to give these energy vampires any of your energy and time. If you're an empath, be highly alert to these types of people.

People can tell I'm glowing from the inside out and that I'm very content. When they see someone like me, they just see someone they can use. I don't allow people to use me anymore. I used to sit and listen to people's bullshit for an hour, but no one gets that time from me these days, not even if they pay me.

I used to go out of my way to greet people, but I no longer do that. If someone greets me, I'll greet them back. Why? Because people's egos are out of control! These days any show of kindness is considered beta or cringe. So, I give the people what they want - NOTHING! Seriously, it's so sad how so many people want to be disrespected and ignored. It sounds counterintuitive, but really, that's what it is. When you ignore them, they latch on to you, chasing validation from you. I don't entertain Debbie downers and attention/pity seekers because when my e-commerce business flooded, the two salesmen I worked with from my two biggest vendors wouldn't even listen to my story of how the storm wreaked havoc on my business. They didn't care! I was so shocked. I was seriously hurt. In one year alone, I purchased roughly $2.5 million worth of products from one salesman and about $1.5 million from the other. Both netted roughly $150,000 each (one had a higher commission rate than the other).

Just imagine you had just one client earning you a six-figure income. And they couldn't give me 5 minutes on the phone? They couldn't even say, "you know what? I know you're going through something really difficult; I will give you a discount on your next order with free shipping to help you get back on your feet." They were arrogant, thought I was easily replaceable, and completely wrote me off. Well, within a year, the salesman that got $2.5 million in orders from me was let go by the company he was working for. And the other salesman's company was no longer trending, and as a result, sales plummeted, and now no one wears that brand.

My e-commerce business focused primarily on licensed sports caps, like the New York Yankees, Chicago Bulls, Tampa Bay Lightning, etc. I also sold streetwear clothing. It wasn't long before people stopped wearing caps as part of their fashion and even created a phrase, "no cap," which means "no lie." Essentially, if you're a liar, you're capping. There's a negative connotation with caps now. Nothing made me happier!

I feel like that was my justice. Now the kids essentially tell each other, "don't wear a cap." I couldn't believe how these salesmen and vendors left me to die. I was loyal to them. Their shipping department would often screw up and send me a ton of extra products worth thousands of dollars. Instead of keeping and reselling the items for 100% profit, I would alert the companies and tell them exactly what was wrong. For example, if a case is supposed to contain 6 units, they sometimes sent a master case of 60 units. I didn't want bad karma and always knew God was watching. Did the salesmen or vendors appreciate it? Obviously not. I had saved them tens of thousands of dollars. Nevertheless, despite how awful it was, I'm still grateful to have experienced everything.

Even though I wanted my business to bounce back from the damage done by Hurricane Sandy, a big part of me wanted to see it fail so that I would never give these salesmen another dime. They taught me a valuable lesson. The lesson is - everything is transactional. Hardly anyone out there is operating from their heart space. People are just chasing the dollar. They saw it as my business got crippled, which probably meant I wouldn't be purchasing products from them for a while or ever again. Hence, they felt it wasn't worth investing 5 minutes into hearing what had happened regarding the storm's destruction. I wasn't trying to dump negative energy on them. I just wanted to tell them the local berm broke and I got 8 inches of water which destroyed 20% of my inventory along with the server.

After that, they would call and email me about new offers, and I'd pick up the phone and say, "Hey, can I call you back?" I would never call back. They'd want my opinion on future releases, and I wouldn't give it to them. They trusted my taste and judgment, but I wasn't about to let them benefit from me after how they treated me. A lot of people are delusional in this world. They want to take from others but don't want to give. And it wasn't just them. A lot of people behaved this way regarding the storm's effect on my business, so I started getting wise to the fakeness in people. I still had a heart of gold, and it took another 10 years before I completely gave up on people and made it an internal policy not to hear other people's problems, especially since I went through such a difficult life.

I think, "well, if I'm not complaining about my situation, why should I listen to other people's small problems?" For example, the lady at Starbucks was in her 70's, still stuck on a man from 50 years ago. The sad reality is, if I had taught her how to get over him, she wouldn't like that. These types of people don't want solutions; they just want attention from others and want to get an emotional reaction out of them. In my case, I just wanted an ear. I just wanted to hear a solution from the salesmen. I didn't want them to say, "aww, you poor thing," I wanted them to say, "don't worry, I'm going to do XYZ to help you out. You've been a great client. It's the least I can do."

You need to be aware that there are people like this in your life. They are weighing you down and holding you back. The reason is this: whatever you feel, that is what the universe will match you up with. For example, suppose I let this lady's story get to me and make me sad, and I let others do the same, and I'm always sad as a result. In that case, the universe will keep presenting me with situations and scenarios to make me sad. This is why you need to nip it in the bud immediately. Instead, you need to associate with those who induce a happy feeling within you. Just make sure you're not dumping anything on those people. If you're feeling happy, the universe will present you with situations that will make you happy. That is why you can't view people as organic and random. You need to take control of who you associate with because you can't leave things to coincidence and randomness. Once you recognize that people have a major influence on you, your well-being, and your life, you will move and behave accordingly.

Before I close out this chapter, I would like to say the following - don't be too available for people in general, and don't show your face frequently. Use absence to create desire for you. People take you for granted when you're always around and treat you as a peasant. You become too common - even though there's only one of you. So, no matter how much you like the person, never spend too much time with them, and always end the convo on a high note. Even if you live in a building with a concierge, don't interact with the staff daily - unless you want to be treated like the Uber Eats guy delivering food to one of the tenants. Absence creates a craving for you in people. Use it to your advantage. That's why it's best to make tons of friends, even if they're surface-level friendships - so you avoid interacting with the same person or people too frequently. Whether you're in a serious relationship or are dating multiple people, you should only meet with each one once a week (max). And if you're in a committed relationship or marriage, don't give your partner your undivided attention 24/7/365. You need to create an absence in your relationship. Otherwise, your partner is going to lose interest and attraction to you. One of my friends got married this year, and he and his wife both work. Their day to spend time together is Saturday. This is perfect. It allows for the other person to miss the other person's presence.

No matter how much you like the person, you must always remember how human psychology operates. Your availability will decrease your perceived value even if you're the kindest, most masculine, most alpha, tallest and funniest person. The other person will assume that your life revolves around them and that they have much power over you.

24

DEFEATING KYPHOSIS (HUNCHING OF THE BACK)

ost of us envision a great life filled with money and material things without ever realizing that health is the most important thing we could ever have. You don't believe me? Talk to some wealthy people who are miserable due to all sorts of health issues, including mental health. Many people live in big mansions but are dissatisfied with life. It's more than dissatisfaction. It's actually suppressed anger. Suppressed anger, according to psychologists, is essentially depression, which is a mental health issue. Imagine you have $100 million in your bank account and are depressed! What's the point? I can guarantee that that person would switch his life with someone genuinely happy and satisfied with life but earning a middle-class salary.

I grew up with all sorts of health issues. From as early as 4 or 5 years old, I remember always asking my mother to rub my middle back. I'm not sure why it was painful. Honestly, for all I know, my mother could have smacked me hard on my back when I was younger. That's the only explanation I can come up with. Who knows? It hurt so much. It hurts today. It's painful to touch. On top of the pain, a suffocating tightness feels like a big rubber band in that area and constantly squeezes me. Just standing or sitting is very uncomfortable. The only way I could get relief was to hunch my back (kyphosis). Unfortunately, I developed a hunchback, making me look weak and short. I tried hard to stand straight, but the ache and pain were too much. One day I was sitting in my car, and I glanced at the side mirror.

When I saw myself in the mirror, I didn't like what I saw. My head was tilting back so that my chin was exposed. I didn't like my appearance, especially being slouched over. It was at that moment (I was 42 years old at the time) I decided to do something about it. I started practicing sitting and standing awareness. I learned how to carry myself properly, and I went to work. Boy, was it hard! Good lord! I would get up in the morning and do whatever I needed to, and then I started practicing good posture all day. I would stand on all 10 toes with the proper posture, which felt painful and exhausting. I had so much pain in my back trying to hold my posture. I would stand for 8 hours straight while maintaining correct posture. It was physically the most difficult thing I've ever done. It was excruciating. The pain was unbearable. I constantly had the sensation of collapsing my back and falling over, but I kept fighting.

On the 2nd day, I noticed my back was still collapsing into a hunchback whenever I wasn't aware of my posture. So, I continued doing what I had done the previous day. Again, it was painful, uncomfortable, and achy, but I was determined. Days, weeks, and even months passed, and my posture still didn't hold. I had to always be aware, and I mean always - from the moment I woke up until I was laying in bed. I was still in agony whenever I was in the proper alignment. Finally, after about 6 months or more, my good posture started to hold without my interference or awareness. I can't tell you how much it changed my life. First of all, a correct posture automatically increases your confidence. This confidence translated into getting respect from everyone, especially doctors and other professionals. Everyone knows how difficult it is to maintain a good posture, even with no back issues. The fact that I could do it despite having kyphosis is an absolute miracle. The benefits of a great posture are priceless. If I had to do it repeatedly, I would do it in a heartbeat.

Another three reasons I would hunch my back were:

Because of an ear infection

Because of a bad case of asthma

An inherently weak core

I had excruciating ear pain from when I was about 5 years old until I was about 12. I guess you could say I had something like tinnitus. I had a throbbing whooshing sound 24/7; It was painful and aggravating. I would moan and cry all day and night for years. I went to several ENTs, and they didn't help. One doctor out in Clifton, NJ, always prescribed Dimetapp. I would look at my mother and try to communicate telekinetically that this doctor was an idiot. How is he prescribing me an over-the-counter cough medication for years, thinking he's helping me.

It was always the same diagnosis. The doctor would look in my right ear and give me the "eww" face, squinting and all. "What's the problem, doctor," I'd ask. He would say, "you have a hole in your ear. Your eardrum is gone, and one of your auditory bones has disintegrated from the infection. This was one of the three hearing bones and happened to be the one in the middle. At 12 yrs old, I had ear surgery. The doctor attempted to replace the eardrum with flesh from the surrounding area. He also put tubes in my left ear. Well, it wasn't long before the "eardrum" he put in fell out with the bleeding and infection. It must have fallen out within the first 2 or 3 days. What a waste. Years later, at 27, I went to a different ENT. The way he explained the procedure made logical sense, so I went through with the surgery. After two weeks, I finally removed the bandages on my ear and head. I couldn't believe my hearing! It was crystal clear and loud. I was so happy! Until one day, the ear drum collapsed within, and I lost a great portion of my hearing in my left ear. I guesstimate I'm hearing about 25% out of it and only about 50% in the right ear (despite a missing eardrum and ear bone).

What does my ear have to do with my hunching? Well, whenever I'd shower, I would be seated in the tub as a young child. Since I was so self-conscious of my ear infection and the doctor told me to avoid getting water in there, I would lower my head, hunching my back. I was trying to avoid water in my ears at all costs. I did this for years, and it contributed to my poor posture. I would do the same thing when showering and standing throughout my adult years. I would hunch over so the water rolled down a different path that would not align with my ears.

Another contributor to my poor posture was my asthma. It was severe, but I'm sure others had it worse. I had to go to the emergency room a few times because I thought I would die due to the lack of oxygen. While walking during an asthma attack, which frequently happened back then, I would hunch over to help expand my lungs to breathe easier. As you can imagine, I prioritized breathing over good posture. I suffered from asthma attacks until I was about 27 when I saw an allergy doctor who prescribed me Advair and Singulair. This combo did wonders for me and essentially cured my asthma. I'm now 43 years old as of writing this chapter (my birthday was yesterday, September 19), and I have never had a single asthma attack since I was 27 years old. I don't even have an asthma pump for emergencies because I don't need it.

Yet another reason for my poor posture was my abnormally weak deep core muscles. I saw a therapist for this once, and she said I practically had zero pelvic floor muscles activated. I have worked extremely hard on my core, yet it is still not as strong as it should be. I've been consistently doing Schroth therapy, and while it helped, it didn't do the job completely. Because I have a weak core, the curve right below the mid back carries the load. These muscles shouldn't carry that load; the core muscles should. This causes an ungodly amount of tightness in my mid to lower back region. It feels like there's a giant rubber band around my torso.

Today people see me gliding through life effortlessly, but they don't know what I have endured all my life. They see my strong energy and strength and don't understand that I was training under fibromyalgia and everything else I went through, not under Cus D'Amato. Many think I was born with a silver spoon in my mouth when in reality, I had to problem-solve all my life and my family was poor, even though I felt wealthy. I had to console myself. I had to fight all my life. I had to defend myself. I had to be the one who told me, "it's ok. It's going to get better someday," because I didn't have anyone to tell me that. I had to develop a tough exterior and pretend nothing could get to me. I would pretend like nothing happened. But deep down, I was ashamed.

How did I deal with all these things hitting me all at once? God/Love. It was the hope that the struggle would pay off in the end via entering paradise after death. In the back of my mind, I would always say, "there's gotta be a God. Something had to have created me. I know there's a God. He said to be patient. I'm going to be patient, even though I'm hurting badly, no matter what." Because of my obedience to God, he made me stronger. Strong enough to carry the load. (If only I could have heard David Goggins yelling, "who's gonna carry the boats, Chris!?" back then) God wanted it that way. I was honored to have had the pleasure of unrolling our family's prayer rug at 12. At first, I was seated on the rug. I was rubbing the rug with my hands imagining I was rubbing on God's shoulder. When I got up to start my first prayer ever, I felt like a portal was open. It felt like I had established a direct link to God Himself. I can't describe how eager I was to worship God. I was glad that Muslims prayed so many times a day because I got to show God my obedience and love for Him often.

I don't exactly fit the image of an obedient servant of God. For example, I use profanity sometimes. I speak the truth even if it might hurt someone. I'm a rebel. I'm ready to fight for my respect and to defend those who can't defend themselves. I crank my music loud in the car. People know this about me and are bothered by the fact that God has been looking out for me. They also get bothered by God's favor being upon me.

My closest relatives noticed this and were always envious of me. They didn't understand why *I*, of all people, was favored by God so much. They didn't see how tight I held on to the rope of God while I was at war with everyone and suffering from health issues. They could never see how many thoughts regarding God I had every day. In his book, "As a Man Thinketh," James Allen points out that what a man thinks about all day is who he becomes. This is so true. But I thought about God all day, does that mean I will become God? The Bible says, "I have said, You are gods; and all of you are the children of the Most High" - Psalms 82:6 KJV. Become God? No. Because I kept God in my mind so much, he showed me through this verse that I *am* God - always was and will always be. Me and you, the you-niverse.

The faith I have today is magnitudes stronger than even 10 years ago. I believe people can reach this level of faith through hard work and perseverance, and plenty of reflection on God. I was blessed to be led to different faiths. I understood Buddha when he said there was no god. I also understood the Atheists when they say the same thing. There is no God in the sky, per se. Although everything is God, including everything in the sky, no one is separate from all of us; that is God alone. In that regard, the Buddhists and Atheists are correct. The sky or the universe is God. God is the 'substance' that life is made of. He is you, I, us, everything, and nothing.

The monotheistic religions claim life after death, in which the person goes to heaven or hell. I was able to reach paradise from Earth before physical death. I reached paradise through many ego deaths and by healing childhood trauma as well as adulthood trauma. The way I did that was by bringing up a specific event where someone grossly mistreated me, and I would allow the emotions to come to the surface. 9 times out of 10, the emotions led to me crying. I first started doing this healing work the day I left Zina. Once I got to my hotel room, I started reflecting. I was lucky to have gotten a free upgrade to a suite. The door between the bedroom and living room served as an extra soundproof barrier. I allowed my body to behave naturally. I would let it all out if I felt the need to wail. I can't begin to explain what a wonderful relief this type of self-work is. This should be mandatory for every human being on the planet. These past hurts keep us held back, unhappy, and tolerant of sub-par relationships.

This healing journey has been going on for nearly a year. Whenever I thought I was healed from a particular event, I found that I wasn't and needed to do more healing for that specific event. Sometimes I needed to do this 3-4 times to completely empty out the bottled-up emotions. When I moved to the current apartment building I lived in, in Edgewater, NJ, I came here with visible stress on my face. Within two weeks or so, the concierge manager commented on how different I was starting to look. She said, "your face is glowing." To which I replied, "that's what happens when you get rid of toxic people." She chuckled when she knew who I was referring to (Zina). She was genuinely happy to see me happier. She had a great attitude.

As the months passed, many of my neighbors watched me transform continuously. They all recognize that I'm a completely different person today than I was a year ago. That is because I've constantly been doing the healing work. Writing this book has been a blessing in disguise. I can't tell you how much healing I've done just by writing out my past pain in this book. I shed many tears while writing this book. In fact, in the beginning, I wasn't so motivated to work on this book because I knew it would stir up my emotions, but I also knew that it was good for me. So, I motivated myself to write a few pages every day. I knew if I could tell myself that the goal was to write just 2 pages a day, it would make it much more appealing to work on.

Journaling is an excellent way for you to let your emotions out. You get the same benefit as I did from writing this book. Write down what happened and when. Who was involved? What did they do? Why did it cause you pain? What specific thing(s) hurt you the most? Do you feel betrayed? One time I cried out when recalling the things my mother did to me. I wailed out, "how could you betray me like that? Your own son! Why!?" Some tears just rolled down my eyes after writing the last sentence. Healing is a continuous process. Deep pain is going to take several sessions to heal. That's ok because you do the bulk of the healing the first three times, allowing the emotions to surface on any trauma.

We erroneously think that if we stop thinking about the matter, it's gone. Wrong! That's what I thought too! Boy, was I wrong. I shoved so much crap back into my body by suppressing my feelings and pretending I wasn't deeply hurt. Again, I had to put on this tough exterior and show everyone they weren't getting to me and that I was a survivor.

Once most people in this world heal their trauma and hurts, we, as a collective species, will be a more joyful civilization. Hard to imagine that, right? We have billions of people roaming the Earth with buried pain. Because of this, they project onto others, which starts new drama and conflict, which continues the cycle of hurt and projections. They also adopt the mindset of hurting others. This, of course, stirs the pot and ultimately causes conflict. If your trauma is healed, a heavy burden will be lifted off your shoulders. This allows you to be in the moment and focus on what's at hand. This allows for happiness, joy, and peace to naturally arise within you since there are no negative blockages. Healed people heal people. And out of this healing, peace, tranquility, contentment, and ease arise.

In order to heal, you need to recall every person, place, or thing that's ever hurt you. Write it all down. You don't have to recall everything in one day but do update your list as the days go by. Try not to miss anything.

For example, even though I've done a ton of healing work, I missed one major person in my life. And I just healed that today, September 22, 2022. I was scrolling through TikTok and saw something that reminded me of my first girlfriend when I was 17. I can't believe I totally forgot about her. She was unforgettable, but I somehow forgot all about her! I met her at Rutgers University. She lived a few doors down from me in our dorm. I recognized Arabic music being played in her room. I didn't know there were two girls behind that door dorming together. So, I knocked on her door, and she answered. I said, "you like Arabic music?" She was so beautiful I didn't recognize her as an Arab. She told me, of course, she did and that she's from Egypt. I found a commonality between us and told her my parents are from Lebanon. We hit it off instantly. When I tell you she was super hot, I mean all the guys were jealous of me and constantly staring at her ass in shock that I got her. She turned heads everywhere we went. I remember we were standing in front of her building in Jersey City, NJ, and a group of guys started yelling from a car on the opposite side of the yellow lines. One guy whistled really loud and another made howling noises like a wolf. We looked at each other and laughed hard. She was drop dead gorgeous and turned heads everywhere we went. She had to be top 3 in all of Rutgers New Brunswick.

She had a vibrant personality and loved to sing and dance. She had silky hair. The girls were envious of her hair. Her sense of humor was incredible. We just loved spending time together, having a great time and laughing. Go to the movies, mall, and beach. She was a God sent after dealing with my mother for 17 years. Unfortunately for me, she got accepted into medical school in EGYPT! She decided to leave Rutgers and pursue that opportunity. I was so bummed out. All I could say to myself was, "nothing good ever lasts for me," not knowing I was casting a spell over myself. Was it love? Maybe, maybe not, but it wasn't just her beautiful face and goddess-like body that I liked. I liked spending time with her. She was a bit immature, but we were still young. I had a lot of growing up to do myself.

I wanted her so badly that I was willing to see if we could make a long-distance relationship work. I'd call her once or twice a week using an international phone card, and we'd talk, but I was so depressed. Her leaving me like that really sent me into my first major depression. I was filled with anxiety as well. Here I was, thinking I had someone special to be beside me through college - someone I could see myself marrying if things continued going well between us. I did the silliest thing! I went and bought a pack of cigarettes to cope with it all. After 5 days or so, I was officially addicted. Seeing that it wasn't helping my situation made matters worse because my breathing suffered, and I stunk. So, what did I do? I told my group of friends that I'd smoke marijuana with them. Previously they've offered, but I always declined. This time they were shocked at what I said. They said, "isn't that against your religion?" To which I said, "yeah, but I don't give a crap right now, I'm stressed."

Marijuana made matters EVEN worse. I was missing a lot of classes because we'd get high and sit in my friend's living room for hours just sitting there stoned, playing Sega Dreamcast. My one friend screwed up so badly that he ended the semester with a 0.00 GPA. It was the worst in Rutgers history, and he laughed about it like he was proud. None of this was helping me. I missed my girlfriend so much. You would never understand how bad I felt after going through 17 years of child abuse at that time and losing this beautiful vibrant soul. To my surprise, I hadn't officially healed from that pain. Although I had forgotten about her, I hadn't let out all the emotions. Today I remembered that pain, and rather than suppressing the feelings, I allowed them to come up as aggressively as they wanted to come out. I couldn't believe the relief I got from it.

Every time you heal from a situation, you lighten your load. The more you heal, the more space you give for happiness and joy. Calmness and tranquility arises. By healing, you're removing all the burdens holding you back without you even realizing why you feel the way you do. So, when you create your list of everyone who did you wrong, backstabbed you, cheated on you, mistreated, or disrespected you, make sure you don't leave anyone or anything out of that list if you want to heal thoroughly. Be sure to include situations like unfortunate breakups.

There's no shame in crying if you're a man or a young

adolescent male. Just cry in private. And if you're a woman, do the same. This is your own personal healing journey thus, no one needs to witness your cries. Let whatever emotions you feel regarding the situation arise and trigger your tears. Wail if you have to, and I recommend you wail. The wailing gives you relief as you breathe in and exhale deeply. The breathing and crying will provide you with a peaceful resolution where you feel your mind has cleansed itself from that pain. You may have to repeat the process to detox yourself fully from that person or event. For example, in my case with my first girlfriend, although I felt major relief today, I may need 1 or more sessions to fully heal from that breakup.

25

THE WARRIOR FROM HELL WEEK

I wasn't always this positive person. With so many terrible things that happened to me as early as a preschooler (I never attended preschool), it was illogical to be optimistic. It seemed like the older I got, the more pessimistic I got - even though I was happy and cracking jokes a lot of the time. I mentioned earlier in the book that I was always cheerful and positive as a young boy. My mother, "family," and "friends" treated me so poorly that I became negative. I was too caught up in logical thinking. I.e., I would think, 'since that thing happened, this must also turn out shitty.' This pessimism dragged on to my adult years. In fact, I was pessimistic until 2020, right before the COVID-19 pandemic started. I know I've stated that I was always smiling and in a good mood, but deep down, I was pessimistic and felt things would always be the same. That I would be mistreated, and I would have to wear a smile and pretend everything was ok.

Around 2020, I came across a warrior, David Goggins. To

this day, I'm so grateful for him, and I used to cry in private when I thought of how his story helped me put things into perspective. His story of resilience and determination gave me the boost I needed. I needed to hear his words. I needed to adopt the military mindset to help me get through my fibromyalgia and overcome my past. His story so moved me, and it gave me hope. This man did the unthinkable. He went through Navy Seals Hell Week training multiple times. The final time he attempted Hell Week, he completed it with fractured limbs. He lost about 100 pounds in 3 months just to be accepted for Hell Week. I urge you to pick up his book, "Can't Hurt Me."

Within weeks, it occurred to me. I hadn't read his book yet. I had only watched some of his online videos where he explains his weight loss and Navy Seals journey. Thus, I wasn't aware at the time that he had a rough upbringing too. I thought to myself, "David Goggins did go through hell, but his hell didn't last nearly as long as mine did (not to take anything away from his amazing feat)." That's when I gained even more motivation. Again, I didn't know at the time what David had gone through all of his life. I started seeing myself as a true warrior - a survivor. But I don't know where I'd be if it weren't for Goggins. I get emotional whenever I think of him. I didn't have anyone on my side but I had his testimony. That was all I needed. He was Godsent, and I pray he is on his best timeline. I pray I get to meet him one day and look him in his eyes and give him a nod while shaking his hand and then give him the hood style hug. This chapter has thus far been very challenging to write. I just cried and wailed before writing my last sentence.

It's a cry of gratitude! As I blew my nose, blood was mixed with my snot which never happens.

I think to myself, "thank you, God, for David Goggins. Thank you." A part of me cries for Goggins' struggles too. I prayed on many occasions for God to protect and bless that man. He gave one of God's favorite children (me) hope and fuel. Peace and blessings be on him forever. And may the rest of his days be filled with great health, joy, tranquility, prosperity and ease.

Around the time of discovering Goggins, I was becoming an omnist. After abandoning Islam, I ventured off into other religions and philosophies. At that time, I gained wisdom from the Buddhists and the Bible. I took all I learned along with Goggins' motivation and started developing a positive mindset. I started telling myself I could do things I wouldn't normally do. For example, when I injured my shoulder, arm, and hip, I started doing push-ups even though my arm and shoulder hadn't healed yet. Since I didn't wear a cast or even a sling when I was supposed to in November 2020, my arm healed somewhat in July 2022. It still hurts today, but not nearly as much as it once did.

I not only did push-ups, but I then started doing burpees, and eventually, I started doing weight resistance training. I performed overhead shoulder presses while my arm was experiencing sharp stabbing pain as if I was stabbed with a knife. It hurt like hell, but I was determined to lose weight and gain muscle. I didn't want to make excuses or postpone until my arm improved. The truth was, my arm should've been healed a long time ago, relatively speaking, and it didn't. I saw this as a permanent thing, so I figured I might as well start weight training and push past the pain.

Positive thinking mixed with a military go-getter mindset emerged at approximately 40 years old. Knowing I was determined, disciplined, and pursuing my goal without making excuses increased my respect for myself. I'd look in the mirror and say, "I'm proud of you. You're doing what hardly anyone is willing to do." This kick-started my self-love and self-care. Something I didn't have during the majority of my marriage and life. Not because I didn't want to but because I was under attack by an evil woman who claimed to be my wife. Coincidentally, I left her a month after starting weight training (7 months after starting my burpee and core workout). The day I left was extremely difficult beyond comprehension. At the time, my fibromyalgia symptoms were about half as severe as they were a year before, but leaving the house still required a lot of strength. As I was getting ready to leave, Zina came in and started fake crying, making things even harder for me. She grabbed my wrists and wouldn't let me go, but I had to find the strength to break free and leave. She even involved our 15-year-old son, who begged me to stay, but I knew I had to do what was right for myself and find the extra strength to leave. That morning I had already done my minor workout at the house, the burpees and core workout. After I left, I checked in at a nearby hotel in Edgewater, NJ. The next morning, as you can imagine, I was heartbroken. But I told myself, "don't stop the workout routines," "and stick to the diet!" So that morning, I did my burpees and core exercises in the hotel room with a distraught mind. What helped me stick to the workout was knowing how it cured my depression and lethargy and made me feel so much better as it released bottled-up energy and loosened me up each day. It gave me more energy and made everyday tasks seem much easier since I was pushing my body to its limit.

By sticking to my workout routines, I gained even more self-respect. A few days later, three police officers showed up at my hotel room. Zina told them I was suicidal, which was a bold lie. I never once mentioned or alluded to it. I let them in. They were very nice to me and commented on my physique. Although I had only been weightlifting for a little over a month, I had been doing burpees for over 7 months, which reflected on my body. I gained even more respect for myself, motivating me to continue working on myself. At that point, my self-care and self-love wasn't anywhere near what it is today, but I was starting to pour energy back into myself. Now that I was separated from Zina, I focused all my attention on myself.

When the cops asked me why I left, I told them in an agitated manner that she was manipulative and controlling and that I suspected infidelity due to the warning signs or red flags. I told them that even if there wasn't infidelity, I would still have left due to the cognitive damage caused by her manipulation tactics and emotional abuse. Her constant playing on my heart caused me real cognitive and mental issues. The police put someone on the phone from the suicide hotline. She asked me what was going on, and I told her. She said she wanted me to go with the officers to the hospital for evaluation. I was so pissed, but I had no choice. I thought to myself, "this freaking bitch already screwed me over, and now this?" When I got to the hospital, they recommended that I volunteer to be admitted for a psych evaluation. I assured the nurse that I was fine and that I would never kill myself. She said if I didn't volunteer, I'd have to stay for a week instead of two days. I told her when the doctor speaks to me, he or she will see that I'm fine. WRONG. I never got to speak with a doctor; they simply admitted me by force.

I ended up staying at the hospital for a whole week. Boy, was I heated. At that point, I hadn't fully committed to filing for divorce, but after this incident, I was determined to x her out of my life for good. I even wanted to go as far as filing a restraining order against her. When I got out, I looked for a place to live. I was such a wreck and so stressed with anxiety that I decided to rent a luxury apartment with an NYC skyline view. I landed an apartment on the 20th floor, so the view was spectacular. When I left the hospital, I had to return to the house and stay there for a few weeks. I pretended that I would stick around but was waiting for my apartment to become available for me to move in.

When she found out, she went ballistic. She was trying everything in her power to sabotage my plans and keep me bound to her. I'm sure she called the apartment building's office to complain about me. Nevertheless, November 7, 2021, rolled by. I remember it like it was yesterday. It fell on a Sunday. I should mention that in the days between the hospital discharge and my move-in date, I was out of the house all day which was definitely unusual. I'd get up, do my workouts, do my work, and when I was done, I'd drive around for hours - I'd go into the city (NYC) daily to kill time. I'd only return to the house about 30 minutes before bedtime. This irritated Zina, and she kept asking where I'd been and why I won't stay at the house anymore. I wouldn't give her an answer. In my mind, she knew why, but she was just pretending like she didn't know.

Once I moved into my new place, I really started my self-love journey, and that's when I upped my self-care game. Mind you, at this point, I had severe social anxiety due to years of isolation (due to fibromyalgia, which I highly suspect was caused by witchcraft). The building I moved into (The Riello in Edgewater, NJ) has over 200 units. It was my best decision because I started making small talk with the neighbors and finally beat my social anxiety. I became so comfortable around people in general. I still have work to do on myself, but at least I'm not nervous around people anymore.

Another eye-opener for me while living here is that most people are generally the same - it doesn't matter their education and income level. In the end, they're just people. They weren't happier or more loving than the low-income people who frequented the Chelsea shop. I felt more loyalty and cheer from the customers than from more than half of my neighbors. Knowing this really updated my personality. I stopped expecting people to reciprocate my energy because they weren't; therefore I stopped giving away my energy to all people in general. I learned a valuable lesson. Now I'm only my truest self with people who like to have fun and go with the flow - everyone else gets a very limited version of me.

Another reason I stopped giving my energy so freely is that people are always skeptical of me. They think to themselves, 'is this guy real? Or is this too good to be true? Is he out to get me? Is this some type of trickery?"

For this reason, I throttle back my personality nowadays. The less energy I give now, the more trust I get. I get why they think like that because so many con artists trick you with a smile. I guess I can't blame them. Besides, I'm sure it's part of our DNA to be on the lookout for fast talkers and extraordinarily nice people. Fortunately for me, I feel a great love within me. Unfortunately, it used to always show up in my personality, which scared off a lot of people. After realizing this, I finally put an end to it. These days I keep the good feeling to myself. Others can feel it subconsciously/energetically, and they're attracted to me because of it. However, they're not attracted to a slightly pepped-up optimist who's showing genuine love. It's scary to them. It's bizarre! No one's like that! Is this some wizardry, they think?

Living at the Riello taught me that living a luxurious life doesn't mean you're going to be happy. Many didn't look too happy with their lives. I rarely saw anyone smiling - not even the penthouse residents! In fact, one tenant had so many units in the building and parking spots that he was always stressed out because it was so much to handle. The man was constantly on the lookout to see if anyone was parked in one of his 30 spaces. And, of course, there were always a few people who parked in his spaces, and he would have to call or go down to the concierge to complain about it. I saw that those spaces were practically never in use, but his stress hormones were sure in overdrive.

I've been living here for 11 months now. I can say it was worth every penny. I not only de-stressed tremendously here but also learned many valuable life lessons you simply don't learn by reading a book. I saw how living a big lifestyle can be extremely stressful and defeats the purpose of living a luxurious life. I learned that people with money are just as insecure as people with little money, perhaps even more. I learned that even people with great riches envy those who are happy and positive with very little. Some would look at me and wonder why I was so happy, and I wasn't even wearing designer brands - a pair of Levi's and $25 sneakers that were a copy of the Converse Chuck Taylors. And my car isn't a Lamborghini Urus but a Ford Explorer. They'd think, "how dare he be happy, and I'm more wealthy than him. Who does he think he is?"

I have love. I have God. What more could a person ask for? That's the ultimate. I already had what they were after! They took the long road. They thought they had to do XYZ, and then they'd feel awesome. Not! When you chase money instead of God, you'll most likely be deprived of pure love because you're having other feelings like stress, clients, deadlines, and hundreds of other business-related issues. Not to say you shouldn't aspire to be wealthy. I'm saying God should be your solid foundation. Money is great, but without God, it can't be truly enjoyed because the person will always feel a void inside him/her. That's why so many turn to hard drugs. They didn't get the feeling they were promised when they hit it big.

I've made TikTok videos on being in a state of love. I tell the viewer to feel 'love' but not to be naive and not to overgive to others. I can't say those are my most popular videos. The world is repulsed by the thought of love (and God). I don't believe it's because they don't like the idea, it's just that they've been hurt before and so they've shut it off and are very skeptical of it. I get it. I went through so many heartbreaks. Each time I reverted to love, I somehow got stronger over time. With each heartbreak, I became more and more of my warrior self.

26

GRATITUDE IS YOUR LATITUDE

*I*f I attribute most of my blessings to something, it must be gratitude. When I was 40 years old, I started a daily habit: gratitude meditation. I can't tell you how much it changed my life. Nothing has ever changed my life so tremendously and magnificently. Before you run off thinking, "ugh, gratitude! That's so cringe. What am I supposed to be grateful for? It's not going to do anything for me!" Think again. I would not waste my time writing about it if it weren't extremely valuable and crucial. I've done plenty of A-B tests and found that when I practice my gratitude meditation, my day goes supernaturally smooth and effortless. Whenever I forgot to do it, my day was chaotic and difficult. Give it a shot before you dismiss it. Don't allow your mind to resist. Your ego will fight you at first because of pessimism and how your life has been thus far. Having the spirit of gratitude will make you joyous and slow down your insatiable desires. When you're not grateful, you need more and more products in your life because your mind is operating from a poor state of mind - poor as in you don't feel you have anything valuable. Truthfully, once you adopt a grateful mind, you will realize you are already blessed and wealthy. And once you feel like that, you will attract more abundance, joy, and health.

Every morning, I get up and head straight to the bathroom. I take my morning piss, wash my hands and face, and brush my teeth. Then I go back to my bed. I lay down, put my right hand over my heart, and put my left hand below my right hand to cover more of my chest area. Doing this brings awareness to your heart. You will connect to your heart chakra, and it will ingrain the affirmations in your heart. While taking slow, deep breaths, purse your lips so that when you exhale, hardly any air exits and your cheeks expand. You should feel your cheeks stretching. This aids in reducing tension in your face and jaw. Start by saying:

I am grateful for my health

I am grateful for my mind

I am grateful for my soul

I am grateful for my body

I am grateful for every atom in my body

I am grateful for every cell in my body

I am grateful for every organ in my body

I am grateful for my brain

I am grateful for my eyes

I am grateful for my senses

I am grateful for my limbs

I am grateful for my fingers

I am grateful for (you can list all the parts of your body)

I am grateful for the soles of my feet

I am grateful for the ability to walk, run, jump, and squat

I am grateful for my father

I am grateful for my mother

I am grateful for my partner

I am grateful for my children

I am grateful for my job or business

I am grateful for my income

And on and on and on...

Think of the pledge of allegiance. Why do you put your hand over your heart? It's so that the pledge of allegiance is tied to you emotionally through the hand over the heart. It's programming. Likewise, we want to program gratitude into our hearts.

I take deep breaths with my eyes closed and I start going down the long list of people, places, and things I'm grateful for. I recommend starting with just 10 items on your list, but you can go wild with it. I go through a long list, starting with my "family," and then I continue with my list of other people, places, and things. The longer I meditate, the more relaxed, happy, and energized I feel. Funny enough, when I was being grateful for certain family members, I didn't know they were snakes. But God was cringing when I did so. It was only a matter of a few months before He exposed them to me, as to say, "don't be grateful for them, they are backstabbers!"

Because we attract what we are, I was attracting a relaxing and joyful life - even if I didn't have anything special happen, I was still joyous. This gratitude meditation is life's cheat code. I don't know how else to convince you of this, but you absolutely must try it out for 30 days. I can't tell you how many people I've tried to get to do it for their benefit, but they don't buy into it.

People assume it's hogwash or a corny thing to do. But, when you are grateful, the universe gives you more opportunities to be grateful. In other words, it presents you with more scenarios, people, and things to be grateful for. I also realized that I had so much to be grateful for and that if I didn't take the time to be grateful for what I already had, I'd never be grateful for anything to come. For instance, some people have a few million dollars and aren't grateful because they have yet reached their desired amount. This is faulty thinking because one is just building a poor habit. That habit will not allow the person to be grateful or happy when they finally hit that dollar amount because they've conditioned their emotions to be ungrateful and desire more.

The desire for vast wealth is to have a sense of security, but most wealthy people will tell you they're fearful that they will lose it all. Rather than being happy with the money they've accumulated, some live in fear rather than in grateful happiness. And so there's always a void within. It's very easy to fill that void. In fact, it doesn't require a single dollar of investment. One simply has to take a break and count their blessings. When was the last time you affirmed that you were grateful for your mind? What about your body? And your soul? When I affirm my gratitude for my body, for instance, I say I am grateful for every cell in my body, every molecule, every organism, every organ, every muscle fiber, every bone, every sense, every ability, etc., get very detailed with it. The more detailed I get, the more things I'm grateful for, and the longer the meditation, the better I feel. This meditation is free and will not ruin your life like drugs and alcohol. You can't be joyous unless you have love flowing through your veins. How can you have love when you don't even appreciate what you have?

The key is to be in a state of gratitude all day. If you can practice being grateful all day, I guarantee you'll live a much better life than you do now. You will steadily increase your vibration, and people will pick up on that and want to work with you and get to know you. I do have to warn you against narcissists. They target high-vibrational people, so be sure you look into the topic and learn the signs of a narcissist. Narcissistic people tend to portray a perfect image and will often mirror your every move while not sharing much about themselves. Just be careful. These people will have you believing you found your king or queen (or best friend) when all you've found is a nutcase with no soul.

Despite attracting these individuals, the time invested into your daily gratitude affirmations is well worth it. It takes as little as 10 minutes. You can even do them again later in the day when you're in your car. Take the time to reflect on what you have. For example, imagine you were blind for 20 years, and then a doctor can restore your vision one day. How grateful would you be? I'd bet you'd be very grateful. But why wait for a scenario like that? Why not be grateful right now? Do you know how many functions and systems exist within your body, and they all function close to perfect? You have so much to be grateful for just within your mind, body, and soul - let alone your friends, family, and worldly possessions. You have to recognize that whatever you desire in this world requires first that you exist in a healthy state.

So what's more important and of higher value: life/existence or the desire within life/existence? Life is required for anything to occur and for any desire to be achieved. You are required. Without you, no desire can exist. Therefore, you must genuinely feel grateful for your life and for being you. Once you make this mental shift, your entire reality will shift.

Being that I have a dysfunctional jaw, you would think I ignore my jaw when I'm doing the grateful affirmations, but no. I affirm, "I am grateful for my jaw." The same goes for my back. Does kyphosis cause me pain and discomfort? Sure, but I still affirm, "I am grateful for my back." And because I affirm these, my jaw and back have improved a lot. I believe it's only a matter of time before they're both completely healed. Author and entrepreneur Gary "Vee" Vaynerchuck, born in Belarus in the former Soviet Union, says, "my energy, every ounce of it, comes from gratitude." I can attest to that.

Being grateful clears out the bad energy. You stop ruminating over nonsense. This allows energy to flow freely within and through you. Being grateful lightens the load, allowing you to be your true authentic self. Furthermore, you will start to respect yourself more because you will subconsciously be proud of yourself for recognizing your blessings. And you'll see the beauty in all things. You already have so much to be grateful for if you just stop and think for a moment. More material things aren't going to make you happier. They're only temporary. You're happy about the purchase, and when you finally have it, you're bored of the thing after a short while, and then you're looking for the next fix. The cure to this addiction is gratitude for what you already have.

Just think about our poor ancestors who had to hunt every morning for food and fight off wild beasts. Today, you and I walk into a gigantic big box store and walk through the aisles casually and safely. We have 20 brands of yogurt, 50 brands of cheeses, and different coffee brands; you get the point. We have plenty of options within arm's reach. If you genuinely ponder on this, you'd agree that these big box stores are truly a miracle. The fact that we have so many options is truly a blessing that most don't fathom or appreciate. After all, food is the biggest source of joy and comfort for most, yet they hardly ever take time to reflect and be grateful for these stores, their employees, stockholders, and the farmers and even the banks.

Since I left Zina, I decided not to cook and, instead, eat Chipotle for dinner since it was the healthiest fast food option, and I was trying to stay within a specific calorie intake. If I had to make the bowl myself at home, I'd have to cook for at least 2 hours. I'd have to buy all the ingredients (many of which will spoil in the coming days). And I'd have to clean and wash dishes. The good people at Chipotle have everything already prepared. All I have to do is go there and tell them what I want, and for less than $10, I have a solid, tasty, and healthy meal that fills my stomach to the brim. Every time I'm about to eat my Chipotle bowl, I thank The Holy Father, The Holy Son, and The Holy Spirit for blessing me with the meal and to bless Chipotle's employees, management, investors, and suppliers. They save me time and help me keep in great physical shape. Why wouldn't I be grateful for them? In fact, I pray that everyone involved in that company prospers more. Believe me, I've broken down in tears on more than one occasion while saying my grace and praying over my food. Tears of gratitude and appreciation. If I had to prepare my dinner, I wouldn't be able to write right now due to lack of time. They provide me with incredible value. Your spirit will be renewed and rejuvenated when you start thinking like this. You will become mighty. Over time, you'll become unstoppable and unbreakable. I can't stress how important it is to be in a state of gratitude. I will only use my time if something is giving me a healthy return on my investment. Gratitude doesn't cost anything; therefore, the returns are astronomical!

Being in a constant state of gratitude will make your day much smoother. You will be taken care of by the grace of God/The Universe. Your problems will resolve themselves or require very little involvement on your part. This is one of my secrets to leading a harmonious, fulfilling life. It's so easy to do, yet only some people want to take 10 minutes out of their day to meditate on the people, places, and things they're grateful for. They'll gladly stand in line for hours and even days for the new iPhone or the latest Nikes. Many write off my recommendation to be grateful as hogwash. They simply think to themselves, 'it's bullshit. Too good to be true. That's so corny. I'm not even grateful. Why should I be grateful? I have nothing to be grateful about. My life sucks."

I'm not saying their lives don't suck. I'm just saying it really only sucks because of how you interpret the situation(s). That and the fact that they don't balance out their "bad lives" with the positive emotions of gratitude. Our words are gods. They have the power to shape our reality. Say "my life sucks" a hundred times, and you'll experience your life spiral out of control within days and weeks. However, say, "I'm grateful to be alive," several times a day, and you will soon start seeing evidence that supports your claim or affirmation.

You must be your own hype man or cheerleader. The way to do that is by using the right internal dialogue. Can you imagine judging your friend and telling them, "your life sucks" several times daily? Do you think that person will stand you? Or would that person cut off all ties with you? If they can cut off ties with you over the words you chose to use, why can't you cut off the words causing strife in your life? The answer is simple: lack of faith. That's not an insult to you. Not at all. It doesn't matter how convinced you are of YHWH; Jesus or Allah is God, chances are you still lack faith in life.

You have to shift your mindset. Shift it from being "woe is me," to "I am so grateful and happy for the sun, water, Earth, wind, trees, insects, and animals...I am so grateful I can think, see, hear, feel, touch, smell, and taste. I am so grateful I can breathe, walk, stand, sit, jump, squat, and lie down. I am so grateful I can speak with others and am understood. I am grateful I love life, and I love to smile. I am grateful regarding my happiness, peace, and joy - the choice is mine, and I choose to be happy, peaceful, and joyous, no matter what." You have to adopt this mindset with an overlay of a militant mindset. You have to have great discipline in maintaining this type of internal dialogue. It must be part of your daily routine - preferably all day, but if you do it first thing in the morning, you'll be golden.

Have you ever invited someone to your place and treated them special, but they didn't seem grateful for everything you've done (i.e., cooked a special meal)? How does that feel? Does it incentivize you to continue inviting this person over? It depends, but probably not. Likewise, God/The Universe has done many amazing things for you, but you never show gratitude. Do you think the gods will give you more things that invoke gratitude? Probably not. Most likely not. You have to give The Creator a reason to bless you exponentially. When

God sees you being consistent with your gratefulness, He will say, "look at him/her…they are so grateful for all they have…let Me bless him/her some more!"

When you adopt this as part of your lifestyle, you will start vibrating higher. And depending on how much work or energy you put into yourself, you will continue vibrating higher and higher over the coming months. The key here is to do the daily gratitude meditation and work on releasing past hurts and trauma by isolating yourself in your room and allowing the emotions regarding that thing that hurt you to surface (i.e., cry it out). Remember to ask yourself why that thing hurt you when releasing the emotions. You'll be surprised that many times there are several things, and you need to recognize and cry those out of your system as well. Remember, you may have to do this several times for each trauma and event to heal from that hurt fully.

By having productive, empowering, and uplifting internal dialogue and a release from the past, you will vibrate at a frequency 99% of people will never experience. And believe me, many of the 1% are not of the financial elite. What does it mean to vibrate higher? It means you're visibly joyous when others see you, even if you don't crack a smile. You become a massively attractive person. What does a massive body in space do? It attracts other bodies of mass. You are in space, too - not just the planets and stars. Therefore, when you vibrate higher and become massive, you will attract a lot of attention because you become everyone's source of sunshine and happiness. You become their medicine. They will go out of their way to ensure you're cared for. Why? Because you set the example. Subconsciously, they know you know how to live, and they can learn a lot from you. Things they can never learn from their college professors. Who wants to be surrounded by a depressed or anxious person? None of us do. But why? It's because we can feel the other person's vibration or feelings. If a person is visibly anxious, you will confirm it through your feeling of anxiety that you picked up on from that person. Now you feel the jitters and have to excuse yourself from that person because you don't enjoy feeling that way. Likewise, if a person is vibing high and is peaceful and joyous, you will feel that. Because of that, you will be incentivized to extend the conversation and invite the person to hang out over some coffee or something. You will definitely want to grab that person's contact and stay in touch.

Vibing high attracts abundance. The first form of abundance is people. It's no wonder HR stands for human resources. Humans *are* resources; the biggest resource. Therefore, people are a form of abundance. When you pay someone $15 an hour, they will give you the bare minimum of what's required on the job. But pay that same person with high vibes and sunshine, and they will give you the maximum for $0. Why is that? It's because energy is valuable. And great/good energy is priceless. Remember, just by them being in your presence as a healed and grateful person, they will feel your energy. It's an experience they can't get anywhere else - not even from Disney or Six Flags.

I can't stress enough what an attitude of gratitude will do for you. In essence, it removes your energy blocks, and you gain access to more energy, allowing you to create more. Increased energy will allow you to perform your work easily. Your workouts will seem like a smooth process. You will notice that you no longer experience lactic acid while training. The key is to always practice gratitude so that when something unfortunate happens, you can rely on the fact that you have plenty and you have your health, food, and a place to sleep. If you consider what a life with an unbearable condition or disease would feel like, you will thank the heavens that you are healthy.

Here's where the trouble lies. We are excited for a limited time when we obtain the shiny object we worked so hard for. Think back on your last car purchase or home purchase. Weren't you filled with happiness and gratitude when you were given the keys? But what ends up happening? The feeling fades away. That's because you no longer focus on the benefits. When you wanted a car or house, you thought about all the benefits that come with it. Once we obtain those benefits, we tend to normalize them and take them for granted. What this leads the person to do is seek out more shiny objects. I mean, it's fine and dandy to keep working towards something, but you should do it with a feeling of being whole and complete - not a feeling of a void within.

The benefit of being grateful is that you are forced to slow down and clear the clutter in your mind. So you see, being grateful has many benefits. By slowing down, you can drastically improve your life and increase productivity. How? How does slowing down speed up productivity? That makes no sense! Here's how. When you slow down your mind, speech, and gait, you free up energy (and create space), your golden resource. Instead of driving yourself insane trying to do 20 things per second, slow down and focus on the one task at hand - ignore everything else. Your mind is much more efficient now that you have freed up energy. It will signal the most efficient movements for your limbs to do the task effortlessly and gracefully.

To extract all the benefits of gratitude, it's important to *feel* grateful. Allow your heart space to activate. Feel the gratitude in your heart; let your heart emit gratitude. You should feel a love within and the urge to shed some tears. If so, you're doing it correctly. You want to vibrate the frequency of gratitude for you (God/Your higher self) to create scenarios that inspire you to continue being grateful. The issue most people have is that they are waiting for something to happen to feel grateful. The trick is to feel grateful, and then something will happen that will validate your gratitude.

If I were given a choice between being able to be and feel grateful or taking the $1 billion, I'd choose the former. No amount of money can make my day go smoothly without having an entire team around me like gratitude can. When I say smoothly, I really mean it. I'd say 97% of the time, I find parking near the entrance of the mall or any shop. That's one example. Why not 100%? It could be that I got there too soon and God wants to realign me with the people in the shop by making me walk further. Everything happens for a reason.

Another example is when someone is performing a service for me, and we run into a situation where it looks like there's no way they can help me, and I keep my mind quiet and don't react to the service person. Suddenly, the person comes up with a solution and now will be able to take care of me. When you're grateful, you share that feeling with others, allowing them to free up their energy. In turn, this allows them to use more resources to figure out how to make everything work.

An example of this would be when I ordered new internet

service at my place of business. The tech showed up. I was genuinely grateful for him and his company. I introduced myself, and we chatted a bit. I asked him if he knew two guys I went to high school with, and he said he knew both, and it made him happy. I let him do his work, and I went about my work. Later, he called me over and said something about a problem connecting my place with internet service because the complex doesn't have Verizon internet service. What did I do? I didn't say, "oh, ok, I understand. I'll just call the office to reschedule then." Here's what I did. Internally, I didn't allow my emotions to change. I stayed neutral. I didn't say a word to the tech. I looked at him and slowly said, "oh really?" And I continued looking at him, ensuring my emotions were completely neutral within.

I kept silent. He was thinking…He looked like the loading bar on software installs. When he got to 100%, he said, "oh, but Dwayne (high school friend) is in the area; I'll just call him and use his bucket truck." Just like that, I had internet that day. Had I interjected immediately and told the tech, "thanks for trying, I'll call the office. Have a nice day. And tell the boys I said hi," I would've had to get back on the phone with customer service, explain the situation, and get a new install date about 3 days later.

Another example, I walked into a barber supply store once and requested a particular hair trimmer. I already had a grateful vibe when I walked in. When the clerk told me, "sorry, we're sold out of those." Did I say, "ok, thank you," and leave? No. I directed my emotions to neutrality and looked at him without a response. To which he said, "hold on, let me check the back for you." What a miracle! He brought me the last one. Not only was

I grateful, but I was non-reactionary and patient. Patience is key, and I will get into it in the next chapter. Now the question is, did that trimmer magically appear? We'll never know, but the fact that I allowed the person to think allowed him to come up with a solution. Had I said, "ok, thank you," and left, he wouldn't have remembered to check in the back. So, remain calm, be grateful, and take it easy.

27

THE GREAT POWER OF SILENCE

*U*nless you've been living under a rock, chances are you've heard of unconditional love. Did you know that that's who you really are? Think about it. Why are you alive right now? Why are you reading this book? It's because you are unconditional love. And you are life. If you weren't life, you wouldn't be alive. You love life unconditionally; it's the reason why you don't commit suicide and why you go to work. You were born with unconditional love. Have you ever observed babies and toddlers? They're a bundle of joy. You were once a baby. You were full of joy. But what happened? Well, the globe is full of people with generational curses. It's full of hurt people who are desperate for control over everyone. Only so many times can a human be hurt before they turn off their love for others. They're not to be blamed. It takes great faith and courage to say, "you know what? I don't give a damn what happened. I'm going to be me. I will be happy because it's the best way to live." We're all unconditional love - it's why the planet is so populated. Do people commit suicide? Sure, they do. Thankfully, the vast majority don't commit suicide. Even an act as terrible as suicide can be viewed as a form of love. The person loves themselves so much they won't allow themselves to be treated so harshly by life anymore or endure pain. Although I don't agree with or recommend suicide, it *can* be viewed as such. If you ever feel suicidal, please contact the professionals who can help you. There's no shame, and you won't be judged. Suicidal thoughts are common in society.

Have you ever heard of unconditional patience? Me neither. I came up with that concept. And it means what it sounds like. Being patient 24/7, 365 days a year. Rather than drawing on patience when a situation calls for it, I've found it best to be in a state of patience all day long. While many think only certain situations call for patience, they often neglect other stuff that also requires patience. Sometimes we're not patient in times when we really should be. So, it makes sense to be in a constant state of patience.

One of the benefits of unconditional patience is you become nonchalant. You can't be moved easily. You don't freak out if a situation gets out of hand. If someone sneaks up behind you to scare you, you'll turn around and look at the individual and ask him if he's alright. Back to the Verizon example in the previous chapter, the state of unconditional patience automatically gives off a non-reactionary vibe. This feeling of unconditional patience allows you to sink deep into peace - sinking deep into your body. The very feeling of being patient allows you to be more in tune with the present moment. It keeps fear at bay.

The magic happens when you operate from unconditional love, patience, and joy; as well as always being in the moment. I guarantee your life will vastly improve. Fake it till you make it. You will be unbothered. Unshakeable. Unmovable. You will vibrate so high that you will attract new people into your life, and the bees will love you. Bees are attracted to highly vibrational people. "But I don't want to get stung!" Don't worry, they won't sting you!

The beauty of unconditional love is that everyone can tell. People appreciate it. They respect it. Of course, some people won't appreciate it, and some will be turned off. But those are the people you want to filter out of your life. Being that my parents are from Lebanon, my skin color is pale. Whenever I encounter people of color, they instantly recognize me as real and treat me as a friend rather than someone they deem a racist. Love is a universal language. Everyone is out desperately searching for it. With so many people walking around with past hurts and trauma, it's no wonder fewer people operate from a state of unconditional love. That's what will set you apart from the majority of people.

Obviously, you don't want to do this for the benefits because then you'd turn it into conditional love. You have to let go and trust that the universe will take care of you for putting out loving energy. You get what you put out; remember that. If you want love, you have to give love. The same goes for money. If you want money, you have to give money. If you want energy, you have to give energy. If you want happiness, then you have to give happiness. That's very important information. You should definitely highlight it and memorize the formula. If you want more of X, give (or be) X. As an extra bonus, remember this: the faster and more you give of anything, the faster and more you get in return. For instance, money - when you get it, the faster you get rid of it, the faster you make money. Here's what I mean. Say you just got a check for $10,000. You can either hold on to it and watch the spending power diminish over time due to normal or high inflation, or you can immediately get rid of it and put it in an investment. The faster you invest, the faster your money will return in excess of what you put out. By this logic, the faster you move money, the more you'll make.

When you balance your feminine and masculine energies and surrender and go with the flow but still know when to take control, you become a force to be reckoned with. Trusting that the universe will let things play out in your favor is such an understanding that liberates one.

Imagine being love. Being in love with yourself. You don't have to seek it from anyone outside of you. You have access 24/7, 365 days/year. Feel the love in your heart and veins so that you emit the signal of love into the world. You're no longer on the hunt for love from the opposite sex and friends. In that sense, you're truly liberated.

Love is one of the most important things that a human can value. Think of how many men out there are looking for love from a woman. It's logical to think a woman will give a man love since another woman gave her son love. However, a woman typically reserves her unconditional love for her offspring. On rare occasions, you'll find a woman who truly loves a man for who he is and not for what he can provide. Unfortunately, Hollywood propaganda had us all fooled with their romantic movies and made-up lies. I'm not saying a man shouldn't be with a woman. I'm saying both men and women should love themselves unconditionally, therefore loving life and everything within it unconditionally. And understanding that things are happening for us, not to us.

Once you embody love, life feels like you're relaxing on a hammock. Just existing all relaxed and feeling good. Don't we all work our butts off so we can go on vacation and hopefully lay on a hammock all day to destress from life? If that's the case, why go through all the hassle of earning money, buying the tickets, booking the hotel, and running up your credit cards when you can be on your hammock right now?

I don't need vacations. I don't need to book a flight and go somewhere; I've become the vacation destination! I always feel like I'm permanently on vacation right here in Northern New Jersey - a state NO ONE comes to visit, lol. Nevertheless, I've become the destination, and people gravitate towards me. Strangers even. I don't have to smile, or people please. They just naturally happily come to me. They cherish my energy. I'm one of the few people they'll encounter that day that will change their life for the better simply by me existing.

Now all of this sounds like a bit of a stretch, right? To those who never experienced it, it sounds outrageous. But enlightened beings know exactly what I'm talking about. When you have the light of love within, you become a star. A star shines bright. It shines its light. Light is knowledge, and it is also love. Love is understanding which requires knowledge and wisdom. We were born as love, which means we were born as knowledge and wisdom as well. We are simply discovering our own knowledge and wisdom. You can only truly love someone if you understand yourself and them and understand where they're coming from and where they've been. That's why we go through trials and tribulations.

My spirit is strengthened by love, patience, and gratitude. The energy I radiate evokes positive responses from most people. The ones that don't are because they're star-struck and feel as if they are in lack. Therefore, they get stuck in their heads. I don't take it personally. I understand where they're coming from. They're so used to the cookie cutters who have copied their personality from someone else. Everyone talks and sounds the same to them. But when they see me, they've never seen anyone like me. Someone who is nurturing and caring yet ready to scrap with anyone. It's bizarre, I must admit.

Those who grew up with me always ask themselves, "why did God choose him? Why not me?" He saw that I was obedient when I was a child, a teenager, a young adult, and even as a grown adult - despite all the trials and tribulations, betrayals, and back stabbings. Despite all the heartbreaks and tears, I kept God as my target.

When I hit rock bottom in 2017, I woke up at 2 am. I went straight to my man cave and pulled out the prayer rug. I had read somewhere that Prophet Muhammad (PBUH) prayed for 4 ½ hours. I wanted to show Allah that I really meant it when I said I wanted to go to the highest level of paradise after death. I prayed the non-obligatory but highly recommended Islamic "Night Prayer" for 4 ½ hours straight. Typically, the Night Prayer only takes about 10-15 minutes. The entire time I was standing and prostrating over and over again. By the end of it, my ankles were swollen. I had to sit down. Then I got up for the obligatory Fajr prayer or morning prayer.

I also heard that if you do a specific "tasbeeh," a prayer using rosary beads for an hour after the fajr prayer, Allah will consider it a pilgrimage to Mecca, Hajj. I never got to visit Mecca, so I thought this was a bargain. Lord knows it takes many hours just to get to Saudi Arabia, and then you have to get on a 12-hour bus ride, deal with the crowds, and possibly die in a stampede. So, I did this extracurricular activity several times and was happy that Allah had written down that I went to Hajj in Mecca several times. To me, I was racking up lots of points with God. I went hard in the paint, so to speak.

That wasn't the end of it. I not only prayed the 5 daily prayers, but I added another 5 prayers that were non-obligatory every day. I read the Quran in Arabic and English for 30 minutes in the morning, 30 minutes at noon (most days), and another 30 minutes at night. In that period, my entire life revolved around God and worshiping Him. How many people will put in this effort while still working and providing for their families? Only a few. On top of all this, I was still learning other topics and subjects. God makes no mistakes. He knew who His choice was.

You can do it too. Nothing is stopping you but you. The people need you. The planet needs you...to increase the vibration. If you want to arrange a meeting with the President of the United States (past or present), do you think merely sending a request will do it? Absolutely not. You have to be someone worthy. You have had to put in a lot of work throughout your life to become the person to meet the president. Of course, sometimes you're part of a school trip and get to meet him, but that's the exception, not the rule. Suppose you went to the Trump tower, rang Trump's bell, and hesitantly asked if you could see him. What would happen? They'd send security after you. However, if you were a fanatical supporter of Trump and it was clear that you were one of his most excited and biggest fans, chances are, he'll let you in, so long as you didn't appear to be mentally ill.

It's the same with God/Universe/Allah/Yahweh/The Father/The Son/Holy Spirit. If one is not The Creator's biggest fan by showing It through devotion and spirit, then they cannot "meet" God. It's because they're not worthy yet. Why would He open up to them and establish a direct line of communication when they don't show Him gratitude, praise, or reflection? I'm not saying all this to make you feel worthless and that I'm better. I'm giving you tough love and showing you the way. I was once in that position too. I only wish someone had told me sooner.

Most people send God a prayer, and if it isn't answered within a certain period, they give up on Him and say, "He doesn't exist." For example, let's say a person prays for $1 million, and weeks and months pass, and the person has yet to become a millionaire. Could it be that God is preparing you for that money? Perhaps you need to learn a thing or two before you gain access to that type of money. Why? So you can retain it and not lose it due to ignorance of financial literacy. Sometimes it could be because you're married to a cheater, and you don't know that. So God wants to delay it until you two get divorced. Other times, He knows it will destroy you and your health.

God is love. If you want to feel God, then you must feel love. If you want to know God, you must gain much knowledge. It's that simple. Once you feel the love, you will attract miracles. Show compassion and consideration. Do loving acts. A simple tip at your local fast food joint or the gas station clerk pumping your gas shows God that you care, and He sees that if He gives you more money, you will spread it around and not just hoard it. Love is recognizing that God is within all people - therefore, we must treat people as sacred beings.

In the Islamic greeting, as-salaam alaykum means peace be upon you (plural). Why would anyone greet a single person with the plural form of you? This is my answer - no sheikh or imam has ever proposed this answer. We always use the plural form because we are greeting the ego of the person and God and the angels. Think of the implications of you knowing that God is within man. You will treat people with greater respect; they will notice that and love you. Besides love, we crave respect, especially men. When you treat someone as if they're important to you, it moves them. You add value to their lives by showing them they're worthy of being treated honorably. Of course, some people are outliers and don't feel they deserve respect.

I must mention this, however. Do not, under any circumstance, allow others to take advantage of you. Do not people please, and do not over-give. I'm not asking you to be lovey-dovey like you're in a fairy tale. I'm asking you to be and feel love. You only show people love once. If they decide to take you for granted or mistreat you, cut them off immediately and ignore them. Next time you see them, give them the cold shoulder - don't even say hi to them. Let them learn their lesson.

That's where some people get me confused. They think because I'm positive that I'm gullible or will tolerate bread-crumbs or even hate. Never. Nowadays, I match other people's energy. If they seem happy to see me, I reciprocate. They need to come correct, or they won't get any energy from me! It's a balancing act, but you must do it - otherwise, people will walk all over you.

As a positive, loving being, you add value to the world. How so? Your light energy motivates and inspires others to do and be better - it also makes them *feel* better. They get those lessons live for free. There are many motivational speakers out there, and they charge top dollar. Meanwhile, you and I are out there giving it out for free. It's valuable energy! You show others that they need to work on themselves and that it can be done with discipline and hard work. They will notice that all of the work you put in yourself has given you an abundant life.

Silence is one of the most, if not the most, underrated abilities we have. It can be used to make us look smart, to ignore a person's question, to allow the other person to think of a solution, to bow out of a debate or confrontation, to manipulate (stonewalling), to deceive, to meditate, to think and create, to send a loud message, to let the other person know that they are extremely dumb, to appear to be a friend, to show disgust, to show anger, attract women, to invalidate someone, to show disapproval, to remain neutral amongst all parties, to reflect, to listen to our inner voice, to relax, to concentrate, to read, to write, to pray from the heart, to run, to sleep, to swim, to slam dunk, to score a touchdown, to play chess, to listen, to get a degree (lectures & exams), a stethoscope check-up, blood pressure check-up, and on and on and on...

Most of us never think of silence that way, but it's powerful and dangerous. You must never use it for manipulation or to deceive others unless someone is plotting against you. Then it's ok to deceive regarding your intentions to protect yourself. And for that matter, don't ever become a manipulator. Karma will come back full circle. It's a universal law. It's good for you to know this information to protect yourself from connivers. However, you should learn how to use it to your advantage. If you're smart, speak only when necessary and be direct using plain English rather than fancy jargon. You do not impress anyone with big words unless you're interacting with doctors, scientists, etc.

You might think it only makes you look smart, but it's also attractive for women. Women don't want a chatty guy as a lover. As a friend? Sure. You can't be boring, but you can't talk her up like you sit with 10 women gossiping all day about celebrities. Showing her, you can be fully present in the moment and not have to say a word without feeling nervous. She'll crave you more for that. Otherwise, you'll just come off as a nervous wreck by being chatty. This is a sign of weakness; women are hardwired to mate with strong providers and protectors. Besides being so talkative in general, one's bound to say a lot of foolish things that they will regret.

I became obsessed with the power of silence because Neuman used this technique to manipulate me and others. He would lie through silence by making me assume it was true or false, depending on the context. He started using it heavily when I was in my 30s and older. There was a lot of bullshit going on with the family, and many times it required him to say something or pass judgment on the situation, but he never did. Ever. It's as if he learned a secret of the universe. Say nothing, and eventually, everything will sort itself out. For, I.e. if different family members were fighting amongst each other, he wouldn't say one of them was at fault even if he knew 100% who was at fault. He'd stand there and say nothing. We'd all get pissed at him because he wasn't being a father. He was running away from the problem without actually running away. A few hours or a day later, he was still on good terms with everyone, while the rest weren't talking to one or more family members. No one would stay mad at him for too long. Once the situation simmers, we usually forget about his lack of fathering. To this day, everyone talks to him even though there's conflict with other family members. You could say that's a good thing, but to me, he went too far with it.

Why's he like that? He did get married at the young age of 17 and came to this country at that age. Lucky for him, rent was pretty cheap back then, while there weren't many big box stores, so the competition wasn't as fierce, and people were spending money like crazy in the 80s. Still, I have to respect him for going through all that and putting food in my stomach and a roof over my head. Sure, he wasn't there for me. And if you think about it, he only enabled my mother by providing her with a place to beat me in private. So it's a double-edged sword.

He's also like that because he needs everyone to like him. So he'll almost never speak his mind if he knows the truth will hurt a person or people. There's nothing wrong if most people or everyone likes you. It's an issue when the person is just being agreeable and super friendly. Now don't get me wrong. When I say he's super friendly, I don't mean he's a softie. He's got some ruggedness, but he's super friendly in that he knows how to invoke a good feeling in you when he wants to impress the person. That's what always pissed me off. He'd make others laugh and feel good, but he just gave me a serious face with hardly any words spoken. I always felt like he was embarrassed that I was his son, mainly because I was chubby and Arab Muslims said I looked Jewish as a kid as if it were a terrible thing! He hated that I bore a lot of resemblance to my mother's side of the family. It's as if it was my choice.

He would always hold back compliments or validations because, in his mind, he wanted to be on the pedestal. I can see if one does it a lot, but to NEVER compliment me my whole life? In his eyes, I already knew, and he didn't want to give me the satisfaction. When there were moments he would have complimented his friends for the same thing, he'd stay silent. And I'd become silent. And then he'd be in my head. "What the heck just happened? Am I a loser? Why do I feel worthless right now?" He didn't understand that he was having the exact opposite effect of an inflated ego. He was tearing me down and making me feel smaller and smaller. Because I had codependency issues, abandonment issues, and a strong need for love, I would stay near him, hoping he would compliment or approve of me and be proud to be my father. Years went by, and he never did. When I started working out again, he never once complimented me when everyone else did: doctors, police officers, strangers, my employees, etc. Everyone but my family!

Mind you, I always gave these people positive energy and great words, but they withheld theirs from me. They are thieves in my eyes because they were stealing my energy. In other words, they'd take what I gave them and never reciprocate with equal value. It's just like going to a store and taking stuff without paying. Sure, I don't mind if you don't give the exact amount of energy, but to hardly give any at all? No way, that's haraam (forbidden). That's stealing, whether they know this or not.

They thought I'd never abandon them. Well, one day, I said enough's enough. I cut them all loose. Blocked their numbers and later changed phone numbers for good measure.

These people thought that by being silent with me, I'd continue supplying them with ideas and help so long as they didn't inflate my ego. In other words, had they inflated my ego, in their opinion, I would abandon them. Well, their fear of me abandoning them is what ultimately caused it. Whenever you fear something, you stand a good chance of attracting the same thing you don't want simply because you keep thinking of what you don't want. If you think about what you want, your mind will attract that thing into the 3D world.

You know, you watch these tv shows growing up, and you see the fathers telling their sons, "come here son, I just want to tell you that I see you're putting in the work, and you're making great progress. Keep going. I'm proud of you." Had he only told me those words, I promise I would have achieved my childhood dream of becoming an astronaut. I was infatuated with the cosmos as a child. I wanted to spacewalk, even though it's risky as heck. I wanted to fly at warp speed. I was really big into sci-fi as a child. I knew sci-fi wasn't entirely real, but I always wanted to walk through a portal in a hot desert. Little did my dad know, his supportive words could've helped create some of my dreams.

I had no cheerleaders. Admittedly, my mother would boast about me to her friends and family when I was young. I later learned that's what narcissists do. I knew she was a bullshitter, so I never took her compliments to heart. I took them as her trying to brag for her own sake. She wants to be seen as a woman who possesses my qualities and traits, such as intellect and empathy. So, in essence, I didn't have anyone to motivate me - AT ALL. The only motivation I ever got was a threat of a beating if my grades didn't improve.

I kind of wish my mother practiced silence. She was *ALWAYS* on the phone on a 3-way call. When I say always, I mean always. She used the phone so much that she screwed up her ears. She had ear pain and infections. I would think, "boy, she sure loves to talk to everyone else. She sounds nice too. Am I that bad? I don't get it. What am I doing wrong here? I go to the supermarket whenever she needs something. I fold the laundry when she tells me to. I work passing out flyers or bagging groceries in the supermarket.

I was so embarrassed working in the supermarket. I felt like a peasant working for tips. The owners made me feel like that too. Even though they weren't paying me, they would treat me and others as if we were thieves. Such idiotic people! We were speeding up the lines, allowing them to process more customers per hour without extra cashiers. It also improved the customer experience. They were assholes. They lost the super-market their father gave them by scamming the government with food stamp fraud and other crap.

I took so many losses in my life and lost count a long time ago. When I was about 7 years old, I had a taser, and some sleazeball about 16 years old offered me to trade it for his cell phone. I agreed. I was so happy. The prick! It wasn't working! I went back to him, but he bullied me, and I just took the loss. I would just think about how all the other kids would bully me, and my mother was never happy with anything I did. I just accepted defeat. I kept incurring loss after loss throughout my life.

Eventually, I learned to say "oh well" and count my blessings. I'd say, "it's ok, I still got A, B, C...it ain't so bad. I'll bounce back." When something unfortunate happened to me, I'd brush it off as if it didn't happen, and I'd focus on something else that's productive or makes me happy. I got really good at using my pain to propel me forward. In other words, as I got older, I wouldn't dwell on the loss and mourn over whatever happened, but instead, I'd stop thinking about it and do something else. I would stay busy.

For example, when I left Zina, I used the disappointment of a failed relationship to fuel my workouts, especially my pull-ups. I unknowingly became a self-made alchemist. I started turning doo-doo into gold. Without anyone teaching me, I was transmuting the negative energies into positive energies. My secret is that I take the L or loss and don't dwell on it. I acknowledge I got screwed or suckered and subconsciously tell myself, "it's ok. Stuff happens."

After I left Zina, she called the police, telling them I was suicidal when I wasn't. She was trying to get a hold of me. Because I was a bit pissed off since I had just left her 2 or 3 days prior, they wanted to evaluate me in the hospital just to make sure I wasn't suicidal due to the break up. I ended up staying there for about a week. The food was terrible! First of all, the portions were inhumanely small. I had to drink extra cartons of milk to make sure I was getting enough calories for the day. That wasn't even the worst part. The chicken they served was boiled with no salt or seasoning, rubbery, and didn't taste like good quality fresh chicken. I didn't belong there, and the staff there were shocked I was even there - but I had no choice but to go through the process. I could've made excuses that week. I could've said I didn't have enough food or that it was unfair. But guess what? I still did my mini-workout, which consisted of burpees and core exercises. I did them Monday - Saturday and rested on Sunday. I didn't have my pre-workout drink or marijuana, and I was barely sleeping 3-4 hours. It was worse than prison in there. We weren't allowed to use our phones.

I had a choice to make. I can lay in my shitty bed and make excuses and get mad. Instead, I did my workouts and talked to the staff and other patients. I gave the patients wisdom and sound life advice, including how to deal with their situations. Someone gave me a copy of the Bible, so I'd read it occasionally. What Zina didn't know is that because she called the police on me and did this to me, I had made up my mind to divorce her and even get a restraining order against her. I wasn't 100% intent on divorcing her until she did that. When I got out, I prepared to move into my new apartment and get away from her. About 2-3 months later (Feb 2022), I pulled the trigger, called a divorce attorney, and got the ball rolling. I decided enough's enough. I'm not going to cry over her, and I'm going to work on myself even more now that I don't have her in my way.

After a breakup, there are two ways to deal with it: you can cry about it and lay on your couch all day or improve yourself. At that time, I was already working out with weights, so I made sure not to miss a single workout. Throughout the entire ordeal, I stuck to my diet and workout schedule. Never fell off the diet, and I never skipped a workout. I used the pain of the breakup to propel me forward. By the summer of 2022, I had the best physique ever. And I had a nice 6 pack (abs) for the first time ever. I could've easily said, "woe is me. My life sucks. I will order a triple cheeseburger and large fries and sit here while I get fatter by the day." However, I didn't. I said I would use that energy to do something with myself.

I started to look great. I took my appearance and fashion more seriously. I always smell great. My vibration kept increasing gradually since the day I left the old house. My face cleared up; my face and skin started to glow. I started posting updates daily on my TikTok (@TheChrisJosh). Zina was and is stalking me on TikTok. She had front-row seats to my level-up and glow-up. I made sure she understood that I never needed her, but that I only wanted her. And I can pick myself up with no help from anyone and rise above any situation - even if I don't have a single family member in my corner, which I didn't.

One of the most valuable skills you can learn to do is transmuting energy. You must understand that negative energy is still energy and you can use it to your advantage. You can use it to spread negativity to your person or use that energy for something productive. You can think of transmutation as retaliation, not always, but sometimes. In the case of Zina, I wasn't achieving my physique as retaliation, although she certainly sees it that way. I was achieving my physique because I wanted to do the best for myself, especially my mental health. I wasn't doing it to build a physique when I started working out. I was doing it because it was helping me with some of the fibromyalgia and ADHD symptoms. It also did wonders for my depression. It helped me gain lots of energy, and it gave me motivation and ambition.

My life today is eons better than when I was married to

Zina. If I knew my life would be this way, I would have left her long ago. I look 10 years younger now than I did with her. My anxiety is COMPLETELY gone. No more depression. No more stress. I got over the social anxiety. I've become the center of attention wherever I go even though it's not my intention. People can't help but notice me. Whether it's because of how I look, or it's something they feel from my aura. Whatever it is, people notice me a lot more than when I was married. Women smile at me and talk to me. Some even stand an inch away from me even though there is 100 ft of space in every direction to signal that they want me to talk to them.

This elevation in my health, appearance and status only occurred because I transmuted the pain into power. Another way I transmuted the pain was to write this book. If I ever wanted to procrastinate, I'd think of Zina and hop on the computer and start writing away. I started a TikTok account (@TheChrisJosh) approximately November 2021, just one month after I left Zina. Unfortunately, she found me on TikTok. She and her family relentlessly reported all of my videos. I was doing great until they found me. Once they found me, I wasn't getting any more views, followers or likes. I tried to weather the storm, but they got my account shadow banned. My intuition told me to hang on for some more time. Then it told me to start a new account. Thankfully I've already surpassed the number of followers on the new account. Once again, I could've thrown in the towel and given up, but I kept pushing forward instead. Yes, I had to start all over again. I got stuck at 2,000 followers for a long time on the first account. I have approximately 64,000 followers on the new account, which hasn't been that long. I'm sure Zina found the new account, but she has no help this time. Her family has seen through her lies and deception and no longer supports her. All the people she slandered my name to have distanced themselves from her as they, too, have seen that I'm nothing like she said I was. They watch my videos too. When people slander your name and go on a smear campaign, the best thing you can do is make valuable content and showcase your personality. It worked for me.

You can transmute the negative energies in your life into something you believe in or enjoy doing, like a good cause or hobby. You can use it to organize your entire life, from your finances to your belongings. You can use that energy to take classes or to start a side hustle. The key is to not think about or dwell on the unfortunate situation but to focus on something else - something productive and fulfilling. Remember, what happened happened. You gotta accept the loss and trust that it happened for a good reason. When one door closes, another one opens.

Remember, you have to heal the hurt, then transmute the pain. Let the emotions come about in your body, and let the tears out. You can make sounds when crying that will help you let it all out. You'll notice that when you're done, you feel a weight lifted off you. You feel more stable, more solidified, and more relaxed. That's because you're getting rid of the trauma. The trauma leaves you shaky and unstable. Once you let it out, you will be visibly calmer and at peace. People will notice that you're more grounded.

I learned to transmute all on my own by accident. After getting beaten down so much, I just learned to accept what happened and move on. There came a time when my ego stopped making a big deal out of the losses. In a way, you could say I was broken down to my bare self. The self that has no name and no body. Whenever an unfortunate thing happened to me, I'd respond the same way a baseball player responds to a ball coming fast at them. I'd pull my "glove" back as the "ball" entered the glove to minimize the impact. Likewise, when something bad happened to me, rather than holding my glove stationary and with brute strength, I'd let myself (the glove) absorb the event (the ball) gracefully.

When I look back at my younger versions, a part of me feels sorry for that young boy or young man. For whatever reason, it seemed like 95% of the people I came across didn't like me and didn't want me around. They wanted to steal from me, take advantage of me, bully me, make fun of me, and hurt me badly, use me as their scapegoat. Today, I understand that, in a way, I caused it all, not on purpose. It was because I was always in fight or flight mode. But I was in fight or flight mode due to the abuse at home. I was always on guard. I was always anxious and afraid due to all the drama at home with my mother and Milton. When you're in fear, you naturally attract fear-inducing scenarios. I didn't know that back then. No one taught me otherwise. My parents didn't teach me anything. They hardly knew anything. My mother only taught me that I better get my grades up in school and earn lots of money. She taught me impatience. She taught me anger. She taught me brute force. She taught me blatantly obvious manipulation. She taught me ungratefulness. She taught me how to curse God. She taught me that people with money are the most honorable in society. She taught me you could steal from Jews because they invaded Lebanon. She taught me hate, jealousy, and envy. She taught me you could make a dua (optional Islamic prayer) after salaat (obligatory Islamic prayer), asking Allah to take away the blessings of her own brother simply because he had more money and was more successful. While she taught me all these things, I didn't keep them in my toolbox. I knew she was a conniving, trifling, no good, sorry excuse of a human being. I would never adopt her ways and views. I used my critical thinking to determine what is appropriate behavior. And for the record, I really don't care what people think of me with regards to me speaking this way of my mother. Truth be told, I have restrained myself greatly. If I let loose about everything she did, I wouldn't be surprised if random strangers pulled her hair out in public every time she stepped out of her house as payback - Zina too. Why? Because they *violated* a pure soul with a heart of gold. All out of envy and jealousy because they weren't me.

Admittedly, I wasn't transmuting much when I lived with my mother for the first 17 years. I was lost and confused. A part of me thought that Allah didn't even know I existed since he had to tend to billions of other people. How could I be noticed by the Most High? Even though I continued my faith in Him and did my 5 daily Islamic prayers, a part of me felt neglected and forgotten by Him.

In my childhood and teenage years, I didn't know how to use negative energies and experiences to my advantage. Therefore, I wasn't growing much during that time. In fact, when I started college, I hadn't read a single book until then as I had terrible focus, making reading a difficult chore. For four decades, I had to re-read the sentence 3-5 times before proceeding to the next sentence. It was that bad. It wasn't until I was finally diagnosed with ADHD when I was about 42 years old and prescribed Wellbutrin that my focus started improving. It wasn't just a focus issue but also a memory issue. Wellbutrin isn't the first choice that doctors prescribe, but due to my trouble sleeping, my doctor couldn't prescribe a stimulant like Adderall.

So, I found a pre-workout drink that helps with focus and energy. I started drinking it at the age of 42, first thing after waking up. I don't even take it prior to working out. Instead, I take it as my morning coffee. The caffeine helps speed up my brain, so I'm not sluggish and unable to hold a conversation. My ADHD was so bad I couldn't keep track of what the other person or I *just* said! I would stop mid-sentence and ask the person in front of me, "wait, what did I just say?" It was impossible to have conversations with anyone, and I only felt comfortable speaking to Neuman and Zina. I'm sure they thought I was slow or even mentally disabled. While the pre-workout and Wellbutrin helped, I wasn't out of the mud. My memory was causing me major issues. You really don't know how valuable memory is until you lose a significant portion of it. Think of a computer with inadequate memory trying to load big software.

After talking to my doctor about my memory, he said it was normal due to my condition, and there wasn't anything I could do about it but wait it out. For about a year, I just accepted it as a fact. However, one day, I thought I should scour the internet for memory-enhancing pills. I found a brand, Prevagen, that was rated highly by others. To my surprise, it improved my memory by at least 5 times. Later I started also taking gingko biloba. Mind you, my memory isn't 100% back. However, I can have fluid conversations now. I don't have to ask the person in front of me, "wait, what did I (or you) just say?" I'm able to generate thought-provoking ideas rapidly. I'm able to be witty and funny now. I can think at lightning speed now. And because my memory and focus improved, I can make videos for social media - something that was absolutely impossible at the end of my marriage.

28

HEALING FROM PAIN CAUSED TO OTHERS

So far in this book, I've only mentioned the things I had to heal from when it comes to people. However, I also had to heal from the pain I caused others. I used the same technique to heal from what others did to me. I would sit in a quiet space and ponder on the evil I've done. I'm not proud of this, but there was a time when I was between high school and college when I hung out with the wrong people. Sure, my high school "friends" were troublemakers, too, but these guys were evil. I was with a pair of twins and their uncle, who had just come home from prison. He must have been at least 10 years older than me. It's like he had something to prove.

We went to one of the main boulevards in our town, and we went to an area that was full of trees intending to smoke marijuana. That's all we intended to do. However, there were two guys there doing the same thing. The uncle pulls us to the side and comes up with a plan to rob them. They had on gold necklaces and cell phones. I went along with it because I didn't want to appear lame. So, we walked over to the 2 guys. It was 4 against 2. We jumped them. They were hurt real bad. We took their phones and jewelry. I thought we were going to split everything among us. WRONG! The uncle said it was all his. I couldn't protest. He was nearly twice my height, weight, and age. Besides, he always had his gun on him. He once pulled it out on me for no reason except to get a laugh. He was a big bully and a loser.

I remembered that day many times throughout my life. However, it wasn't until I learned how to heal that I decided to let my true emotions regarding that situation surface. I was wailing. I thought about those 2 kids. What did we jump them for? Jealousy. Because they appeared to be flamboyant. What's funny was when the uncle went to pawn the chains, they were fake! He was visibly upset about it and wanted to go back and beat them some more. The day I healed myself from this, my soul was trying to reach those two kids' souls to apologize to them. To tell them that I never meant to hurt them and that I was caught up in peer pressure. I imagined they were right there in front of me, giving them a genuine hug. It was just cruel. I cried out to the universe. Not so much for forgiveness, although I sought it. I cried out because I was genuinely sorry for what I did.

My violence and carefree attitude are what the entire high school loved about me. They knew I was always ready for a brawl, even though I wasn't the biggest or strongest. I had one of the biggest and most fearless hearts, mainly because I was hit so often as a child, I wasn't afraid of getting hit in a brawl. Besides healing from the incident where we jumped those two kids, I started recalling all the hurt I caused others. One by one.

Each time, I let the emotions come up to the surface, and I'd start tearing up. It was such a huge relief. I went through many boxes of tissues! Each time I healed something, my brain felt more and more stable and relaxed. It got to the point where people couldn't move me anymore. I was less and less reactionary as a result. I was sinking deeper and deeper into peace and tranquility.

Many of us have done others wrong, but we pretend we didn't. Some have bullied others extensively and feel no remorse for what they did. The thing is, even if they don't believe God was watching the whole time, *they* witnessed what they did. And in the Bible, it is said that man was created in the image of God. And in Psalms 82:6, it is said, "I have said, Ye are gods; and all of you are children of the most High...." Therefore, God was watching the whole time! And you better believe we are judging ourselves, which is why we have an unfortunate sequence of events. It's because our subconscious mind knows we did wrong, generating scenarios to match that vibration.

It's extremely important that you not only heal from what others have done to you but also from what you've done to others. You must work through the trauma, ask God for forgiveness, and believe you have been forgiven. You must forgive yourself, knowing you were ignorant when you did what you did. All of this healing sends you into a higher vibration and higher timeline. You become visibly tension-free. People start to notice you're glowing from the inside out. They can tell you're carefree and relaxed. Nothing is weighing you down anymore; you release the guilt and shame. After all, we're human and bound to make mistakes. The key is owning up to whatever you did and releasing it.

You have to analyze some of the things you're putting up with and not releasing. Is there something you're bearing or tolerating in your life but have lots of unspoken resentment about? If so, then you should really address that thing(s). Healing is a daily practice. That's what I've realized. You can't just do healing work today and forget about it for a month. You won't progress fast enough that way. You need to dedicate 30 minutes a day to healing your pains. That might seem like a lot of time, but you can go more than that easily - as long as you have the time. The more you heal, the more solidified you feel. You become more and more grounded in your body and your mind and definitely in your soul.

Why is healing so important? Because health is wealth. Wealth comes in many forms: energy, youthfulness, material, spiritual, knowledge, and a favorable life. The healed version of you attracts many people, including both healed and unhealed, which means you will enjoy much better relationships because you will be perceived as a high-value person. You provide inspiration, motivation, and good energy, which many crave. Have you ever looked at a depressed person, ready to blow his mind, and said, "geez, that guy looks fun, let me go and talk to him?" I doubt it, but I wouldn't be surprised if you have. On the other hand, if you see someone that's happy (may not be smiling, but you can tell the person is in a great mood), you get intrigued and want to go up to them and talk to them to get some of that good energy.

Earlier, I mentioned how I got through all the health issues and went on a tangent without properly giving God His due praise. He made everything tolerable for me. Of course, it's just as challenging to me as it would be for anyone else. He's taught me how to shift my mind within and find a space where the senses aren't as sensitive. I could cut through the pain and rise higher than the pain. Most aren't aware, but we humans can shift our point of view within our minds to deviate from perception sensitivity, especially pain. In a sense, you become numb to the pain. That's not to say you wouldn't feel a burn or a hack. It just means your tolerance for pain and discomfort increases. The things that would immobilize someone else don't affect your day-to-day activities as much as you'd think they should.

I attribute many of my achievements to the lessons I learned while quitting smoking cigarettes. I "only" smoked for 3 years, but boy, was I hooked! I consistently smoked 2-3 packs of regular Marlboro reds daily. I'd often pull out the next cigarette while I had one already lit. I'd use it to light the next one, a true chain smoker. I didn't like the habit. It's so disgusting. I was duped by people making it look cool. It tasted nasty. I smelled like it too. My fingers were yellow. My clothes stank. I had had enough. The worst part was the hot and humid summer days in Northern New Jersey and New York City, where I could barely breathe. I would wheeze like I just dove into a pile of dust. I tried quitting approximately 10 times. Each time I tried, I felt more and more defeated. I kept thinking, "this is impossible to quit, no wonder so many people are hooked."

My intuition inspired me to do the following. Go to a local Rite-Aid and purchase cigarette filters. The kind you put on at the orange end of the cigarette (the cigarette's filter). It traps a lot of tar and nicotine, essentially reducing the amount of nicotine your body absorbs. This made it feel like I cut down significantly even though I was still smoking 2-3 packs a day. I tapered gradually. Every few days, I'd take away 1 or more cigarettes. Eventually, I got down to a pack a day of regular Marlboros. So, I switched over to light. And then ultra-light. And one by one, I eliminated all cigarettes. It's no easy feat! Tapering was super difficult, but it was my only realistic option. I did it without nicotine patches or gum.

When I quit smoking, I had bizarre dreams for a year. My hands automatically pat my pockets, looking for the pack and lighter for months. I once dreamed I was having a Streetfighter-type fight with a giant cigarette. It was like Neo vs. Agent Smith in the Matrix. The cigarette was fast as heck! I never saw the ending of the fight in the dream, but I'll tell you, I won. It's been 20 ½ years since I smoked. I never even took a casual puff after I quit. And I never vaped nicotine either.

Being able to achieve this was a major milestone. Even bigger than I initially thought. Because of this experience, I easily quit alcohol cold turkey in 2011. The experience proved that I could accomplish difficult goals if I thought it through and took consistent action on my plan. It made me realize I'm in control and can say no to anything. Whenever a challenge presented itself, I'd always refer back to the time I quit smoking, and it gave me the confidence to go after the challenge. The key was to break down the challenge into smaller, more realistic milestones.

Right before I left Zina, I stopped giving a damn what others thought of me. I couldn't care less at that point. I decided I would live my life on my terms and no longer live my life per others' standard of living. This attitude allowed me to put my foot down and leave her. She begged me to stay, but I was no longer boo boo the fool. Twenty years was enough. I saw what I needed to see, and there was nothing she could say or do to make me unsee things. I couldn't give her more of what she already didn't appreciate. Even though I am multifaceted and have accomplished much more than the average person - a lot more than her father and brother -she treated me as if I was average or even below average. Her manipulative ways of acting out on me to position herself on the pedestal. (I understand that psych majors don't learn dark, manipulative tactics, but I believe she studied psych thinking she'd learn manipulation).

In her deranged mind, I'd chase her forever if she treated me that way. Little did she know then that I was secretly studying psychology (non-university psychology), amongst many other topics. I got hip to what she was doing to me. Once I learned about narcissism and started carefully analyzing her behavior, I knew it was time to kick her to the curb. With her arrogant attitude, she told her family when I left, "oh, I'm not worried. He'll be back." A week passed. Two weeks passed. "That's odd," she thought. Usually, the husband comes crawling back at week two. Two months passed, and still no word. Six months passed - now she was starting to worry but still had a cocky attitude that I'll be back. Well, it's been over 12 months, and I never returned.

As of this writing, November 2022, she's been sending messages to Neuman asking me to go back. I guess her theory of me going back to her was disproven. I used to go to the house to visit my then 15-year-old son for about 1 ½ months after I left her, but I stopped going because she's a conniver. She promised she would not interfere with me going to see Hunter, but she lured me in so she could talk a slick game about getting back together. It worked. I gave her a chance to redeem herself. But I couldn't help but notice she only lusted after me and had no love or compassion towards me. She was sex-bombing me for two weeks until I cut her off for good this time.

I had to make a painful decision. Do I continue going to the house and dealing with her bullshit, or do I completely cut ties? After thinking about it for a while, I decided not to go to the house anymore. I feared eventually, she would antagonize me and even resort to physical violence. It hurt me that I wouldn't go to the house every evening to see my son for an hour or two. There is a nice park one block away from the house. It happens to be across the street from Hunter's high school. I asked my son if we could meet at the park since he goes to school on his own. He would not agree to it. His mother told him not to. She wanted to use him to get me back in the house. He'd say, "I don't want to leave the house because I'm in a wheelchair, come to the house." I declined and said, "how about I take you to Starbucks and get you your favorite drink." To which he declined.

One day, after not going to the house for weeks, the kids begged me to go and hang out with them because they missed me. They said their mother would not be in the house because she would run a few errands. I went and spent about

1 ½ hours with them. It was dinner time, and I told them I'd see them another day. They begged me to stay. They said, "order your food and have it sent here; we want to eat with you." So I ordered food for my kids and I from Chipotle. When placing the order, Hunter left the sunroom and texted his mother. Before the food even arrived, the police showed up. It was on a Sunday. Two officers said they wanted to speak to me. Magically, Neuman appeared. Obvious setup. It was more than

apparent that something was going on between my "father" and ex. I don't know what claim she made exactly, but I had to speak to someone at the suicide hotline.

The two cops were very cordial towards me, talking to me casually while the person at the suicide hotline said they'd call back. Anyways, the lady called back, and we spoke. I told her I had left Zina and was only there to see my children. I told her I had left the house and was living alone now. I told her that I was planning on divorcing her. After speaking with me for about 5-10 minutes, she and the officers concluded I was perfectly fine. I told the woman on the phone, "this is the 3rd time she has done this to me. Why is she allowed to do this to me?" The woman on the phone said, "I will note in your file that you are not suicidal and have been in contact with your therapist and that your therapist also says you're doing great."

Zina was in the hallway. She heard the conversation. To her and Neuman's disappointment, I was free to go, and they weren't going to be able to do this to me anymore as the lady noted my file that I was perfectly fine and said they would not be allowed to do this to me anymore. Neuman is a sleazeball. I regret ever helping take him out of bankruptcy twice. I regret putting my neck on the line for him by letting him put all his business expenses and inventory purchases on my credit cards. He backstabbed me in the worst ways.

Zina tried her best to use the kids against me. My daughter goes to NYU and dorms there. I often told her I'd like to visit her for just 5 minutes on the weekend. I just wanted to hug, kiss, and give her some money for her expenses. But upon consulting with her mother, she made excuses. Let's be honest. Who doesn't have 5 minutes for their own father? I was willing to travel a minimum of 2 hours round trip to see her for a measly 5 minutes, and she kept turning me down. All she was required to do was walk down the stairs of her dorm and say hi to me. It was blatantly obvious that their mother was pulling their strings.

I knew what Zina was doing by using the children. "It's ok," I told myself. "I'm not going to let her manipulate me with the kids. If they don't want to talk to me, that's fine. I'm already used to not talking to close family members." I told myself, "I cut off my own biological mother. I can handle this. My children will wake up one day and realize that I really did a lot for them throughout their lives. They'll understand that I gave them a life most fathers couldn't and wouldn't. One day they'll understand that I *had* to leave for my own sanity."

She was controlling what they texted me. I knew that because they'd both text me at the same time using bologna like, "Thank you for sharing your feelings." That was all. They never used to communicate like this prior to me leaving their mother. They continued doing this for a year. Finally, I sent both of them a message, "stop communicating in this cold way. You never talk like this. I've already mentioned this, and you keep doing this. If you can't communicate authentically like you always used to, then I will no longer text you." Their response was silence. "Ok, fine," I thought. "So be it."

One day, when they're adults, they're going to remember the lifestyle I provided the family, and they're going to realize that they were living amongst the 1%. I bought them a house on a 100x100' lot. They each had a big room. We had three vehicles and three fridges. They regularly had expensive cuts of meat. They had Amazon packages flooding the house every day. I'd like to see if they can do that for themselves. I hope they can, and I pray they can, but they will see that it's not doable for millions of Americans. I'd be lying if I said it didn't hurt that they didn't talk to me. But what can I do? Submit and go back to the house? NEVER!

29

MY 15 YEAR OLD SENSEI

I was devastated when I learned Hunter was born with Spinal Muscular Atrophy, or SMA. The best way to describe it is that he has very low muscle tone throughout his whole body, and his core is very weak. Because of this, his feet collapsed (pronated), and he couldn't walk properly. He was walking from ages 1 ½ to about 5 years old. However, he wasn't stable at all. If you so much as walked by him, he'd fall. A slight tap on the shoulder would cause him to tower over and hit the ground. He fell dozens of times each day and always dusted himself off and got right back up with a kool-aid smile. He always had a big radiant, and refreshing smile. At school, the teachers and staff referred to him as Mr. Sunshine. He was walking like a penguin on two pronated feet. Like the movie, his mother and I called him Happy Feet. And we also called him Mr. Sunshine because that's what the staff at the school referred to him as. It broke my heart to see this boy struggling all his life. It broke my heart that we couldn't wear leather gloves and play catch in the backyard together. I always dreamt of that experience when I was younger. Unfortunately, it wasn't in the cards for us to play catch together.

The doctors and therapists told us what to expect with this condition. We were always monitoring his spine for scoliosis. Due to his weak core, his spine wasn't supported as it should be. This made his spine collapse and curve. He started doing Schroth therapy to strengthen his core to stabilize his back.

The therapy helped keep his scoliosis curve at 50 degrees for a long time. However, once he had a big growth spurt, it got worse. The experts all said corrective surgery should be done before the curve gets too large because the surgery would be much more difficult then. Scoliosis is dangerous because the spine forms an "S" shape (side to side), crushing vital organs and leading to fatal death.

We decided to go with the surgery, which was performed in August 2021. It was a 7-8 hour procedure. As mentioned in Chapter 14, Sally and Hannah called a day before the surgery pretending to care. They never once visited him or called prior - in his whole life. Now all of a sudden, they were concerned. When they found me to be optimistic and unbothered, it infuri-ated them. I didn't know their apparent regard for him was disingenuous at the time, and I was authentically optimistic. This hurt their ego. They never called or texted after that, which made me realize that they were just calling to hear me in distraught and panic. When I didn't provide them with that satisfaction, they ghosted me. They never called, texted, or visited my son after the surgery. In fact, they never followed up after that call to see how he was doing. They never contacted me, either. Good riddance. I will *never* allow them back into my life, even if they went on their spiritual journey and woke up. That was one of the cruelest things I've ever witnessed in all of my life. I regard them as savages with no civility or wisdom.

When Hunter came out of the operating room and was moved into the ICU, I was moved emotionally and spiritually. An avalanche of emotions roared within me. Chills burst within my body as if exploding from the core of a sphere and extending way beyond the sphere. I was so happy to see him, yet so affected. He looked all drowsy, and his lips doubled in size. "My poor son," I thought. How I wish I could trade places with my little booger. While I sat in the ICU with him, all I heard were constant chimes from the equipment. It drove us all crazy.

Suddenly I remembered something. I don't know when or how, but I remember being in his exact predicament. I'm not sure if it was a dream or some internal knowledge, but I was 100% sure I had seen things from his perspective before. This is called remote viewing. It's one of my spiritual abilities/gifts. I remember my back being solid and feeling like I had a cast on my back. I remember moaning with aches. I remembered time going by so slow. When did I experience this? I don't know. Perhaps one of the times I was put under anesthesia, I had this experience/vision. I'm unsure if it was a dream because I clearly remember going through the experience for a considerable time. It was so weird! It's as if God put me in his shoes to see what he was going through. I cried. I cried because I knew what he was going through. I love him so much.

What is thoroughly impressive is that he didn't push the morphine button. If I'm not mistaken, he was told he could push it every 10 minutes. I constantly reminded him, "baba, you gotta push the button. It's for your pain." But he would hardly press it. I don't know how he was able to endure the pain.

I learned so much from him. I learned patience. Even though I had plenty of patience before his surgery, I gained great patience from that experience. He taught me to accept things as they are and not complain. He stayed at Columbia Presbyterian hospital in New York City for 1 ½ weeks. The food was atrocious there. It was worse than prison food. After that, they moved him to Bristol-Myers Squibb Children's Hospital in New Brunswick, NJ, where he stayed for 2 ½ weeks to do therapy and recover. There, the food was pretty good. They gave him a full menu full of tasty food. This kid never complained or cried throughout the process - not even when he got out of the surgery. He was a little worried prior, but I told him that the anesthesiologist would count down from 10 to 1, and he'll go to sleep and won't feel a thing. That was comforting for him. When they took him away for the surgery, he wasn't worried at all. Oh, how I love that son of mine! Only a real father would know about this love and how heartbreaking it is that he and his sister don't talk to me. What can I do but remain strong? God created me to be strong. To withstand a bomb going off right in front of me, figuratively.

30

FREQUENCIES & VIBRATIONS

*B*eing born into Shi'ite Islam, we knew nothing about frequencies and vibrations. All we knew was we had to pray 5 times daily, refrain from alcohol and pork, and fast during Ramadan. We didn't know who God was. We said it was Allah, but no one knew who Allah was or is. We had no idea how to use the mind to create a desirable or favorable reality. I would have forced myself out of fear and anxiety if I had known. The reason is that because I was anxious and in fear, life was presenting situations that perpetuated those two states of being. Without my knowing, I was feeding the cycle perpetually.

When I first learned about the frequency or vibration scale, I learned that fear and anxiety were at the bottom. These states were the worst to be in. That is what hell is. It's a state of fear, and I didn't know that. I didn't know it was the feeling that was producing reality. Once I learned that from the Buddhists, I immediately changed my attitude. Then, I understood Franklin

D Roosevelt's famous line, "the only thing we have to fear is fear itself." It was true. I started to fear feeling fearful, for I knew the life it brought about and wanted nothing to do with it.

When people see you in fear, they smell blood. And when they smell blood, they attack! You're an easy target, an easy laugh. People had no regard for my state of being and my psyche. No one stopped and said, "no, that's not right. Leave him alone. He's actually a good kid." People can be so cruel. These days, I carry the vibration of courage and brute fearlessness. People get out of my way when I walk through now. I always have a weapon on me and in my car at all times. I'm ready for anything. I'm a one-man army. But guess what? I never have to deploy a weapon because my high frequency doesn't allow any of the stuff that used to happen to me anymore.

Whereas I was bullied as a young boy, I'm now viewed as someone to be taken seriously and one to take lessons from. People can see in my eyes that I'm not playing around. Sure, I'm at peace, and that's the state I'm usually in, but I've made a deal with myself. That I'm not going to let anything slide. I'm going to defend myself immediately and every time. I will start by dismantling my opponent with my tongue. Should it escalate to a physical fight, I'm trained and ready. I'm a different type of Buddhist!

With this fearless attitude, I yearn to be amongst an actual tiger and lion. I know that if I present myself confidently with no sign of fear, they will want to play a little and have fun with me. I guarantee you, if you put me with a tiger and lion with the mentality I had as a child, I'd be mauled in a microsecond.

I always ask myself, was my mother an abuser for 20 years,

or was she just an abuser when I was 4 years old, but my fear perpetuated it? Nevertheless, I can't give her a pass. She was old enough to know you shouldn't maltreat a child like that. It shouldn't take me to stop living in fear for her to stop her abuse. After all, it's because of her I was living in fear. And she got satisfaction out of breaking me down into crumbs. She felt powerful and in control. She had an evil but satisfied look to her when I'd be on the ground wailing, and she was swinging the belt buckle at me. She got off seeing an innocent child beaten like a rag doll.

I'm kind, but I'm no doormat, and I'm no wuss. I treat people I first meet with respect. Once I sense they're taking me as someone replaceable, I no longer give them any energy. For example, there are people I've met and had hour-long conversations with. Once they start acting immature or think they're more important than me, I never converse with them again. And each time they see me, they want to flag me down so I can talk to them, but I no longer give second chances. Once you show me your true colors, there's no coming back from that. Being that I'm 43 years old, I'd much rather converse with people in their 60's and up. Other than that, I like to connect with motivated entrepreneurs and people from the tech industry. I love talking to mature, smart people who are genuine and are not playing games.

It's been hard to make friends. Most men get jealous and become competitive, which I have no time or patience for. And just talking to women casually is mistaken as flirting. So what if women think I'm flirting with them? The woman thinks I'm flirting and expects me to ask her out and get her number. And when I don't, she gets visibly upset. Of course, I didn't realize this until after I left Zina and started talking to women again. Once I realized what was happening, I had to change my policy. I would no longer talk to women I don't intend to ask out. This saves me a headache. Women have retaliated against me, thinking I was playing mind games with them. One woman retaliated in a major way which I won't even discuss. It was the worst retaliation ever. I kid you not, all I did was speak to her with some enthusiasm. No malice intended whatsoever. When I didn't ask for her number, she looked at me like I was cruel. She then took action a few days later.

I've been told by many people I look like the actor Jason Statham, and Johnny Sins, the pornstar actor. Now, I'm no Brad Pitt and truth be told, I'm not stuck up at all, and I'm not attractive to every woman. However, the women who find Jason Statham attractive tell me I look like him and they behave in an enthusiastic and animalistic way towards me. So, while there are plenty of women who might not find me attractive, the ones that do are huge fans of me.

And it's not just women who say I look like Jason Statham. Men also tell me that and they get zealous and start talking about his movies. I gotta admit, I do like the comparisons. A lot of men don't want me at their parties or around them because the attention goes on me and they want to be the center of attention instead. That's especially true if they're around their girlfriend or wife. However, I respect people and would never make a move on a woman already in a committed relationship. I wouldn't like it if it happened to me.

I kid you not. Once, I was in my building's elevator, and there was a very attractive woman; I stood in front of her, waiting for the elevator to take us up to the lobby. I just minded my business. I didn't want to talk to her because I had seen her with a man prior. When she noticed I wouldn't talk to her, she made a bratty noise and stomped her foot to get my attention. I was laughing on the inside. I said, "oh boy, here we go again." So I chopped it up with her. She happily told me her name, and I gave her mine. Fast forward months later, I saw her again and said, "I haven't seen you around; I thought you moved." She smiled and said she was in her apartment most of the time. I apologized for forgetting her name, and she said it again. I replied, "my name is…." She said, "Chris." I was surprised she still remembered my name.

Anyways, I could've asked her out, but the fact that she was with a man and was trying to get my attention turned me off. I'm not one of those guys that sleep with just anyone. I did that in college, and it wasn't fulfilling. It felt like when you overindulge in food. Sure, you ate some good food, but you don't feel right. Same thing with sex and women. Sure, you had sex with a good-looking woman, but casual sex doesn't feel right to me. Besides, sex is a spiritual experience. I learned that there's an energy transfer that goes on during sex, and if your partner has had many partners, you will adopt their energies, traits, and personalities.

Life is all about setting boundaries, I learned in my later years. Because I've set up my boundaries and decided I will always enforce them, people automatically feel that. As a result, they think twice before speaking and ensure not to insult my intelligence. Besides setting up boundaries, you should also speak up for yourself. Use your voice to get what you want. Don't be shy. If you're ordering food where they make it for you and feel like the person didn't put enough on your plate, speak up and ask for more. Don't fret about what that person might think. Who gives a shit? I don't have a problem saying "put more" when the Chipotle worker puts scoops of rice in my bowl. I'll say "put more" 3 times if I feel it's not enough. I don't give a rat's ass about what the worker thinks. Maybe they think, "the nerve of this guy." Who cares! Go after what you want, period. I once went to a different Chipotle location than I normally visit, and the person hardly put any rice. I kept saying, put more, until she said, "that's it, that's all I can give you."

I looked at her and said, "you know what, forget it then!" As I walked out, I thought, "crap, I don't want to drive to the usual location and waste 30-45 minutes." So I turned around and approached the employee, and with visible irritability, I demanded to speak with the manager. From their point of view, I must have looked hostile. I told the manager his employee was trying to shortchange me. He asked what happened, and I told him I asked for a normal amount of rice, and she gave me half. He told me not to worry and that he'll prepare my bowl. He told the employee in Spanish, "it's just rice, you can put extra - it doesn't matter." And I added my adlib and said, "yeah, it's rice, it doesn't matter. It's not like I asked for extra meat."

The reason I don't care is not that I don't respect the worker or because I'm trying to take advantage of the company, it's because I want what I paid for, and I feel I'm standing up for the truth. The truth here is food is measured in weight and volume. The average bowl should have a certain weight. If the weight is under, then the worker and restaurant are committing fraud in my eyes. That is why I feel no shame to say, "put more repeatedly," and neither should you.

Sometimes we don't want to speak our minds because it

might ruffle some feathers. Of course, we shouldn't say *every-thing* that's on our minds, but some things must be said. You should be able to determine that, step up, and speak up. If you don't speak up for the truth, you will always live wearing a false mask. And worse is, if most people don't speak up for the truth, we will find our rights being stripped away to bare bones.

One area of your life where you definitely need to speak your mind is when it comes to your romantic relationship. Some men, for example, are so addicted to sex that they will not speak up when their partner cheats on them. Trading our respect for pleasure is degrading and negatively impacts your mind, body, and soul. You can tell yourself whatever you want; at the end of the day, you lose respect for yourself by not speaking up. And so does your partner. Your silence is their green light to continue the infidelity while taking advantage of you financially.

Words are powerful. When you speak up, you have the power to change reality altogether. Words can be uplifting and uniting, but they can also be destructive and divisive. We're aware of this subconsciously. That's why most of us shy away from speaking our minds. We know that once those words leave our mouths, the energy in our environment will change. People are going to be taken aback. Some will resent you for breaking them out of their fantasy life. People would rather live a false life as if it were a made-up dream. Many people escape reality this way. But if no one speaks up against the pedophile, he will continue victimizing children, for example. If no one speaks up about the people cutting in line, you'll never get to the front of the line. Sure, you'll be confrontational, but it's necessary.

Speaking your mind is important but don't step into a relationship with someone who already exhibits traits you don't like. That person is not a good fit for you, and they're for someone else. You can't pretend that you accept the person as is and then start "speaking your mind" regarding how they dress. That's not right. Find someone who already dresses the way you like. Of course, if they always dress a certain way and suddenly dress more scandalously, then speak up because that's not what you signed up for. But even then, you will cause resentment in her. You're better off deciding whether you accept her for how she now dresses. If you have to constantly bicker about it, it's time to pack up and leave if you're not ok with it because people don't like being controlled and told what to do. People outgrow each other.

While speaking your mind can get you in trouble, sometimes you have to bite the bullet. I faced major backlash from my mother for speaking up against her ignorant ways. How dare I point out her injustices. How dare I call her out on her manipulation. She made me pay for it.

Fibromyalgia was the hardest thing I've ever physically dealt with, and it's one of the hardest mental things I've faced. Although I was tapped out at one point, the experience proved to be training, training for a better life. I didn't see the light at the end of the tunnel then, as I thought the condition would get worse over time. But to my surprise, when I started affirming "I am healthy" repeatedly, I started to get better within a couple of months. I was filled with gratitude for the relief! The experience made me incredibly strong. Because you have to imagine…one of the feelings you have with fibromyalgia is that an 800 lb gorilla is hanging on to your neck and shoulders. It feels like you're pushing an invisible wall everywhere you walk. Everything was a physical struggle. I was overwhelmed with lethargy, lack of energy, and motivation. I was drained.

When I started seeing my fibromyalgia doctor, he said I was the worst case he's ever seen and advised me to stay in bed permanently. To which I said, "yeah, right." Once I broke free from the mental and emotional chains Zina had on me, my symptoms subsided greatly. Now, as a result of the condition, I'm much stronger mentally, physically, emotionally, and spiritually. When gym goers wonder how I keep up my pace by putting in the volume of sets that I do without hardly breaking a sweat and only taking 5 second breaks (as of November 2022), it's because I'm a fibromyalgia survivor - no gym workout will compare by a long shot.

Dealing with narcissistic abuse from two women did a number on me and caused me great distress. Mentally, it was unbearable. I've mentioned it before, but had it not been for fear of hell as punishment for suicide, I would have even ended my life several years before I became a teenager. I had no choice but to accept everything that happened to me and deal with it. I prayed a lot. My prayer may not have been answered as soon as I wanted, but eventually, God blessed me with the tools I needed to heal and grow with a loving, kind heart and not be bitter about my experience. That is the true miracle of God. He took this innocent boy under his wing. He guided him all the way. He consoled him when no one else was there. He kept supplying love into his veins. Nothing could keep this young boy down. Sure, he'd cry himself to sleep, but he'd be back to smiling, cracking jokes, and laughing ASAP. He endured harsh treatment into his teenage years and adulthood yet still shows kindness to others when he has every reason to be a total crab. That person is me. How is that possible?

I confused everyone around me. That was one of the reasons I was envied. No matter what they did to me, they couldn't keep me down. They absolutely hated that. And they always upped the ante. They thought I was in competition with them. That I was always setting out to outshine them, but I was honestly just being me. I looked at life differently than they did. We didn't interpret the same things and situations the same way. I always saw things from a higher point of view; I suppose that's due to ADHD and autism.

I always had the feeling of love. I didn't know that was what love was supposed to feel like. I was looking for love from my parents and others, not knowing I already had love within me. It was the thing that made the bad times bearable. That feeling is what was soothing me and having a cooling effect on me from within. It's the reason why I couldn't be bitter. And the reason I would continue smiling, laughing, joking, and having fun.

That feeling still resides in me today. That is God. He was with me the whole time when I thought I didn't have anyone. You have access to this love, *unconditional* love. You need to understand that a reason to love is not required at all. Love should be your default state of being. That's when you'll see the miracles. I'm not saying to be all snuggly with people but come from a place of meaning well for yourself and others instead of a mindset of manipulation for your benefit only.

It is said that if you give God something, He returns it multiplied. If God is within man, shouldn't you give something to men? A genuine, kind gesture can go a long way. It doesn't have to be big. Just the thought alone can cause the person to want to return the favor multiplied, just like God, because God is within man; therefore, man *is* God. Get it? God is more than man; God is everything and everywhere, nothing and nowhere. Suppose you approach people with the mindset that you're dealing with royalty. In that case, you will communicate, on all levels, including body language, in such a way that prompts the other person to like you and reciprocate the energy (not all people, of course). None of this is fake or manipulation, but it's being authentic. We can never deny that we aren't love. We can try, but we know it's false. Because why else are you alive? Why do you go to work? Because of love. You love life and the pleasures of life regardless of the pains and struggles. It's love that's keeping you alive without acknowledging that you are love, and without living in and out of love, you won't be fully alive.

Many have given up on love because they think it's given to them by people. But that's not the case at all. You're the one creating the emotion within yourself, and it's not being transferred from another person. It is simply something that you like about that person that *allows* you to feel love. In other words, you've put conditions on love. Only if XYZ happens, *then* I'll feel love or be loving.

Some men and women may be repulsed by someone operating from love, but that's ok. You're never going to please everyone anyway. You might as well filter out those who are not for your highest and greatest good. Just because you're authentic and kind does not mean you're less of a man or woman. As a matter of fact, you're a super-man/super-woman. More than a man/woman. You are a man/woman who is tapped into Source/God/Spirit, which is love. And when you have Source/God/Spirit within you, you have a great power helping you.

Once you understand this, why would you ever want to experience anything *but* unconditional love? That's the question I asked myself as a young boy. And to me, it was a no-brainer; why *would* I be bitter and become a complete asshole? What good is that going to do? I'm going to feel crappy all the time that way.

You *are* love. It's not gay for a man to affirm he is love. Not that I have anything against gay people. They are wonderful people and deserve equal rights and treatment. Love is an honorable and masculine trait. For isn't a man who protects a woman and is willing to sacrifice his life an act of love? There's a stark difference between operating out of love while being completely genuine versus fake love, where you're overly expressing yourself to others to manipulate them (i.e., love bombing). When you're authentic, loving, and feeling grounded, you become an incredible force to be reckoned with. This is the side of love Hollywood will probably never show you.

Love yourself right now! Don't wait for someone to come into your life to feel love. Turn that unconditional love on and throw away the key. If you encounter a jackass, don't look for the key to turn it off. You just need thick skin and allow negativity to glide off you like water droplets on a rainy day. Don't allow anyone or any circumstance to make you turn your back on love. That is your power! That is your vitality, your prosperity, and your youthfulness.

31

FROM AVERAGE TO WOUNDED WARRIOR

I hope my story will help you pick yourself up, dust yourself and keep pushing forward. I was just a boy with average height, average looks, and chubby. Back then, I wasn't attractive. I was the target for many. I was outnumbered. I was the butt of every joke. I was broken down, humiliated, and straight violated daily. I had no one to go to. I often ran to the phone to call the police on my mother, and she would rip it out of the wall and take the line out of the phone jack. Then she'd proceed to beat me more for even attempting to do that.

I'm living proof that the human mind can withstand tremendous pressure as long as you still believe in Jesus Christ/Spirit/God/Allah/Yahweh/Krishna/Universe. This right here is key. The way I learned to deal with bad news or negativity thrown my way is to imagine that energy coming towards me like a baseball about to be caught by a player's glove. In the same way, the player moves his glove back while the ball enters the glove to reduce the impact. I handle the energy coming towards me. I absorb it in a feather-like manner. I don't allow the energy to smack me head-on - that's too painful!

Next time you're feeling down, just remember that little boy trapped in hell, and everywhere he went had to deal with disrespect and abuse. Just remember that little boy kept pushing forward. Yes, he cried a lot but always found a reason to smile. Despite the hell he was living, he always went out and did things he loved. When you're ready to give up, think of that 9-year-old boy who plotted to kill himself. Remember how *he* remembered God each time and aborted the mission. Remember that an average boy grew up to be an above-average (wounded) warrior who now inspires the masses. You can always improve. You can always become more patient and resilient. Above all, you can always talk to God and ask for relief.

Sure, the beatings and humiliation didn't stop after I prayed, but He made me strong enough to endure it all, and in the end, it turned me into a savage with a kind, loving heart. When life gets difficult for you, remember that you have that inner power that you exercise all the time. You have that patience. You have that tolerance to pain. You can parent yourself. You have the power to laugh after you've just cried. You just have to tell yourself, "I got this. I've been through it all. I'm not backing down. I'll be able to work through this. Relax; take it slow. Think a little slower. Move a little slower. Focus. It's ok. I took a loss. No big deal. I'll bounce back. Besides, I still have a lot going for me. I'm grateful I still have XYZ...."

In order to be mentally tough, you must be able to freeze for a while mentally. You must be non-reactionary to the undesired outcomes and scenarios in your life. In the face of your losses, you must stand erect and let the losses flow right through you. Let the losses not make an impact on your ego. Do not allow these two to get to know each other, for they'll never leave your house (your mind). Your mind will show you the footage of what happened from all the cameras it has set up so you can see the event from hundreds of viewpoints, aka ruminating thoughts. This is what your mind essentially does when it ruminates over a loss. A loss isn't just referring to death. It includes things like a loss on an investment, loss of a relationship, something embarrassing that happened to you, etc.

You must decide you no longer want to see your losses from hundreds of viewpoints. In fact, ask your mind if there are any lessons in the situation. If there is, learn and move on. If there isn't, move on. Thinking of a loss begets more losses. After all, what you think about all day is what comes about. Rather, it's in your best interest to reflect on your wins. That's not to say you'll never be disappointed again, but disappointments will drastically decrease. And when a disappointment occurs, you'll process it immediately and clear your mind. Above all, you'll know that the disappointment was necessary and for your highest and greatest good. You just gotta trust the process.

I had to be strong as a child. Not that I didn't cry, but I had to be mentally strong. I had to reason with myself and console myself. I had to be strong enough to move past it and laugh here and there. I had to hide from myself and pretend I wasn't being constantly violated, disrespected, and humiliated. That was such an awful feeling. It made me feel like a coward, but there wasn't anything I could do! I was seriously outnumbered. It was essentially everyone against me, save a few pure souls. Admittedly, I didn't like to ignore injustice whenever I witnessed it. That's why I had so many school fights. I fought on behalf of my mother like you have no idea. Each time I'd ask myself, "why the heck am I fighting for her when she abuses me?" Because no one knew I was being abused (because I never talked about it - not even to my then close friends' parents). I couldn't let anyone get away with it because I'd look like a wuss in front of the kids. So here I am going through, on most days, three fights a day for a woman that was always fighting me. Make that make sense.

So you might be asking, "so you're saying I should just endure everything? Is that your solution?" What I'm saying here is that no matter how awful your situation is, someone else is going through worse. It's the same with me. I'm sure some people go through worse shit than me. I'm also saying that what you're going through is life's way of teaching you important lessons. I'm also saying that you will always experience more fear if you live in fear. Let God handle your problems; ask him to strengthen you, and let your love and light shine from within. Trust that you are on the right path. Start believing you are worthy. Start declaring, "I am grateful that I am grateful." Look yourself in the mirror, point at the person in front of you, and tell that person, "I'm freaking proud of you."

The same people who did me wrong, "family & friends," are all watching my social media and are learning from me now. They're all wondering how they screwed up big with me. They're flabbergasted by my transformation. They will forever be haunted by the things they did to me. Some have tried to weasel their way back into my life, but I will never allow them back in, no matter how much they praise me. Once someone shows their true colors, it's over. Sure, I forgave everyone (for my own sake), but I'm no martyr to allow them back in.

All that I mentioned that I went through as a child was no harder than my adult years. The only difference was I wasn't being physically abused but instead, psychologically and emotionally; Zina was doing a number on me covertly. The loss of my e-commerce business was a catastrophe. When I decided to heal from it a decade later, I couldn't even describe my bottled-up emotions regarding the situation. It was like someone took a sledgehammer and hit me directly on top of the head, crushing me down to the surface. Everything I worked for was gone in one night! The thought of starting all over was overwhelming, daunting, and, quite honestly, extremely discouraging because of the sheer amount of work involved in starting a new business.

The 9 years I worked in Chelsea, Manhattan was extremely terrible - this was one of my worst periods. I've never dealt with anything harder. Who am I kidding? I dealt with lots of difficult things. Anyone who shopped on 28th street and Broadway in Manhattan circa 2001-2009 will tell you that the district was a literal zoo. There was always someone getting knocked out in the street. Cops would shut down the whole street because of gunshots or hostage situations. And when that happened, we'd have to go inside the store and lock the front door in case the shooter ran loose.

The customers were an absolute NIGHTMARE to deal with, and these were people who were fed up with life. Hurt people hurt people. Many came from neighboring boroughs, mostly from projects and ghettos. You could not let your ego get in the way of working at that store. If I had let my ego get in the way, like in grammar school and high school, I would've had 20 fights a day, and that's just being conservative! Nothing but assholes. There's a difference between an asshole and a major asshole. A major asshole is one you really have to fight. The problem is, we had at least one major asshole walk into the store daily, 7 days a week. My solution came about after rationalizing that it would be wise to allow 1 major asshole per day. But the 2nd major asshole that walks in the store will be hit with a 2 piece combo. It proved to be a good policy. Luckily it was just 1 major asshole per day. Although this was tied to one of my hardest eras, it was in this era that I developed a lot of patience and diplomacy. I learned to get along with everyone from every state and every country. Many of our customers were in a local gang: bloods, crips, latin kings, ñietas, ms13, etc. Most showed me love. The bloods that hustled in front of the store would rush in the store if they heard anyone getting loud with me, ready to beat the person up.

Just don't give up. And don't judge your situation as all bad. Yeah, times get rough, but diamonds have to undergo pressure. Do you want to shine like a diamond? Do you want to be recognized and respected? Then you must go through the pressure. If you feel like the walls are caving in on you, you have to orient your body so that you create space within those tight walls. In your mind, you have to be able to shift "you" into another space within your mind. A space where things are calm and safe - not where you're currently at, a space full of panic and anxiety.

We're all born frail. We become kids, then teenagers, and so on...Society has taught us that you've reached your ultimate peak after college. That's not true at all. There is so much valuable information about self-growth that *needs* to be learned. You are more than a man or woman. You can reach godhood. You can reach warrior status.

The key to plowing through your problems is to not give a damn and understand that just because logic dictates, it doesn't mean the scenario will pan out that way. Be grateful and trust that all is well and that everything will work out. You must trust the universe and its process. Problems have always existed. Things like health issues, money problems, relationship problems, and many more have always been around; chances are, they will always be here.

If we are to give a damn about everything we deem as wrong, we will never give ourselves a chance to just enjoy life. When you fly out of the country for vacation, what's the purpose of it? It's to get away so you can care less about all that's happening at home, right? How about if I told you that you could achieve the same feeling by giving less concern about problems? No alcohol or drugs are needed. If you ponder on everything that's going right and relax a little, you'll start to see things work out in your favor. You have to always remember that you're alive and you have your health. Sure, you might have $75k in student debt, but what will thinking about it do? All you're doing is thinking about debt, and what you think about all day is what you'll get, more debt.

You should instead have faith that your loans will be taken care of. I'm not saying to stop going to work. All I'm saying is with faith, you'll be surprised how that loan gets satisfied. Sometimes when we have a lot of problems, it feels like we're in a river of crap. Everywhere we look, it's crappy and gloomy. You're constantly thinking about how awful it is being trapped in it. Rather than get overly excited about the situation, float on your back and enjoy yourself while in that river of crap. Because of your attitude and faith that all will work out, soon you will be out of that river. And you will have got out with plenty of important lessons that you need for the next chapter of your life.

As I'm sitting here writing, my jaw is tight and spasmed as usual, and my back is exhausted because the wrong muscles keep my body up, so I'm very uncomfortable and tight. If I think about them, they will bother me more and more. I'll start to notice more things that are causing me pain and discomfort. Soon, I'll be on the couch or bed incapacitated. So, what did I learn to do one day? I said to myself, "I don't give a damn about my jaw or my back, screw it." And I would include my jaw and back in my gratitude meditation. "I am grateful for my jaw. I am grateful for my back." Since I started affirming my gratitude, they have both improved in a real way, but I still have some ways to go.

That's how I learned how to deal with all of my problems. I simply said, "oh well. I'll just take this loss and move on. At least I'm alive and breathing. I have a bed and food for the day. I'm safe and healthy." This worked when I cut people off too - people who took advantage of my kindness and those who purposely wanted to tear me down and keep me beneath them.

As I stated, problems have always been around. And in this economy, you'll always have debt, so why stress over it? It's nearly impossible to live today without at least *some* debt. The key is to not think about it too much. Because you need to free up your mental space for new ideas; ideas that might turn into a business and bring you generational wealth to pay off that debt. You can't think of new ideas if you're constantly thinking about all of your problems. Your conscious mind can only process so much, and if you've preoccupied it with problems and negativity, then there's no room for solutions and positivity.

I dealt with many problems all at once, and I didn't even have anyone to guide me or give me words of encouragement. I had a choice to make. Do I lay down and die or clear my mind and charge forward? I did the latter. I refused to quit no matter how many relationships I lost, including my mother, how my health was, who wasn't beside me, what debt I had, or who hated me. I kept my chin up, continued gaining knowledge and wisdom, and remained peaceful, humble, and loving. That's how you become a wounded warrior. To go through all the trials, tribulations, heartbreaks, betrayals, ridicule, and attacks and come out victorious with a smile on your face tells the whole world what you're made of, God's love! Love is God's armor. Have you ever seen a genuinely good person out in public? Does anyone ever bother that person? Hardly ever. Because that person's vibration doesn't attract that. A brawl can occur right where they are, and chances are that person will not be negatively affected or hit.

Just stop caring about your problems so much and trust in God. Tell Him, "I know you will handle my problems for me, God. I leave my problems to you." And just go on with your life. Find things to be happy about. Sitting in your car, be grateful from time to time. Say, "Thank you for my car. I appreciate its safety features and the radio." Look for reasons to be happy. They're all around you, just like all the reasons not to be happy. You have to see life as a television. You can choose the happy channel or the depressed channel, or the anxiety channel. Whatever you want, it's up to you. But if you're smart, as I'm sure you are, you'd choose the happy or joy channel - those are the best channels! You'll notice that when you set the channel to joy, you'll see lots of content that will make you joyous. In other words, because you're joyous, life will put you in situations that will cause you to remain joyous.

So, imagine you set the channel to miserable. Life will keep dishing out terrible situations to maintain your feeling of misery. It has no choice; that's the channel you're on. Therefore, you need to be aware that A) there are many different channels and B) you have the remote control; nothing is by chance.

Spread good vibes, always. When someone makes eye contact with you, give them a pleasant smile, not necessarily showing teeth. Drop them a tip when you go to a fast food joint with a tip jar. You will make the workers' day, even if it's just a dollar. You'll lift up their spirits. When you're driving down the street, from time to time, ask God to bless everyone on that street. Whatever you give, you receive. In order to get your blessings, you must give them. It's like when you give someone anger; chances are they will fire back with anger. You are the source. Whatever you put out, that's what you'll get back.

Everything is energy. If you are smiling on the inside and happy on the inside, your energy will be felt by others even if you have a resting bitch face. Practice this, and you will spread lots of good vibes for which people will adore you. Remember, many people are going through difficult times, but not everyone knows how to deal with them as you do now. So, when you step into their lives, you become a source of light and comfort. They will love you and appreciate you for that because that is truly priceless. You can't go to any market and purchase good vibes. Understand that this elevates your status and your worth in people's eyes. People will go out of their way for you. And I'm not telling you this for you to be manipulative. After all, you are putting in the work and spreading goodness. There's nothing wrong with the fact that some might choose to show you a bit of favoritism for the value you added to their life. Accept it, be grateful, and continue to be a light source for others. Your strength will make those around you stronger. They will see you as an example, giving them hope that they can overcome their challenges.

32

THE OTHER VOICE

This morning, October 19, 2022, I had an epiphany at 2:30 am at my building's gym as I was stretching and doing some yoga before I started my workout. I realized I have at least two inner voices. One is my intuition through which the universe communicates, and the other is me or my ego. When my intuition declared, "I love working out," it expected the other voice to repeat after it. When it did, it wasn't satisfied with the energy the other inner voice was using. The intuition voice scolded the other voice and said, "say it with conviction!" The other voice had to repeat it several times, each time changing it a bit to appease the intuition voice. Finally, the other voice said it with as much force and conviction as the intuition voice.

This is an exercise I will now employ to program my subconscious mind effectively. Imagine the other voice yelling like an army sergeant at the top of its lungs. Declare, "today's already a great freaking day," with enthusiasm and conviction.

Send a clear message to the universe on how the day is and is going to be. The universe will show you that you are correct by presenting you with a great day. Be sure to do this daily in the morning, but you can also do affirmations throughout the day.

SOME OF MY favorite declarations or affirmations:
- I love life
- I am healthy
- I love my life
- I love who I am
- I am grateful that I am grateful
- I am love
- I am strong
- I am energetic
- I am enthusiastic
- I am passionate
- I am happy
- I am peace
- I am wealthy
- I am worthy
- I am intelligent

Never wait for someone to tell you who you are when you can say who you are right now. If you've been working out for six months or more and some of your so-called "family" and "friends" don't tell you who you are, a dedicated achiever who gets results, don't fret over it because you can stand in front of a mirror and tell yourself "I am a dedicated achiever who gets results." Don't you find that liberating? To not seek outside validation? What makes the other person more qualified to define who you are? Has God/Universe given them authority to define others? No.

If you're a musician, what does your inner voice sound like regarding that? Is it timid? Is it unsure if you're really a musician? If the answer is yes to these questions, then you need to grab the idea of being a musician by its horns, so to speak, and while yanking it violently, you scream, "I am a real musician, you heard me!?!?!" The other voice will be thrilled you finally said it with passion and conviction. Now your subconscious goes to work to support your claim. It's going to give you the right resources and plenty of creativity. That's how you enter the subconscious mind. It's not the only way, but it's a sure way. You must knock the door down, so to speak. That's why you're grabbing the idea by its horns and being so forceful. You are sending a very clear message to your whole being - that you're not messing around here - you really mean it when you say you're a musician!

You can utilize this concept in the shower. For instance, say you want to affirm, "I am freaking feeling great!" or "I am feeling great (if you want to keep it PG)." While in the shower, with the door closed, scream that declaration at the absolute top of your lungs - like you'll lose your voice after this scream. This act will energize your body and completely shift your mood. It's like a jolt to your system. And just like that, you're already feeling better and will continue to feel better throughout the day. You can also do other affirmations or declarations, such as "I freaking love this life!" And don't be greedy with the Ric Flair "woooooo!" Hype yourself up. It's priceless.

And if you're in your car and need to lift your spirits, scream at the top of your lungs, as mentioned in the previous paragraph, "I feel amazing!" and "I love myself!" You'll immediately shift your energy. One thing, though. I wouldn't advise doing it at a red light on a really busy street. No one's going to believe you're on the phone, but who cares! Do it if you feel like it! Besides these practices, you can also shift your energy by the way you move your body.

I do this prior to my workouts. I start by stretching my hamstrings, groins, calves (via downward dog), quads, shoulders, lats, obliques, etc. I then rotate my torso from left to right for about 30 seconds to loosen my body up. After that, I start to bounce around like a boxer which also helps to loosen me up. I then shake my hands as if they were wet, trying to shake off the water droplets. This will loosen your forearms and remove stagnant energy. Next, I stomp my feet while wearing a flat-soled shoe. At times one by one, and at other times, I jump and stomp with both feet hard, but not hard enough to cause harm to your ankles. This will wake your body up, especially your lower body, and give you a more energetic feeling. And while you're at it, clap your hands hard a few times. All of this is going to wake your spirit up. Now your muscles have been stretched. You feel more relaxed, and your joints feel lubricated due to the torso twists. And all the clapping and stomping have you in a more energetic mood. All of this removes the negative energy trapped in your body, which is why you feel better. You will always have an amazing day if you practice this every morning.

Not having educated parents ended up being good for me. Because I knew they couldn't teach me much, I had to look elsewhere to learn. I'm fortunate to have had that realization as a young boy. The alternative was to stay stagnant and hope things change. I decided to learn from others. It didn't matter what the person looked like; I was learning from everyone. I learned from Christians, Buddhists, Jews, Muslims, atheists, black, white, yellow, red, young, old, male, and female. I even learned from plants, animals and insects. I had to learn how to live. It was like looking up Youtube videos on how to parent myself. Eventually, I learned enough to be one of my own spiritual leaders. I gained so much knowledge from so many fields, and I could see the bigger picture and arrive at conclusions no one else has.

My workout regimen was self-guided by my intuition. It told me, "do this, and next, do that...." I didn't copy anyone's routine. I did whatever my gut told me to do, no questions asked. It guided me to weight lift only 2 times a week instead of the norm, which is 3-6 days a week. That voice always guiding me was my intuition - my direct line to Spirit/Source/God/Christ/Universe. I always thought these were my thoughts, but one day I realized I have two voices in my head. It feels like you're talking to yourself, which is really what is going on. One being me and the other being my intuition (Higher Self, God, Source). It usually works like this. The "me" voice will ask a question like "how should I go about such and such...?" I'll wait briefly, and the reply will come from my intuition's voice. Learn to discern the voices in your head and learn to trust your intuition. The more you reflect on God and act according to His scriptures, the stronger your intuition will become and more accurate.

When I wanted to start dieting, I asked my intuition, "how should I go about this?" And it replied, "make sure half your calories are coming from protein, 35% from carbohydrates, and

15% from healthy fats." I asked it what foods to eat as well. At first, I doubted the plan because dinner didn't consist of beef, chicken, or fish but consisted of tofu in the form of sofritas at Chipotle. How will I put on muscle by eating tofu and greek yogurt? Lo and behold, I built more muscle naturally than anyone I know has in the past year (who isn't on steroids). Of course, I worked consistently hard, but the workout and diet go hand in hand. I've lifted weights, eaten like a carnivore, and never put on as much muscle as I did this past year. My intuition correctly guided me as I became shredded with a nice 6 pack - the first time in my life. When I used to follow the recommendations from the bodybuilding forums regarding diet and working out, I never saw the amazing results I achieved this time around, listening to my intuition.

Many of us aren't even aware of our inner power, called intuition. It's your gut feeling. It's been said the stomach is a 2nd brain. No wonder the thoughts coming from the gut are intelligent and guiding. That's why eating just the right amount of food is important because when you bombard your stomach with endless calories and grease, you impair the signal coming from your intuition. Your body's resources are being used constantly for digestion, and the feeling provided by the food is overshadowing your intuition's voice.

Furthermore, you will learn to dismiss your intuition if you are eating out of control. As it constantly nudges you and reminds you that you shouldn't eat so much, you subconsciously fight it off and tell it to piss off. Do this enough times, and you develop an automatic response that ignores your intuition, and now you've essentially cut yourself off from the Divine. It's no wonder Allah prescribed fasting to the Muslims.

This book aims to give you a glimpse into my life and how I overcame the odds. I really shouldn't be alive today, and that's no exaggeration. By my faith in God, I am still here. Through that feeling of unconditional love, I could weather a terrible storm and live to talk about it. I wanted to share a story of perseverance, hope, and persistence with you. People laughed at me for believing in God. The kids would call me "sheikh" because I fasted in Ramadan and did my prayers, and would abstain from things that are haraam or forbidden. In my adult years, I was mocked by so-called family members because I still had faith in God despite all that I'd been through and my state of health when they were mocking me. Today, they no longer laugh. Today they are believers. They know without a shadow of a doubt that God is real. I'm the proof. They know there's no way a human being can endure all that and rise to the top with effortless grace without help from the Divine. They now want to know how exactly I did it. Many are envious still. They are in awe because I have been guided while they weren't. But I spent countless hours reflecting on God, obeying His orders (I wasn't always perfect, I've committed sins, too), studying his different religions and nations, living through unconditional love and patience, living humbly, and assisting others.

While my adversaries were partying at night, smoking hookah, and drinking tea. I was getting closer to God through knowledge. The more knowledge I had, the more I understood. The more I understood, the more love flowed within me. And love is God. I was laughed at for being a hermit, but I already knew how most people are fake and unreliable. I gambled on God, and it paid off big time. I say it was a gamble because the results weren't instant. People did have the right to laugh at me for believing for so long despite a hard life. Shit, even I questioned it at times, "God, when will things turn around for me? You know I hardly complain to you because I know you have to witness the horror that goes on on Earth, and I don't want to burden God with my complaints on top of that, but when will it be my turn, God?"

Whatever you're going through right now, consider it as training. Be sure to learn the lessons along the way. Every soul must pass through hell. We must undergo intense pressure to reveal our strong character. At times, the trials and tribulations will lead you to believe that you are eternally cursed when in actuality, you're being blessed, albeit through hardships and pain. Just like pleasure teaches us what we like, pain also does the same. And certain lessons can only be learned through pain. If you ever intend to learn the truth, then be prepared for a harsh life. As the saying goes, the truth hurts. I know this because I set that intention as a young boy. I was so intrigued about creation; I wanted to know everything about it. I wanted the truth about everything in life, including the reason for living.

If you're thinking, "well, I don't have a relationship with God, and I've been committing sins left and right all my life," remember, God forgives. It's never too late to forgive yourself and get back on the horse. Dedicate time to reflect on The Creator and the creation. Do things with the intent of making sure it's a win-win for everyone involved. Don't take advantage of people. If you need something, ask - don't steal or go behind a person's back because of your ego. You can connect to God/Spirit/Christ/Universe/Allah/Yahweh, and you need to put in sincere and consistent effort. What you think about all day, you become. If you think about God all day, you will become a god.

One truth I stumbled upon was that the reason for living is to witness how great I am and we are. You and I are one consciousness acting out as multiple people. We get to witness what we're all great at. Seeing everyone as a reflection of you becomes a spectacle of you watching how great you are through different people, including greats like Nikola Tesla and Michael Jordan. When you look at life through this lens, you will become enamored with how incredible you (consciousness) are. Tesla and Jordan cannot exist without you. They are within you. Consciousness was divided into a multitude of people so that we can see the different attributes and gifts in an enjoyable way through living and observing.

Society, ads, and the media leave you feeling worthless and unimportant. I'm here to change all of that. You are worthy. You are worthy enough to meet God through knowledge and strict obedience. You are worthy enough to present yourself as you are. Of course, you should always look your best. But you don't need to copy someone else's personality and style. Be yourself. You are worthy of being accepted for your individuality and originality. It's not only reserved for celebrities.

Does life ever get any easier? Things will continue happening, but after a while, you build up enough strength to endure anything. And when you focus on what's important, you won't see most of the bullshit that occurs because you'll filter it out from your reality. So, while life doesn't technically get easier, *your* life will *feel* easier. After you've gone through your own trials and tribulations by weathering the storms, you'll start moving through obstacles gracefully. It feels like the scene in the "Matrix" where Neo calmly looks at the bullets and plucks them out of the air one by one with zero fear. When you can walk through life fearlessly, with self-belief and strength, you'll dodge a lot of bullets. Life will undoubtedly feel easier. As a result, your experience of life will be so much better!

You want to meet God, but how can you do that? It's quite simple, God is already within you. God is the spirit that Allah (God) blew into Adam and Jesus (peace be upon them). Jesus didn't have children, but Adam did. Don't you see that God's spirit was passed down to Adam's children and all the way down to you? What do you think is holding you upright and causing all of your bodily functions to move in perfect order? Everything is God. You just so happen to be in your ego. Your ego is a made up construct. It's absolutely amazing how the Most High can hide from Himself in plain sight!

Now that I've healed my childhood traumas and inner wounds, all I went through was worth it. Tears roll down my eyes as I write this. Tears of gratefulness, resilience, love, and contentment. I'm a survivor. I'm a warrior. A once wounded warrior who's now healed and warning the young warriors what they're up against so it doesn't do a number on them like it did to me.

I look back, and I have to, in a way, regrettably, be grateful for the following: the relentless child abuse, bad back, bruxism, the school fights, the bullies, the jealous family, Hunter's disability, the failed marriage, the betrayals, the successful e-commerce business that was destroyed by Hurricane Sandy, the fibromyalgia, and all the losses, amongst other things. On their own, some of these things can take out a horse, but all of these things combined, along with a bunch of other things that I haven't mentioned, are absolutely monstrous. It's a massive, massive undertaking. One that surely required an undertaker, but my faith in God somehow kept my head above the cemetery.

Today, I'm hardwired to constantly connect to Source/God. There's not a moment that I unplug. My faith is so strong, nothing can break it. I walk with fearlessness because God will always have my back. Even when something looks unfortunate, I know if I am patient enough, I'll see why it had to happen the way it did and that it's actually good for me. Other times, things look gloomy and I remain still within and everything subsides and works out in my favor. How do you connect to Source? Through your mind. But how? It's so easy! All you have to do is think about Him often.

Show Him you mean business by going above and *beyond* what He requires of you in His different scriptures. For example, to my fellow Muslim brothers and sisters, you must be consistent with your 5 daily prayers and not miss any, and you must consistently be on time, *especially* the morning prayer, fajr. You are having a meeting with your Creator. Say salaat/prayer is at 1 pm. If you had a meeting with Elon Musk, would you attend the meeting at 1 pm or, at the latest, 12:50 pm? I bet you'd be there at 12 pm or even earlier. That's fine, but be sure you give the same level of respect to God. Be at the prayer mat 10 minutes before and do dhikr (remembering God with a prayer bead or by hand).

Further, consistently do the night prayer before the fajr prayer. Although you're "only" required to pray 5 times a day, show God how serious you are and do an additional 1-5 prayers often. The key to all of this is to be consistent. When

Allah sees you are not only following orders but also being punctual and taking it as seriously as a heart attack. Furthermore, you're doing more than He asked. And you're doing this day in, day out, month in, month out. It won't be long before God says, "you know what? This person isn't going to stop. I'll elevate him or her and bring them to me now."

Become God's #1 fan. Everything he's putting you through is training. Do football players abandon their coaches because they put them through the ringer? Of course not! They thank them! Mind you, some coaches berate and curse at their players!

One bonus tip I want to share that improved my life is taking it easy and remaining relaxed. Prophet Muhammad (PBUH) once said, "take it easy, and all will be easy." I never forgot that. For example, I don't chaotically multi-task with great speed because that increases anxiety, and nothing seems to go smoothly that way. Rather, I've found that if I keep it cool and take my time doing what I have to do, it gets done smoothly and quicker, believe it or not. You should try it. When you think, speak, walk, or do anything, make sure your mind is very calm and you're not having multiple thoughts tripping over each other.

Take your time; ingrain that in your mind. Adopt that way of living. If anyone tries to rush you, tell them to piss off. Nothing is worth running around like a chicken with its head cut off. It drains you and causes you frustration. It affects your belief system because you start believing life is hard. When you believe that, life miraculously gets harder.

Some people rush to squeeze in some extra production. But is it really worth it? You're trading your good life for a bad one.

Sure, you might have 5-10% more money (maybe), but you're stressed out to the max now. Besides, money's always losing its value. Investments are always getting lost, too, except for some good ones. My point is, why would you trade a tranquil life with clarity and focus for a stressful one that allows you to buy a couple more things at the big box store or even at the car dealership?

If you walk with unshakeable faith, unconditional love, and unconditional patience in a calm manner while always remaining in the present moment, you've entered the closest place to heaven/paradise here on Earth right now. Furthermore, don't look for external validation. Who cares what others think about you? Why is someone else's opinion of you above your own opinion of yourself? Don't you know who you are? If you're a doctor, do you care if others might think you're not? Does validating you as a doctor make you more of a doctor? All the validation seeking does is preoccupy your mind with silliness. Free up your mind for other thoughts, productive ones.

My struggles became my benchmark. Each time I went through something, I always returned to my memory, recalled my worst struggles, and compared them to the new ones. Most of the time, the new struggle was easy compared to what I had already gone through.

When I had to decide whether or not to leave my first wife (at the time of this writing, I've only had one wife), I thought long and hard about my two children, ages 19 and 16 now as of this writing. How was it going to affect them? Surely it will be difficult, without a doubt. I had to recall my upbringing with an abusive mother. I rationalized that due to what I went through with my mother for so many years, my children could handle this painful experience. After all, they have lived a trauma-free life for most of their lives. I never spanked them. I never verbally assaulted them. I treated them like adults, even when they were toddlers. I provided a comfortable life for the two. They never had to endure what I did growing up, which started at 3 years old. If you consider sending a 3-year-old in New York City across the street to buy his mother a pack of cigarettes from the corner store. The physical abuse started at 4 when she dumped an entire pot of pasta on my head because I didn't want to eat. A year later, the beatings started. From a psychological standpoint, they hadn't undergone even a small fraction of a percent of what I had to. So, I concluded they could handle it, although it would be difficult. Being that trauma is relevant since this was their first major ordeal, I knew they would be fine nevertheless. And I also thought to myself that this is an experience they needed to get stronger and deal with a common problem most families face: divorce.

Life can be difficult, requiring unconditional patience and unwavering trust in the universe. The struggle is what makes life "real." The mental, physical, emotional, and spiritual struggle separates the real world from the video games. The struggle allows one to actively participate in life and experience something different.

Rather than running away from struggles, dealing with them head-on is best. The more you deal with struggles, the less they will affect you. You should want your biggest calamity to occur ASAP so that everything else that occurs after is simple in comparison.

Going to the gym and working out is a struggle at first. After a few months, the workouts start to feel easier as you build up muscle and endurance. And thanks to your struggle in the gym, everything outside the gym starts to feel easy. Lifting things, running errands, doing work, and running a business becomes easier due to the struggles in the gym, along with the energy you develop. Everything is easy in comparison. That's why it pays to run towards your struggles rather than avoid them. You need to pick your battles wisely. Some struggles are better left alone, if possible. But embrace the ones you can't avoid and try to figure out how you will benefit from them.

I've lived one hell of a life. My editor was flabbergasted at my story. She asked me, very skeptically, "did all of this really happen to you? Is the story really about you?" Others have learned parts of my story and they become angry at why I had to go through all of this. Many are just as shocked and in disbelief like my editor. People are amazed at my attitude when they learn about my abusive mother. They ask me, "wow, how can you still smile after all of that?" To which I think in my head, "if they only knew what else I had to go through!" People always ask me, "how did you do it? How did you survive? How can you still have a loving spirit? How did you keep leveling up, even when you were completely isolated?" And I'm always left in a dilemma. If I tell them it was God, they refuse to accept that. If I tell them, "well then, it was me," they say, "you must work with the devil." It's sad that some people won't give credit to God or me but give it to the devil instead.

The truth is, it was God and me together. And yes, the devil was involved too. After all, he's the one that inspired those around me to come against me and violate me. I always had this smart, mature, guiding voice within me. The difference between me and most is that I listened to my intuition. And I kept it real. I stayed authentic. I refused to conform to the fakeness that everyone had adopted. When you're authentic, God will come to your aid, guaranteed. When you support the truth, the truth (God/Universe) will support you.

Today, I respect the devil for doing his part. Evil, I've come to learn, is a necessary evil, pun intended. Without it, we will never learn some of the biggest lessons in life. Evil is why many don't believe in God, but it's exactly why they should believe in God. For if the Devil exists, then God must exist as well.

Look at Satan as your life coach who puts you through intense workouts. These aren't ordinary workouts! With these workouts, liquid not only exits through your pores but also through your tear ducts. Thank you Devil. No matter what you've done, I love you. You helped turn me into a fearless warrior. That is why sometimes I wear a Satanic pendant. People say, "oh he worships the devil!" No. I worship the Almighty God. I wear Satanic pendants for two reasons. Number one, it's to taunt Satan; to make a statement that says, "you thought you could defeat me, but *I* defeated you!" And number two, as a sign of respect for pushing me to my limits. For a loving being, such as a loving relative or friend, he or she will never push you to the edge and cause you such pain. But Satan took the fall for humanity's progress. In a sense, it's like he sacrificed his name and reputation so the rest of us can advance and grow. For that, I respect and love him and I always pray to God to please guide him to love and cause him to abandon his evil ways and grant him paradise. God forgives, that's why I forgive. Me, God and you are One and we're all on the same team. The team of life and experiences.

THE END...OR NOT

With divine guidance, I was led to heal from my mother's and father's wounds. I highly recommend you do the same, whether you're a man, woman, boy, or girl. I handled each one separately. For example, I would think about my mother and how she mishandled and abused me. I tried to think of all the different scenarios. I let all the emotions come out. I kept repeating the process till the very thought of her no longer affected me. The thought of any detail regarding her abusive ways towards me no longer influenced my emotions. I did the same with Neuman. Even though the suspected betrayal didn't get to me, I was still guided to reflect on Neuman and how he treated me throughout my life and allow the emotions to arise within me. And I repeated the process until it no longer affected me.

I even set out to heal from the fact that my children no longer speak to me. After desperately trying to contact them for more than a year, I decided a change was needed. Like Albert

Einstein once famously said, "Insanity is doing the same thing over and over and expecting different results." I decided to no longer reach out to them since they didn't respond. I hope that they will take action and reach out to me since I no longer reach out to them. I'm trying something different because I really do want to be in their lives again. Me reaching out daily for over a year hasn't worked, so I figured a change was needed. I still support them and their mother financially. I would even if the courts weren't involved.

The last time I saw my doctor, he asked about my situation with Zina and the children. I told him I had maintained zero contact with Zina since I last saw him. He said, "good." He knows she has a narcissistic personality disorder and that no contact is the best way to handle that type of individual. And I told him I'd accepted that my children no longer talk to me. I told the doctor, "If they never talk to me again, that's perfectly fine. I'm not going to lose sleep over it." To which he applauded me with favorable body language and facial expression and said, "that's the best way to handle it." Of course, I cried about the loss of my relationship with my children. I cried several times (all in private). It's gotten to the point that the thought of this fact no longer has an emotional impact on me, and I'm perfectly OK with them never talking to me or seeing me ever again. What doesn't kill you makes you stronger. This is my personal story of overcoming many challenges and accepting the severance of many people, including those I love(d), while remaining optimistic and God-abiding. There's hardly an hour that passes by that I don't remember God (love). This is how I've always been since I was a child, always remembering God. There's no moment when love *isn't* flowing through every vein in my body. It is the reason I choose to see things from a loving standpoint, with understanding and empathy. All praises are due to The Most High, God/Allah/The Father/Jesus Christ/Yahweh/Spirit/Universe/The gods (in no particular order).

The most important thing to do while healing is to forgive. Forgive yourself and forgive those who have hurt you. That's what I did. One day, I was laying on my couch, and I felt an overwhelming feeling of love in my chest and I caved in. I told God, "just give them (my abusers, haters, and enemies) what you give me. Every blessing you're giving and will give me, give it to them too. Give it to my enemies." I was reluctant to say that prayer because I didn't feel like they deserved any blessings, but the love within me took over. An intense amount of emotions erupted within, and I shed some tears. It was a huge relief. It was as if to say to God, "I give up. I surrender. I will no longer hold animosity toward them. And to prove it, God, I'm asking you to bless them like you bless me." I didn't expect to feel the weight of the world to be lifted off of me like that. It was just an instinct to do it. When the emotions erupted, and the tears rolled down, I reluctantly said again, "Bless them, God, bless them like you've blessed me!" (Signaling with my hand as if to say 'go away'). That is the day I fully surrendered to the Most High God, vibrating the highest I've ever, and healed many wounds on January 19, 2023.

Remember, I was just an average boy, teenager, and man, but I had above average belief in God and tried my very best to follow His scriptures; and learn about all of His religions, including famous philosophies like Buddhism; and thus, above average love ran through my veins consistently throughout my entire life. I went from an average, overlooked underdog to a warrior and a testimony to God. I literally had no one; no one liked or loved me. No one wanted to be with me except my good friend, Hunter, who I named my son after - ironically they both couldn't walk and both are so loveable. I was alone with The Creator. That was more than enough. You, too, can triumph against all odds. Embrace God. Embrace love. Forgive the demons, for they are your coaches and trainers. Forgive everyone who has hurt you. You and I need them to grow mentally, physically, emotionally, and spiritually. And never forget that because the devil exists, God also exists. And because hate exists, love also exists. And God is love. Operate from love, and you will experience unending miracles. You are love; you are God. There is only one God - It's all of existence and all that is within. With love, Chris Josh.

Before you put your book away...

Please take a few moments to write a review on the platform you ordered your book from. Recommending the book to family, friends and colleagues is also much appreciated. Your review is very important to me because most people decide if they're going to read a book based on reviews like yours. Thank you!

My Other Work:

Book: "How to Access Your Divine Energy"

Book: "How Champions Talk to Themselves"

Audio Program: Develop a strong, positive mindset that attracts financial success, love, health, confidence, and much more with the "Positive Self-Talk" audio program available to stream instantly only at ChrisJosh.com/Power

Visit **www.ChrisJosh.com/Subscribe** today and subscribe to the emails, so you can stay in touch with Chris Josh and be the first to know about future releases and offers.

Social Media

TikTok: @TheChrisJosh
Instagram: @TheChrisJosh
Youtube: @TheChrisJosh
Facebook: Facebook.com/TheChrisJosh
Twitter: @RealChrisJosh
Clapper: @ChrisJosh

Blog

ChrisJosh.com/Blog

APPENDIX: THE SHADOW SELF WORKBOOK

Healing is very important because if you remain unhealed, it will block your blessings, abundance and finances. It will also wreak havoc on the most important thing - your mental, emotional and physical health. It will also interfere with your relationships and the ability to connect with new people. Therefore, your network will suffer. When you're unhealed, you're less attractive than if you were fully healed. So, understand the importance of healing and why you must work on yourself daily in order to address all the deep-rooted pain caused by people, places and things.

Journaling Exercise:

Each day, set aside 10 minutes to relive the betrayal(s), abuse, and/or bullying by writing down each event. You can write down about one betrayer, abuser or bully each day. Be sure to write the following details: what exactly the person did to you, how much it hurt you and why it hurt you. This will get you emotional – that's ok. That's the point. You want to let those emotions that have been buried in your body and subconscious mind to come to the surface, so you can experience them and finally release them.

You will have to write about the same person and event several times, so don't just write about them once or even twice. Be sure to save your writings so you can read them the next day. Each day you write about a person or event, read what you wrote the next day. This will speed up the healing process.

Forgiveness Letter:

Unfortunately, when we've been wronged by a person, that person usually feels no remorse and their ego is too big to admit wrong and apologize to you. You'll be waiting a very long time for that apology, so here's what you're going to do.

Imagine you are the betrayer, abuser or bully and write a letter to yourself. Start with "Dear (your name), I would like to sincerely apologize for hurting you. I know what I did was wrong and there's no excuse for it. You were a great friend/relative/partner and I should have never treated you so poorly. You are a rare individual and I have yet to come across someone as kind and genuine as you. I know your life is much better without me in it to hurt you. I know I don't deserve to be in your life again and I don't blame you. I just wanted to give you my sincere apologies and I learned my lesson – I will never take advantage of another good human being again. Sincerely, (their name)."

Of course, you can add specifics regarding what the person

did to you and you can add more details to the letter. Create a letter for each person who hurt you. This will bring much needed closure. You can save the letters and read them again later.

Releasing Exercise:

Sit somewhere quiet in your home, preferably when no one is there. Or if that's not possible, lay in your bed with the door locked. Dedicate 15-30 minutes (or more if you'd like) to this exercise. Recall one of your betrayers, abusers, and/or bullies. Bring up the negative memories and feel the associated emotions related to the person and event(s). You may cry and that's ok – just don't cry in front of others and if you feel like bawling, cry into a pillow to fully release the deep seated emotions. Ask that person, "why did you do that to me?" Say, "I was nothing but good to you! You took advantage of me. You're such a bad human being. I used to do XYZ for you. I was there for you when no one else was and that's how you repay me?"

You can add more questions as you feel necessary. This is a great way to bring relief and resolve, as well as closure. You will have to repeat the process multiple times for each person. However, you will find that each time you repeat the process, the emotions get less and less intense. You will feel lighter, more mentally stable and at peace each time.

Forgiveness Exercise:

Forgiveness is very crucial for your healing. Forgiving a person who hurt you sounds counterintuitive. However, it's going to release any revengeful sentiments and thoughts.

Now, let's be clear here. Forgiving someone doesn't mean

what they did was right. And it certainly doesn't mean you forget what they did and allow them back into your life. You're forgiving the person or people for your own mental health and peace.

Sit somewhere quiet and fully decide on forgiving the person or people. You must be very intentional and not half-ass it – you have to really mean it. Say, "I forgive you. It's ok because I know what you did to me, helped me grow as a person. I'm grateful for the lesson(s). It's because of what you did to me that I'm stronger and wiser now." Release any desire for retaliation. Release the wish for the Most High God to punish them. Tell God, "I forgive him/her/them. Bless them like you bless me. Whatever you're going to bless me with, bless them too." You may get really emotional after this. Let it all out.

Shadow Self Questions:

1. **What about the betrayal bothers you the most? What are some other things that bother you? Be very specific**. For example, if it was a cheating partner, you might say, "I thought they were mine." But you must understand that they're not your property. At the end of the day, they have free will and you must accept their actions and know that it has nothing to do with you and everything to do with them. Know that they have not healed many aspects of their shadow self and that it is not your job to heal them or tolerate their disrespectful behavior. Take it as a lesson – learn from it and remember the red flags

and move on. And know what you will no longer accept from a partner, relative or friend.

1. **Did they have childhood trauma? Did they have unresolved trauma?** If so, know that it had nothing to do with you. You were <u>not</u> inadequate for that person or those people.

1. **Did that person have family issues growing up? Did one or both parents abandon them in some way or spend very little time with them? Did this person ever express lack of attention from their parents, siblings, and/or family?** Understand that these issues will cause a person to constantly seek attention and validation from many people – usually from the opposite sex. You should now see that their lack of integrity has nothing to do with who you are, the type of person you are, or how you treated them.

1. **Did you assume they would always do right by you? Did you expect them to be moral and perfect? What gave you that impression? Did you think they upheld the same moral code as you?** Understand that many people do not adhere to authenticity or a moral code. You must accept that it is out of your control. You can't force someone to be honest and God-fearing.

1. **Do you think betrayal is something you should tolerate? If yes, why do you feel that you deserve**

this type of treatment? And if not, you must release the emotions, forgive them, forgive yourself and forgive the situation. Be grateful for the lesson and that the betrayal happened sooner than later.

1. **What question(s) do you have for your betrayer? Is there an answer they can give to make your relationship go back to the way it was?** If not, then it's over and you must move on. Let all the emotions arise within you and release them.

1. **What lessons did you learn from this experience? Did you learn the red flags? Did you learn what you don't want in a person?**

1. **Did this person's actions change the way you trust others? Or have you gained the power of discernment to be able to know who is worthy of your trust?**

1. **Do you feel shame because of the betrayal? If so, why?** Understand that many times the victim (you) truly didn't deserve what happened to them. Though your ego might be hurt, it's actually steering you towards God (love). And that is priceless. And just because you're the victim in the situation, it doesn't mean you have to walk around with the victim mindset!! Be strong. You are the victor because you got rid of a person who doesn't serve your highest and greatest good.

1. **Do you feel any guilt?** You must forgive yourself and the other person and truly let go. Feeling guilt implies you did something wrong, when in fact you did nothing wrong. You feel guilty because you think the betrayal is your fault when it's not. In fact, the other person made you feel that way through manipulation.

1. **Did the situation make you angry?** It's completely natural and normal to be upset. However, you must not suppress or repress your anger or else it will turn into depression, and you will essentially be immobilized and unmotivated to do anything. Allow the emotions of anger to arise within you and feel those emotions. Let them out. Go outside and sprint as hard as you can a few times. Burn away the angry energy. Scream at the top of your lungs in rage if you must (you can scream into a pillow if you don't want to wake up your neighbors or look crazy outside).

1. **Did what happened affect your self-worth?** When we get disrespected, abused and betrayed, we believe it's because we're not valuable enough to be treated with great reverence. Understand that the other person has their own issues and that they don't know the value of a great person when they see one. It's like someone who goes to a shop expecting to buy something that costs $500 for $15. They don't see the worth of that thing and what it can do for them. Know your worth and tell yourself, "I am worthy. I

know my worth. Anyone who can't see my worth will not be part of my life."

1. **Did you feel the other person was always competing or in secret competition with you?** This is because you possess something or several things on the inside that they cannot emulate or purchase. They are not in touch with their heart space and they are all up in their ego. They may have always thought they and/or their family were superior to everyone else and you broke that illusion. In a weird way, they were trying to redeem themselves (and their family). A person who truly loves you will be proud of you and will celebrate you every chance they get. Stay away from competitive people. They do not want to see you happy or successful. You would think the person has a vested interest in seeing you succeed, especially if they depend on you. But sadly, some people just don't see the world that way. Leave these people in the dust and move on. They will never change. They will constantly try to one up you and tear you down.

1. **Has your confidence and self-esteem taken a hit?** Stop ruminating over the situation. Accept what happened, forgive and let go. Detach from that situation. Let all the different emotions arise within you and experience them fully – allow yourself to cry, scream or even laugh if needed. Look in the mirror

and tell yourself, "I love you. I respect you. I honor you. I'm proud of you. I'm glad I'm me. God loves me. People love me. People respect me. I attract high caliber people who appreciate me. I love myself for not tolerating bullshit people. My inner child is happy."

1. **How was your relationship with your parents, siblings and family? Did they respect and honor you? Or did they berate you and show a lack of respect?** It's important to heal this so that you no longer attract people who disrespect you. Acknowledge the past and accept it. Let any related emotions come about and experience them fully. Let go and use the experiences to know what you now want from an individual you allow into your life. Understand that you deserve love as you are. You deserve respect so long as you give it.

1. **Do you have strong boundaries? Do you let others know when they cross them?** It's extremely important to have your boundaries and enforce them. Never feel like you have to apologize to anyone when you let them know they overstepped your boundaries. Take time to write down all your boundaries. This process may take days as you think of what boundaries you are going to set. Refer to your list of boundaries daily for 3 weeks and periodically after that time period. If someone does

something you don't like, simply say, "I don't like what you just did. Don't do that again," sternly – not gently and not apologetically. If they cross your boundary again, cut them off. When you internalize your boundaries and you know for a fact you will always enforce them, people will be able to tell you mean business and that you're not someone to play around with.

1. **Were you abused in any way?** Abuse is never easy. It can come in many forms: physical, sexual, emotional, mental and spiritual. It's very important to move away from shame, guilt, anger, and fear. Understand that it's over now. You now protect yourself and no one can hurt you anymore. As hard as it may seem, you simply have to make peace with your past and just accept how everything panned out – unless you are able to bring that person to justice. Ponder on the lessons that can be extracted from these negative experiences. Have you become stronger and wiser as a result?

1. **Do you people please?** You must understand that more than 99% of the world do not respect a people pleaser and most will walk all over that person. If someone isn't showing you interest or respect, do not increase your people pleasing "mechanism." Walk away! You'll find the right people in due time. Never ever try hard to get someone to like you – even if it's a member of the opposite sex that you really like.

Only entertain the people who accept you at your baseline.

1. **Were you bullied in the past? How did it make you feel? Be very specific.** You may find that it made you feel several things. Sit with those emotions and experience them – let the emotions out and then let go. You will no longer tolerate disrespect. Understand that from time to time you will run into an unhealed person who will not show the respect you deserve. That's ok. Let it be the last time that person gets to interact with you. And do not let that person back in, regardless if they're sorry or not. They will always see you as the person they bullied and they will never truly respect you.

1. **Are you in full control of your emotions or do you allow your emotions to be on autopilot? Do you always react to what others do or say?** Learn to be non-reactionary. Stay neutral within. Don't always give people a reaction. You don't owe anyone anything! If people are constantly bombarding you with bad news or their troubles, you need to part ways in order to protect your peace. Your emotions should always be either neutral or positive.

1. **Is there a person in your life who influences your emotions heavily? Are they more in control of your emotions than you are? Is there someone around you who starts the conversation on a high**

note but quickly interjects negativity into the conversation in order to get your reaction? You must be in the driver's seat of your emotions. Do not allow people to play with your emotions. Cut ties with negative and toxic people – even if you're related to each other or they are your life partner.

ABOUT THE AUTHOR

Chris Josh is a spiritual healer, motivational speaker, and a writer. He is the author of three books: City of Serpents, How to Access Your Divine Energy, and How Champions Talk to Themselves. He also created a powerful audio program called "Positive Self Talk." He has also written a short eBook: How to Become Your Higher Self. He currently lives in Englewood, NJ.

Made in the USA
Thornton, CO
06/24/24 22:23:34

99a3bb7d-0eab-46d6-a5dd-3125545c3410R02